Preaching Better

Practical Suggestions for Homilists

Ken Untener
Bishop of Saginaw

Paulist Press
New York/Mahwah, N.J.

Cover design by Moe Berman

Interior design by Millennium Wordpress

Library of Congress Cataloging-in-Publication Data

Untener, Ken,   1937–
    Preaching better : practical suggestions for homilists / Ken Untener.
        p.   cm.
    Includes bibliographical references.
    ISBN 0–8091–3849–2
    1. Preaching. 2. Catholic preaching. I. Title.
BV4211.2.U55   1999
251–dc21   98–48870
                                                                                                        CIP

Published by Paulist Press
997 Macarthur Boulevard
Mahwah, New Jersey 07430

www.paulistpress.com

Printed and bound in the
United States of America

Contents

INTRODUCTION

How All This Got Started

Practice doesn't make perfect; it makes permanent.

———————————

This book comes from the ground up. It will help to know the background.

Phase I: "Feedback from the Folks"

Beginning in 1975, I taught homiletics part-time at St. John's Seminary just outside Detroit. My only qualifications were a graduate degree in theology and 12 years of preaching.

I bought a pocket notebook and began to ask people (Columbo style) what they liked or didn't like about homilies. I asked only "the people in the pew," that is, folks who were not in ministry and, as far as I could tell, had no particular axe to grind. I did it every chance I had—with friends, strangers, at dinner tables, at parties, on airplanes. They talked; I wrote.

Surprising how willing people were (and are) to talk about this. Others who overheard would chime in.

I've kept up the practice and by now have collected thousands of comments. Along the way, I've sorted them into about 25 basic categories.

1

The convergence is remarkable.[1] (One category quickly began to outdistance the others as "numero uno." I'll identify it when we come to that chapter.)

These gathered comments plus my reflections on them are the heart of this book. But there is more.

Phase II: "The Saginaw Program"

In 1993, I finally got the nerve to implement a plan that had been percolating in my brain for several years. The Saginaw Presbyteral Council unanimously endorsed it, even volunteered to go first.

It works this way. I go through the list of priests and choose four, plus a deacon or lay homilist. Then I send each a letter telling him or her to tape (live) an upcoming weekend homily and send it to me.[2] It is not optional. I also tape one of my own homilies and add it to the batch.

My secretary duplicates each tape as it comes in, types up a transcript, and sends each of us a copy of all of the tapes and transcripts. (My secretary is going straight to heaven.)

A date is set for all to gather at my office for two hours, in preparation for which each listens to the tapes and makes notes.

At the two-hour session, we do what golfers do after a match. We compliment, console, offer tips, and try to figure out how we can preach better. This leads into wide-ranging discussions about the joys and sorrows of preaching, what works and what doesn't, and what a homily is supposed to be in the first place. I am not the teacher. I am the gatherer—my homily is one of the six in the packet.[3]

Honesty is the key. I remind them that this is a once-in-a-lifetime opportunity to hear some straight talk from a cross-section of experienced peers. On the whole, honesty prevails and we have wonderful conversations, at times from the depths of our souls. We're talking after all about the heart of our ministry, which is the shaping of the community through the Word of God.

---

[1] Readers may want to experiment with this themselves. It can be done easily in any informal setting. Simply ask, "By the way, what do you most like or dislike in a homily?" It is guaranteed to enliven any conversation.

[2] The priests are taken in alphabetical order, with some adjustments to help the mix of the group.

[3] We don't relisten to the tapes during this two-hour session. It would be too time consuming. We have our own notes from having listened to them previously, and we also have the transcripts in front of us.

When we finish the two-hour session, each of us receives a blank tape to record another weekend homily, we all go home, and the whole process begins again. We do it four times.[4]

It is not our expectation that after each session we will show improvement: The intent is that these four sessions will begin a trajectory of improvement that will continue far into the future.

When we're approaching the fourth and last session, I start the next group, and the next, and so on. It has continued now for more than four years. When in about two more years we've finished, we'll start again.

That is a rough sketch of the program, but there are some important other features.

Our director of communications, a veteran journalist, joins us for part of each session. Beforehand, she selects two transcripts and edits them, using her experience as copy editor of a newspaper. She passes out copies of the marked-up texts and goes over them, explaining her reasons for the changes.

The written word, of course, differs from the spoken word. She takes that into account, listening to the taped homily before editing it. She doesn't claim to be a homilist or a theologian; she is a journalist and applies this skill to our homilies for whatever it's worth.

It's worth a lot. Trust me. It's an eye-opener to see your homily edited.[5]

Also participating in each group is a woman who is both a systematic theologian and an experienced spiritual director. Not regularly a homilist or liturgical minister, she too identifies with those on the receiving end of homilies and also brings her theological/spiritual expertise to the discussion. The presence of these two nonpreaching professional women is a great asset to the group.

There is one more part of the process. A person in a neighboring diocese has lined up a number of lay people who are willing to participate by mail. Prior to each session, six of these lay people receive one tape each, listen to it, and send in their comments on a provided form.

---

[4]Some may wonder why we don't use videos instead of audio tapes. It would have some advantages, but making, duplicating, and then watching the videos becomes complicated. We didn't want the best to become the enemy of the good. As Chesterton said, "If something is worth doing, it's worth doing imperfectly."

[5]In the opening session of each group, my homily is always the first victim, and the editor and I have an understanding that mine will be approached with particular ferocity. This usually rids the group of inhibitions about honesty.

Because they have never heard the homilist before, their feedback is particularly striking when it echoes some of the same comments raised in our group.

That's our "Saginaw program." It's not an introductory course for beginners. It's "hands-on" work with experienced homilists who are trying to help one another improve this art called preaching.

Hands-on Help

No one preaches to full potential, and none of us improves simply by doing it over and over. Practice doesn't make perfect: It makes permanent.

Professionals in almost every field engage in something like this, formally or informally. Professional musicians help one another all the time; so do professional golfers. Authors are critiqued whether they like it or not. The National Football League uses videos to review the referees and linesmen after every single game.

Commercial pilots are an interesting example: Once a year, each pilot joins several other pilots for a program to review and improve their flying ability. Part of it is sort of hands-on because they use a flight simulator, but during the year, they have another review that truly is hands-on. Without advance notice, a "check pilot" climbs into the cockpit and says, "I'm going to ride with you. Just do what you normally do."[6]

A commercial pilot once told me of an even stronger motivation to improve. There are always two pilots in the cockpit, and generally they divide up the stages of a flight. "Pilots take pride in their flying ability," he said, "and the presence of another pilot makes you want to do the best you can when it's your turn to fly. Plus, we try to help one another."

That's what we try to do in our groups: help one another to preach as well as we can and to keep improving.

I'm not opposed to workshops on homiletics—the more the better—but besides that, we need hands-on work. To critique a simulated homily on videotape can be helpful, like a pilot in a simulator or a golfer on the driving range. It's another thing to critique a regular homily given in a parish under actual conditions.[7]

---

[6]These check pilots, by the way, are voted into the job by the pilots from among their own.

[7]At the end of the final session with each group, I invite their feedback on the whole process. This has been positive and helpful. Their consensus is that success hinges on three essentials: (1) it has to be mandatory; (2) the tapes must be of "live" homilies; (3) whoever leads the group has to be a regular homilist whose taped homily is part of the process.

Because I'm part of every group, I've been up to my ears in taped homilies and discussions about homilies. (By now I've had more than 85 of my own homilies analyzed.) I've learned a lot, and I try to pass on from group to group some of the best things we learned along the way.

That is what this book aims to do for all who read it.[8]

Most homilists work hard at preaching, and I have the highest regard for them. Only those who preach know how difficult it is. From my own struggles and failings, I know well the challenge. My hope is that the following chapters, born of the experience of hundreds who are in the same boat, will be helpful.

---

[8]Our homily groups are best when they are characterized by straight talk. This book is straight talk for experienced homilists. Such veterans can decide for themselves whether something is on target. If it sounds at times as though I am setting forth absolutes, know that they are simply offered for whatever they are worth. The ministry of preaching is an art, and there aren't many absolutes in art.

CHAPTER ONE

An "Attitude"

"I will give them a new heart and put
a new spirit within them." (Ezekiel 11:19)

Writing a homily can seem like homework, an assigned paper due almost every week. Such tasks seldom stir our hearts.

The first step, and probably the biggest step, toward improving homilies is to put that attitude aside. We need a new heart, a new spirit.

This change of heart is not a mind game. It is bedrock reality. A few moments of reflection are all it takes to realize what we are about when preparing a homily.

Consider the following:

1. When preparing a homily we participate in *the same action of the Spirit that formed the scriptural text itself.*

That may seem quite a stretch, but the NCCB document *Fulfilled in Your Hearing* is not hesitant about it:

> If the words of scripture are divinely inspired, as we believe them to be, then divine inspiration must be at work when those words are made alive and contemporary to the believing community in and through our ministry.[1]

---

[1] *Fulfilled in Your Hearing* (1982), published by the NCCB Committee on Priestly Life and Ministry, pp. 10–11. Cf. also "The Interpretation of the Bible in the Church," published in 1993 by

Nor is Raymond Brown hesitant about it. He points out that when the apostolic eyewitnesses interpreted the message of Jesus in the face of new situations, they did not do this simply by remembering what Jesus did and said; after all, they had been among those who "saw but did not understand." After the resurrection/ascension, it was the *gift of the Spirit* that taught them the meaning of what they had seen. This was the fulfillment of what Jesus had told them:

> I have much more to tell you but you cannot bear it now. But when he comes, the Spirit of truth, he will guide you to all truth. (Jn 16:13)

Brown notes that the promised Paraclete did not cease this activity when the apostolic age ended. We Christians of later generations are no further removed from the ministry of Jesus than were the earlier Christians. The Paraclete dwells within us just as the Paraclete dwelt within the eyewitnesses after the resurrection/ascension, recalling and giving new meaning to what Jesus said.[2]

2. When preparing a homily, we are composing *part of the liturgy.*

The homily is part of the liturgy. We'd get that right on a multiple-choice test, but in practice, we easily overlook it because a homily SEEMS so much like a talk, a speech, or a lesson given on the occasion of a liturgy. To make matters more difficult, for many generations, "sermons" usually WERE talks, speeches, or lessons given on the occasion of a liturgy.

We are gradually returning to an awareness that in a homily we prepare and proclaim, under the guidance of the Spirit, something that is actually part of the liturgy itself. One thinks of early presiders preparing and proclaiming the eucharistic prayer: They knew they were doing something sacred. The same sense should be within us as we prepare (and give) a homily.[3]

---

the Pontifical Biblical Commission. "The first disciples of Jesus knew that they did not have the capacity right away to understand the full reality of what they had received in all its aspects. As they persevered in their life as a community, they experienced an ever-deepening and progressive clarification of the revelation they received. They recognized in this the influence and action of 'the Spirit of truth,' which Christ had promised them, to guide them to the fullness of the truth (Jn 16:12-13). Likewise the church today journeys onward, sustained by the promise of Christ: 'The Paraclete, the Holy Spirit, which the Father will send in my name, will teach you all things and will make you recall all that I have said to you.'"(Jn 14:26)

[2]Cf. Brown, *The Gospel According to John,* Anchor Bible, vol. 29 (New York: Doubleday, 1966, pp. 1141-42).

[3]The documents of the church are clear on this. "The homily, therefore, is to be highly

3. When giving the homily, we stand with God speaking to the people.

In the homily, the homilist is pointed in a different direction than is the celebrant in the eucharistic prayer.

- In the eucharistic prayer, the celebrant "stands facing God" and speaks to God on behalf of the people.[4]
- In the homily, the homilist "stands facing the people" and speaks to the people on behalf of God.[5]

When you think about it in this light, which is the more awesome task? Well, each is awesome in its own way. But while we recognize the sacredness of what the presider is about in the eucharistic prayer, we're a long way from sensing the sacredness of what the homilist is about in the homily. (In recent years there has been increasing stress on the *importance* of the homily. I would like to see equal stress on its *sacredness*.)

A Prayerful and Enjoyable Work

We need to find ways to make the preparation of homilies prayerful and enjoyable.

Much of my spiritual formation didn't associate those two words: *prayerful* and *enjoyable*. The limited prayer forms I learned didn't seem to include *enjoyment*.

Both words apply here. We enter into a special relationship with the Holy Spirit when preparing a homily, and that already puts us in a *prayerful* mode. We are engaged in one of the most effective and central activities of our ministry, and that is *enjoyable*, fulfilling.

Find ways to make preparation *prayerful*. A lit candle can help; the TV doesn't. Often, prayerful thoughts crop up along the way. Pray them. There's no rush. Besides, time spent on homily preparation should "count" for prayer. Preparing a homily may be hard work, but it is also holy work.

---

esteemed as part of the liturgy itself." (Const. on Liturgy, #52) This is not new information for most homilists. What might be new are the full implications.

[4]The General Instruction of the Roman Missal says this about the eucharistic prayer: "The priest...*unites (the people) with himself in the prayer he addresses in their name to the Father through Jesus Christ.* (54) (emphasis added)

[5]An awareness of this difference can greatly help the proclamation of the eucharistic prayer as well as the homily.

Find ways to make it *enjoyable* too—good space, a time that is not rushed, resources close at hand.[6] It is enjoyable to settle in with scripture. (Note that starting early in the week can help both the prayer and the enjoyment.)

We who are in pastoral work need time for spiritual exercises, but it is a mistake to situate all of these outside our pastoral tasks. Our regular round of activities has already built into it opportunities for prayer, reflection, and attentiveness to the Spirit.

Writing homilies is one of these prayerful, holy works.

---

[6]In her best-selling book *Inner Simplicity*, Elaine St. James talks about creating your own sanctuary: "It could be your own room, or even a small corner of a room.... This will be where you'll meditate, contemplate, do nothing, think, read, heal yourself, enjoy the silence, and do your journal writing.... Do whatever you need to do to make it special and sacred." (New York: Hyperion, 1995, pp 65–66). We ought to have a space like that where, among other things, we prepare our homilies.

CHAPTER TWO

What Is a Homily?

"...In receiving the word of God from hearing
us, you received not a human word but...
the word of God." (1 Thessalonians, 2:13)

Just what is a homily anyway? We've wrestled with this in group after group, and gradually I have come to see homilies differently. This has been far and away the biggest effect upon me.[1]

In years gone by, I pictured the homilist as a cook who looks to see what's in the pantry and the refrigerator (the readings), comes up with a menu (the "main thought"), puts the meal together (the homily), and then serves it.

What I've become more conscious of is that the homilist comes into a kitchen that is filled with the smell of something already cooking, and it is the Lord who is doing it. The liturgy is the Lord's meal all the way around: the menu, the cooking, the serving. We are helpers.

The task of all liturgical ministers, including the homilist, is to help the flow of what *Christ* is doing, for Christ is the leader of all liturgical prayer. The first thing we must do when preparing a homily (or planning a liturgy) is to stand humbly before the Lord.[2]

---

[1] Defining a homily can become abstract, complicated. I find it more concrete to get at this by asking: "What is the role of the homilist?"

[2] Those who select and minister liturgical music are among those who need to take careful note

The Threefold Task of a Homilist

If this is true, then the role of the homilist comes down to three tasks: (1) to discern what the Lord is doing/speaking through this event, (2) to help illuminate this for the assembly, and (3) to do all this on behalf of the church.

1. <u>To Discern What the Lord Is Doing/Speaking Through This Event</u>

God's Word doesn't live in a book. It comes alive within the entire event...which is the convergence of:

these scripture texts (on Sundays there are four texts: three readings plus the psalm)

this liturgical setting (season, feast, occasion)

this historical time and place (all that is going on in our world and church right now)

these people (the real-life circumstances of the people to whom we preach)

This involves exegesis, but it is more than that. We are trying to discern how this text *functions* here and now. Someone once commented to me that homilists so often seem to preach a "historical Jesus"; that is, they explain Jesus "back then." But Jesus isn't back then; Jesus is alive ...and not simply living in retirement. Jesus is here-and-now acting upon us, particularly in liturgy. Something is "combusting" in the combination of these scriptures and this event, and we who preach must discover it and help open it up for the people of God.

The Word of God at liturgy is always live, never a rerun. When the scriptures are proclaimed, we are not listening to something God *once* said. We are listening to God speaking *live* to us now. This is Catholic doctrine,[3] but I fear that we don't take it seriously enough.

---

of this. Lay people who participate in the musical selection process (e.g., for weddings or funerals) usually need some brief catechesis on this before getting down to specifics.

[3]The "live" character of the scriptures proclaimed at liturgy is taught clearly in the Vatican II Constitution on the Liturgy and in the General Instruction of the Roman Missal:

"He [Christ] is present in his Word, since it is *he himself who speaks* when the holy Scriptures are read in the Church." (Const. on Liturgy, #7; emphasis added)

"When the Scriptures are read in the Church, *God Himself is speaking to his people,* and Christ, present in his own word, *is proclaiming the Gospel....*" (General Instruction of the Roman Missal #9; emphasis added)

"In the readings...*God is speaking to his people,* opening up to them the mystery of redemption

The living character of the Word means not only that God *is* speaking to us live, but also that God's Word is *enlivening.*[4] It is a graced word that has a quickening power. It is more than a word that is true and points us in the right direction. It is, to use traditional terminology, an "efficacious sign" that brings about the redemption to which it points. It shapes individuals. It shapes the church.

When Jesus says, "It is the spirit that gives life," he immediately speaks about his *words:* "The *words* I have spoken to you are spirit and life." (Jn 6:63) Several verses later, Peter says, "Master, to whom shall we go? You have the *words* of eternal *life.*"

Saint Paul says, "For I am not ashamed of the gospel. It is *the power of God* for the salvation of everyone who believes." (Rom 1:16; emphasis added)

The flow of this graced, living, quickening word is what we homilists try to discern.

2. To Help Illuminate This for the Assembly

Having attempted to discern what the Lord is speaking to us through this event, the second task of the homilist is to help illuminate this for the assembly.[5]

We homilists need to remember that a great deal has already been happening before the homily. Songs, symbols, prayers, and the Word of God have been flowing upon all of us. Our task is to help the flow of what is already taking place. We are not making it happen; we are helping it happen.

> For just as from the heavens
>   the rain and snow come down
> And do not return there
>   till they have watered the earth,
>   making it fertile and fruitful...
> So shall my word be
>   that goes forth from my mouth;

---

and salvation, and nourishing their spirit; *Christ is present to the faithful* through his own word." (Ibid., #33; emphasis added)

[4] In John's Bread-of-Life section (Chapter 6), a great deal of the focus is on the Word, and it is a living word. Jesus speaks of himself as the "living" bread that comes down from heaven. (Cf. Brown, *The Gospel According to John*, Anchor Bible, vol. 29 [New York: Doubleday, 1966, pp. 255–304].)

[5] One might ask, "Why even have a homily? Why not just proclaim the Word and sit down?" Because we believe that the reception of the Word can be helped, assisted. We believe that God acts through others, in this case those who preach. The ministry of the homilist is an important part of our liturgical tradition.

It shall not return to me void,
    but shall do my will,
    achieving the end for which I sent it.
                (Is 55:10–11)

We minister gifts that are not our own, gifts that have more formative power than our eloquence.[6]

3. <u>To Do All This on Behalf of the Church</u>

When we preach a homily, we do so *on behalf of the church.* It is not as though we who preach are the recipients of personal revelations or function as freelance spokespersons for God.

We participate in the gift of the Spirit given to the church. We are sharing not simply our faith, but the faith of the whole church. That is why a homily is different from giving personal witness. There can be a time and a place for that, but a homily is wider than personal witness.

Homilists have to be attentive to the faith of the whole church as they discern what the Lord is speaking in this event. We have to express this in a way that is personal (i.e., from the heart), but not in a way that limits the breadth of the message to the width of our own personal experience.[7]

Some Corollaries

If one truly ministers the Word of God in the way we've been describing, there are a number of corollaries.

---

[6]The homily is more than the external application of an old text to the contemporary scene: It is a faithful ministry of the living Word that emerges with new meaning "for us and for our salvation." The Pontifical Biblical Commission in its 1993 document entitled *The Interpretation of the Bible in the Church* speaks of *actualization* (i.e., discovering what the text has to say at the present time) and *inculturation* (i.e., situating the text in a specific community with its culture).

On Actualization: "The Church, indeed, does not regard the Bible simply as a collection of historical documents dealing with its own origins; it receives the Bible as word of God, addressed both to itself and to the entire world *at the present time.*" (PBC, IV, emphasis added) "Actualization is necessary because, although their message is of lasting value, the biblical texts have been composed with respect to circumstances of the past and in language conditioned by a variety of times and seasons. To reveal their significance for men and women of today, it is necessary to apply their message to contemporary circumstances and to express it in language adapted to the present time." (PBC IV A 1)

On Inculturation: "Inculturation is not a one-way process; it involves 'mutual enrichment.' On the one hand, the treasures contained in diverse cultures allow the word of God to produce new fruits and, on the other hand, the light of the word allows for a certain selectivity with respect to what cultures have to offer: Harmful elements can be left aside and the development of valuable ones encouraged." (PBC IV B)

[7]Cf. Chapter 18 on the need for homilies to be personal.

- **The preparation process can be more enjoyable.**

There is a sense of freedom. No longer is it a weekly task to come up with an original talk; instead, we participate in and help with something that is already taking place and is very good. The proclaimed scriptures are flowing, and we are trying to help them along. Discerning the flow will require study, prayer, interpretation; presenting it will require some creativity. But there is not so much depending on ME.

- **We never have to worry about running dry.**

Our own stories and files of material are like the oil reserves with only a fixed quantity, but the scriptures are living waters that never run dry, and the life of the community is not static. Endless riches continually open up when the living word engages with life.

- **We don't have to come up with a new topic every Sunday.**

We can feel more at home preaching several Sundays in a row on the same thought; for example, during the Easter season, the emphasis is on the Spirit, a neglected part of our preaching. (We tend to emphasize the earthly ministry of Jesus.) If we preach about the Spirit one Sunday, the next week we might say, "I've already done that. I have to come up with a new topic." Not true. I can speak about the same topic and even spin out the same basic truth over and over with a freshness each time. Homilies on successive Sundays are not individual talks; they are illuminations of the live scriptures happening each Sunday.

- **Great homilies are within the reach of homilists who are not great speakers.**

Attention is less focused on the homilist, more on the Word of God. Our respect and love for the Word will show through and have an effect. The focus will be more on the God-given insight rather than on the homily or the homilist. Rather than the people being taken with the homily or the homilist, it's more important that they be taken with what the Lord is speaking to us. A good homily still requires basic speaking skills, but these are within reach. We don't have to be gifted raconteurs, entertainers, or even extroverts.

- **Our homilies will have much more diversity.**

When we use the text as a touchstone for something we want to say or for something that strikes us in prayer, each individual homilist— depending on temperament, special interests, where he or she is on the enneagram, Myers-Briggs, and so forth—tends to gravitate toward topics to which he or she is naturally inclined: interpersonal relationships, social justice, doctrinal teachings.

On the other hand, if we stand humbly before the text and listen to what God is saying to us through this event, we are less apt to give homilies whose sameness of theme is due to our own inherent inclinations. At times, the Lord will lead us where we do not want to go. (Cf. Jn 21:19)

- **We will preach more directly about God, Jesus Christ, the Spirit.**

I have discovered that people often think that in our preaching we are more focused on the church than on Jesus Christ and his teachings. Think for example of how often people ask us a question by saying something like: "By the way, what does the church teach about such and such?" Seldom do they say, "What does the Lord teach about such and such?"[8]

- **We will preach the basic truths of our faith.**

Scripture will be our guide (not a touchstone for our own thoughts). It will take us to the depths of revealed truths and to the depths of human life. Left to our own choice of topics, some of our most fundamental truths will be neglected either because they seem too obvious or too difficult.

This, I believe, has been a great neglect for some time. We don't preach the fundamental truths—God, the Holy Spirit, redemption, grace. Not long ago, I asked a group of grade-school youngsters (K through 8) to tell me about Jesus. They talked about his birth, his miracles, and how he helped people. When I pressed them as to whether Jesus was *God,* I was surprised to see most of them shake their heads no. Our first reaction might be to blame this on religious-education programs. But what about our preaching?

One of the problems in today's church is that we've been busy arguing about altar girls, inclusive language, who can be called a pastoral minister...and the good news of the core truths *on which we all agree* is neglected. (That's one mistake the fundamentalist preachers have not made.)

- **The effect of such homilies will tend to be long term.**

Generally speaking, these kinds of homilies won't individually seem

---

[8]Commenting on the institutions of Christendom just before the Reformation, Pelikan makes an observation that all homilists might keep in mind: "Intended as windows through which we might catch a glimpse of the Eternal, they [the institutions of Christendom] had become opaque, so that the faithful looked *at* them rather than *through* them. The structures of the Church were supposed to act as vehicles for the spirit—both for the Spirit of God and for the human spirit.... Captive in ecclesiastical structures that no longer served as channels of divine life and means of divine grace, the spiritual power of the Christian gospel pressed to be released." (J. Pelikan, *Spirit Versus Structures: Luther and the Institutions of the Church* [New York: Harper and Row, 1968, p. 30]; emphasis added)

as sensational. They won't sound as innovative or clever. The effect will be cumulative, formative, and the result of continued exposure to the living Word of God, much like steadily praying the scriptures in *lectio divina.* And the effect will be powerful, for the Word of God is powerful. People will begin to listen to the readings more receptively. The people will be less taken with the homily, and more taken with the deep-down insight that broods in their souls. Their appreciation will tend to be quietly long term rather than instantly ecstatic.

The effects of eating healthily are not strikingly manifest after the first day or week of doing so, nor would we react to every fine meal by calling it sensational. Only over the long haul do we sense the effects of eating well. The same is true of fine homilies.

A Closing Thought

It is not the power of the homilist but the power of the Word of God that shapes the church and shapes the individual believer. The *skill* of the homilist comes into play, but it is a skill used to minister the Word of God, not our own thoughts.

Pastoral leaders who wish to affect, change, and form their people will do so most of all not by their own persuasiveness or cleverness, not by programs, policies, or organizational ability, but by truly ministering the living word of God—letting this "sacrament" pour its light upon the community and illumine life.

Imagine what would happen if, in churches around the world, the formative power of the Word of God were turned loose.

In the Capernaum synagogue, Jesus took on a shouting unclean spirit, and commanded it to leave the man. It did. The people "were all amazed and said to one another, 'What is there about his word?'"

What is there about his Word? There is everything about his Word. It is a graced Word that accomplishes more than truckloads of our own.

CHAPTER THREE

What Isn't Quite a Homily

"He's interesting, even entertaining, but it doesn't come from him. It's all cut-and-paste."[1]

———————————

A good way to get hold of what we've said so far is to contrast it with other approaches. Here, in caricature, are five types of homilies that take an approach other than "engaging the living scriptures to discern what God is speaking to us here and now."

1. Old homilies heated up in the microwave

We've all done this. We take an old homily and simply reheat it for the occasion.

This is not to say that we can't use anything we've ever used before, but there's a difference between drawing upon former insights and simply repeating a performance.

Mission appeals are a common example. Not all of them do this, but some mission preachers use the same stock homily for months (even years) and artificially connect it with the scripture readings each weekend.[2] Such reruns are not true homilies *if* a homily is the ministry of the

———————————

[1] Feedback from one of the folks.

[2] But mission appeals aren't the only examples. There are also stock confirmation homilies, stock wedding homilies, and more. These are really not homilies if we agree that the role of the homilist is to discern what the Lord is saying to us live here and now in the convergence of these scripture readings and this setting.

18

living Word of God, which is always fresh—and fresh, by the way, not only for the people, but also for the homilist.

2. "Carryouts"

Some homilies are freshly cooked for this occasion, but the food wasn't cooked in this kitchen. It came from somewhere else and is linked to the scriptures post factum. It may be a terrific movie we just saw and are determined to use as the core of this weekend's homily, even though we haven't yet looked over the scriptures, or it may be a talk predetermined apart from discerning the scriptures, for example, Stewardship Sunday.[3]

Whatever the type, such homilies do not come from "this kitchen," that is, what the Lord is cooking in these scripture readings at this event. They come from somewhere else and are connected to the readings after the fact.[4]

3. Homilies "triggered by" but not "flowing from" the scripture readings

There many ways in which homilies are triggered by scripture.

It can happen when we pray the scriptures of the coming Sunday. Praying the scriptures allows for a much freer use of the text, far beyond its objective meaning. We read with total freedom, allowing the Spirit to guide us to thoughts occasioned by, but not necessarily in, the text.

---

[3]Once, in materials I received for Respect Life Sunday, there was a sample homily. The cover letter indicated that it could be used on any of the Sundays of October because four different endings were provided.

[4]In his book *A Handful of Dust*, Evelyn Waugh has a humorous account of the local vicar in an English village who had previously served many years in India:

"His sermons had been composed in his more active days for delivery at the garrison chapel; he had done nothing to adapt them to the changed conditions of his ministry and they mostly concluded with some reference to home and dear ones far away. The villagers did not find this in any way surprising. Few of the things said in church seemed to have any particular reference to themselves." (New York: Dell Publishing, 1965, pp. 33–35)

Later in the book, he talks about one of the vicar's Christmas sermons: "It was one to which his parishioners were particularly attached. 'How difficult it is for us to realize that this is indeed Christmas. Instead of the glowing log fire and windows tight shuttered against the drifting snow, we have only the harsh glare of the alien sun; instead of the happy circle of loved faces, of home and family, we have the uncomprehending stares of the subjugated, though no doubt grateful heathen. Instead of the placid ox and ass of Bethlehem, we have for companions the ravening tiger and exotic camel, the furtive jackal and the ponderous elephant....' Tony and most of Tony's guests felt that it was an integral part of their Christmas festivities; one with which they would find it very hard to dispense. 'The ravening tiger and the exotic camel' had long been bywords in the family, of frequent recurrence in all their games." (Op. cit., pp. 62–63)

A word or phrase catches us and triggers thoughts that take us down a particular path of prayer. That is an excellent way to pray, but we should keep in mind the difference between this and the homilist's task of discerning what God is saying to *all of us* (the assembly) through these scripture readings.

Another way in which homilies are triggered by the scriptures rather than discerned from them happens when we are looking the readings over (not necessarily praying them) and are struck by something that gives us a great idea for a homily. For example, the gospel includes this passage:

> Jesus said to them, "Come and see." So they went and saw where he was staying...and they stayed with him that day. It was about four in the afternoon. (Jn 1:38–39)

We are struck by the mention of "four in the afternoon" and decide to talk about our use of time in this busy world. Although the mention of time is indeed in the text, it's a bit of a stretch to say that this is the flow of the text.[5]

4. Homilies that are built on an accommodated sense of scripture

The "accommodated sense" is a meaning *given to* the text rather than what the text objectively means. In many respects, it is closely related to #3 just above.

We read in Mark: "As he passed by the Sea of Galilee, he saw Simon and his brother Andrew casting their nets into the sea." (1:16) One might wish to take the word *casting* and talk about their willingness to cast their cares upon the Lord and then build a homily on trust in the Lord, and so on.

While the accommodated sense can have a place in reflections and meditations, it is not what is meant by the homilist's interpretation of the word and discernment of what God is speaking to the whole community. In his NJBC article on the accommodated sense, Raymond Brown says this about preaching:

> Preachers may find accommodation easy and may resort to it rather than taking the trouble to draw a relevant message from the literal sense of Scripture. They are then in danger of substituting their own ingenuity for God's word.... But, in general, now that we have come to recognize the tremendous wealth of the literal

---

[5]One of the tip-offs to the fact that we are using scripture this way is that we stop reading the gospel as soon as we get the idea, without finishing the reading or necessarily looking at the other readings.

sense of Scripture, a sound exposition of that sense will render far more service than ingenious accommodation.[6]

5. "Teachings" vs. homilies

Every good homily teaches in the sense that something is learned. Here, however, we're talking about homilies whose main objective is to convey *information* about scripture, doctrine, or church practices.[7] The assigned readings provide wonderful opportunities to teach, and if there is something of the teacher in us, we want to take advantage of it.

For example, on the 29th Sunday, C Cycle, the second reading has the phrase, "All scripture is inspired by God." (2 Tm 3:16) This, the biblical root of our doctrine on inspiration, could easily lead into a talk explaining what we mean and do not mean by *inspiration*.

If, however, a homily is a ministry to help the flow of what God is saying to us through this event, then we have to resist the temptation to use the homily to teach *about* the scriptures, or *about* doctrines. No matter how good our teaching might be, ministering the real presence of the graced Word of God will have more powerful effects.[8]

It should be noted that the above approaches need not result in a "bad" message; the message taken by itself may be excellent. The problem is that such homilies fail to draw upon the power of the graced Word of God that is happening now, is fresh, and is for all of us. Such homilies become *our* word linked with part of the text rather than a ministry of *God's* Word flowing from the entire event.

---

[6]New Jerome Biblical Commentary, 71:79. Another example of the accommodated sense is given by Pope John Paul II in his encyclical *Redemptoris Mater* when he quotes this text from Colossians: "Your life is hidden with Christ in God." (3:3) The objective meaning of the text is the share that Christians have with the risen Christ. In the encyclical, the pope cites it in developing his reflections on Mary living with Jesus during the years of his "hidden life." This is clearly an accommodated sense. Such usage is legitimate in reflections, in meditations, and in the context of this encyclical, but is not proper for homilies. (Cf. Fitzmyer, *Louvain Studies 20* [1995, pp. 139–140].)

[7]"...the ministers of the Word have as their principal task, not simply to impart instruction but also to assist the faithful to understand and discern *what the Word of God is saying to them* in their hearts when they hear and reflect upon the Scriptures." (Pontifical Biblical Commission, *The Interpretation of the Bible in the Church*, 1993, III B 3, emphasis added)

[8]To illustrate the difference between teaching and homilizing, imagine being asked to preach at a gathering of famous theologians and scripture scholars. A natural reaction might be to beg off or at least to suffer intimidation. But why? A person qualified to preach is qualified to preach to these people. You're not teaching them (you couldn't). You're not writing a talk for them to admire. You have the scripture readings. You are a minister of what they carry within. You are a waiter. What is there to worry about?

CHAPTER FOUR

The Beginnings of Homilies

"Tell them to go right to the middle of it."[1]

The first thing to say about beginnings is that homilies don't need one, that is, a specialized piece called a beginning. Some talks do, but homilies don't. Keep in mind that the liturgy already had a beginning (the gathering rite).

In public-speaking courses, it is common to suggest an attention getter; thus the stock joke or anecdote that predictably begins most talks.

In a homily, the last thing we need is an attention getter. Everything preceding the homily is an attention getter: the people stand, sing alleluias, listen to the gospel, sit down, and hang on our first words. The trick isn't to *get* their attention; it's to *hold on to* the attention we've already got.[2]

The best way to do this is usually to "go right to the middle of it." Our reluctance to do that may stem from the fear that we won't have anything left to say. We feel we have to hold back on the heart of our homily and

---

[1] The dinner host mentioned to a guest that I was writing a book on preaching and asked if he had any suggestions. He thought for a moment and simply said: "Tell them to go right to the middle of it."

[2] It may happen that the assembly is "dead," distanced, nothing happening between us and them. We may need to do something to strike a spark of life. A short quip might do it. That, however, is quite different from a planned full-fledged story, and it should be the exception.

lead into it gradually. But many people feel that we should go more quickly into the heart of the homily. Here is a sample of their comments.

Feedback from the Folks

- "I like the way he gets right into it."
- "I'm tired of long beginnings."
- "Get to the point."[3]
- "Get *me* into it right from the start."
- "She gets too wrapped up in the stories she tells at the beginning and goes on too long with lots of unnecessary details."
- "The start-ups are pretty interesting, although there's not much 'religious' about them. After that it gets boring."
- "He starts by retelling the story we just heard in the gospel. It drives me crazy!"

What We've Learned

In our homily sessions, we noticed three common problems with beginnings:

1. Too sloppy

Our first few sentences are often flabby, puffy, and filled with unnecessary verbiage. The people are hanging on our first words, and we're meandering along.

Some homilies are like the takeoff of a plane: the long slow taxi from the gate to the runway, the gradual roll toward takeoff, and finally the lift-off from the ground. The takeoff image should apply, not to the homily, but to the gathering rite—the people arriving and gradually assembling together and then lifting themselves up to the Lord in the gathering song.[4]

2. Too long

Our opening material is usually easy to talk about, so we chat on and enjoy it. If it's a story, we milk it. Wordy beginnings dull the point of the message and waste the people's attention when it is sharpest. The concern here is not the length of the homily; it's the sharpness.

---

[3] This phrase, almost word for word, was echoed repeatedly.
[4] Perhaps the launching of a rocket would be a better image for a homily.

3. A separate piece unto itself

Many a beginning is artificially linked to the rest of the homily and throws no light on our core thought. It doesn't need the rest of the homily, and the rest of the homily doesn't need it. A good test of a beginning is to see if the material could easily fit later in the homily. If not, it is probably unnecessary.[5]

Some Examples

Here are some excerpts from actual homilies:

> As some of you know, I was away last weekend. I spent a few days visiting some good friends of mine in Chicago. Someone asked me about my golf game. Well, it isn't worth talking about, I'll clue you. Nothing to brag about. But one of the things we did that certainly for me was a reflection on the gospel we hear this weekend, and I hope I can convey the impact of it with you. On Sunday evening three of us drove...

The edited version:

> Last Sunday evening, three of us drove....

Another example:

> On Sunday and part of Monday and Tuesday, I was up north with some friends I'd known for a long time; and even though the ice wasn't too thick, there were people out on the ice fishing. It was so nice out, I went outside, and a couple of the men with a couple of children, late in the afternoon, came back from fishing and were walking by the house, and so I said, "Hi. How was the fishing?" And they said, "Not very good. We just got a few nibbles." A couple of weeks ago some people directly to the south of here—a father and son, and another man and I'm not sure who else—had been fishing for a good week, and they caught almost nothing. They had some nibbles too but not a whole lot. It was a lot like those fishermen in the gospel....

The edited version:

> I was recently up north, and people were out fishing on the ice. Late in the afternoon, a couple of fishermen were walking back, and I asked them, "How was the fishing?" They said, "Not very

---

[5]For an example of this, see pp. 73-74.

good. We just got a few nibbles." It was a lot like those fishermen in the gospel....

Another example:

All of us know that change is difficult, and I realize that the older I get, the harder it seems, but it's true. I think all people tend to find change—at least many kinds of change—difficult. In a way, that's strange because we have had to live through more changes in our lifetime, in our era, than human beings have ever had to experience in their whole lives. So change has been a constant thing for us, and still it can be difficult, and today's readings tell us that change....

The edited version:

Change is difficult. The older I get, the harder it seems. That's strange because we've had to live through more changes in our lifetime than any human beings in history. Today's readings tell us that change....

Another example:

It's good to be back with you again. Father Bill benevolently gave us deacons the month of July off, so it's good to be here again. Also, I got a rude awakening at the 5:00 mass last evening with Father Bob, who is so tall, and I certainly found out what Mutt and Jeff felt like in the world, so Father Bill, it's good to be with you eyeball to eyeball today. And we did promise Father Bob that we'll help him in any way we can...but it's up to you to improve his golf game.

We hear in this weekend's scriptures the universality of God's love, mercy, and care of all people. I was thinking back to just a few weeks ago to the two weeks of the Olympics: How wonderful was the universality of sportsmanship....

The edited version:

I was thinking back to the Olympics just a few weeks ago, and how wonderful was the universality of sportsmanship....

A Lesson from Music

Writing a homily is something like writing a song. Some songs have a first part, and some don't. If they do, it's not a separate piece. The words and chord structure are closely connected with the rest of the song. For example here are the words to the first part of "White Christmas":

> The sun is shining,
> The grass is green,
> The orange and palm trees sway.
> There's never been such a day
> In Beverly Hills, L.A.
> But it's December the 24th.
> And I am longing to be up north.

This leads perfectly into the rest of the song.[6]

Some Tips

1. <u>When Writing a Homily, Don't Begin with the Beginning.</u>
The toughest part of the writing stage of homily preparation is getting started. Don't waste time trying to write the beginning. It would be like an author starting a book by working on the Foreword.

Better to start in the middle by trying to sketch your core thought. You can figure out later what your first words will be...and blessed be the homilist whose first words go right into the core thought. (Remember that great tip: "Tell them to go right to the middle of it.")

2. <u>Don't Use a Formal Beginning.</u>
I refer here to the Sign of the Cross, or "My dear friends in Christ," or "Your Eminence, Cardinal (_____), Archbishops, Bishops, Monsignori, Reverend Fathers, and so forth."

Such beginnings overlook the fact that there was a gathering rite. They also reinforce the impression that the homily is a separate talk rather than part of the flow of the liturgy.[7]

---

[6]Interesting that this first part is cut in most recordings. Even good first parts are often expendable. Note also that there are many well-known songs that don't have a first part (e.g., "I Whistle a Happy Tune" and "You'll Never Walk Alone"). Both of these were in Broadway plays and didn't need a first part because they flowed right out of what was already taking place—which is precisely what a homily is supposed to do.

[7]Note the response of the Congregation for the Sacraments and Divine Worship: "QUESTION: Is it advisable to invite the faithful to bless themselves before or after the homily, to address a salutation

3. Don't Make the Beginning More Interesting than the Rest of the Homily.

I say this tongue in cheek. What I'm really saying is, "Make the rest of the homily as interesting as the beginning." (This becomes difficult if the beginning is the sensational attention-getter type that doesn't really connect with the rest of the homily. When we cross the bridge into the real homily, the people are still enjoying the unconnected first part.)

It is particularly fatal if, after a clever beginning, we say, "As we heard in our (first reading, or gospel)...." People take this as a code phrase for, "Now here comes the boring religious stuff."[8]

4. Don't Begin by Retelling the Gospel.

Retelling the gospel came up repeatedly, and it was a sore point, far more than I realized. Avoid it at all costs, not only at the beginning but anywhere in the homily. (We'll treat this more extensively in Chapter Twenty-Six entitled "Ten Demons.")

5. Don't Begin by Telling What Happened When You Found Out You Were to Give This Homily or While You Were Preparing It.

This is standard filler material at the beginning for those who are nervous and/or not skilled in public speaking. It is done so frequently in talks that it is trite. Imagine if Tom Brokaw were on vacation and the substitute anchor began the newscast by saying, "When I found out that I was to give the newscast tonight, my first thought was what I would choose for an opening story. Then when I started to go through the material, it occurred to me that perhaps I would begin instead with the kind of story that is most often left out. But then I thought it over and decided that the best way to start would be to..." and so on. Not a chance.

The same goes for a homily. Listeners say to themselves, "I'm not here to find out how you felt when you were asked to give the homily or what happened while you were writing it. I want to hear the homily."

---

to them, for example, 'Praised be Jesus Christ'? REPLY: It all depends on lawful local custom. But generally speaking it is inadvisable to continue such customs because they have their origin in preaching *outside mass*. The homily is *part* of the liturgy; the people have already blessed themselves and received the greeting at the beginning of mass. It is better, then, not to have a repetition before or after the homily." (Notitiae 9 [1973] 178; Cf. also *Fulfilled in Your Hearing*, p. 23.)

[8]When writing Chapter 17 on "Jargon," I reviewed homily transcripts looking for positive examples of concrete, real-life language. It was striking that the highest percentage of concrete language was toward the beginning of homilies.

What it comes down to is this: The homily is a continuation of the flow of the graced Word of God. The beginning shouldn't interrupt the flow. A quip, a joke, comments about how I reacted when asked to give the homily, a formal acknowledgment of various people present—all these interrupt the action. The word was flowing, and it needs to keep flowing.[9]

---

[9]There are exceptions, times when you have to do *something* to break the ice because it is an occasion when many are strangers to one another and/or to you (for example, at an ecumenical service in the neighboring Methodist church.) Ideally, rapport with the assembly can be established by some exchange with the assembly before the service begins, but that is not always within our control.

CHAPTER FIVE

Endings

Ending a homily is like trying to get out of a canoe.

The ending is the least-prepared part of most homilies, so much so that I have come up with this rule: "Don't ever begin to preach a homily unless you know what your last two sentences are going to be."

We have the illusion that the homily will end itself: After all, we know where our material ends, and when we get there, well we'll just "end." It doesn't work that way. Ending a homily is tricky business, like trying to get out of a canoe.

A class ends itself. We've finished our material and say, "Well, let's call it quits for today. We'll pick up tomorrow where we left off."

But we can't end a homily that way because it's part of the liturgy and has a certain ritual quality. We have to round it off nicely; sometimes, in trying to round it off, we end up going round and round.

A bad ending can do serious damage to a good homily. It's a shame because it doesn't have to be that way, and it's easily fixable.

Winging an Ending?

Going into an ending unprepared is like going into a haunted house without a flashlight. The demons are lurking there ready to leap out: repetition, church-speak, filler, a new thought.

Ad-libbed endings are the dreaded part of many homilies. As one of the folks commented, "It's painful watching him trying to end."[1]

Feedback from the Folks

People talked more often about endings than beginnings, and their comments zeroed in on the same few concerns:

- "The thing I like about our priest is that he doesn't take forever to wrap it up."
- "We know when he's done, but that doesn't mean he stops. We stop listening but he keeps going around in circles."
- "Oh how I wish homilies would have clean endings."
- "What drives me crazy are false endings. They use words like *finally* or *and so,* but then you watch them pick up steam and get into something else."
- "When he says what he has to say, he ends it, and that's that."

Some Tips

1. It's Not Hard to Write an Ending.

Writing an ending is not nearly as hard as developing the core thought (which we've already done). We don't have to start from scratch and create an ending out of thin air. All we have to do is to finish off nicely what we already have.

2. The Ending Can Be Quite Brief.

Generally, the shorter the better: The best endings are clean and crisp.

I was recently at a Eucharist for a group of religious. The homilist had an excellent core thought and developed it well. Then he paused, extended his arms toward them, and said, "That's the witness of your life, and we're grateful for it."

---

[1] An interesting sidelight is that the same problem with ad-libbed endings happens when at the beginning of a meeting people are asked to give their names and say a few words about themselves. For some reason, these minispeeches are tricky to end. One person after another gives a few autobiographical details, and then we watch them try to get out of the canoe. After introducing themselves, a typical ending is this:

"And so...I guess that's pretty much who I am...at least it's as much as I guess I want to say [nervous laugh]...and I guess it tells you why I'm here, although sometimes I'm not sure myself. [by now barely audible] But anyway, you've heard it and...well...I could say more but I guess that's enough and so, ah [mumbling to the next person to speak] I guess it's, ah...your turn."

Just 11 words. It was a wonderful ending.

3. <u>Don't Ever Sound Like You're Ending When You're Not Ending.</u>

When I was 15 years old, I was coxswain of an 8-oared rowing crew on the Detroit River. (They want someone light, like a jockey, so sometimes the coxswain is much younger than the crew.) We practiced every day, rowing 4 or 5 miles. One time, we were clipping along at a good pace, and the crew needed a rest. I told them we'd take one, but first I wanted 10 of the hardest strokes they could muster. I began to count them off: "Hit it for ONE. Hit it for TWO...." They were going along so well that I decided to do more than 10.

Now, a crew can't stop unless they all stop at the same time. Otherwise, with the boat moving so fast, with their seats sliding forward and back on each stroke, and with those long oars, there'd be some injuries. So they had to keep going until I gave the command which, after quite a few extra strokes, I did.

They were too exhausted to speak, but managed: "You little %$#@! You say it's going to be 10 strokes, we kill ourselves to hit it hard for 10 strokes, and then you decide to KEEP GOING. Try that again and you're %$#@! overboard."

I try to remember that in homilies: Don't ever say you're ending (or sound like you're ending) and not end.

4. <u>If You Think of an Additional Observation or Clarification Toward the End, Put It Out of Your Mind.</u>

If you are winding down and an additional thought comes your way, never ever try to work it in. The people sense what is happening and grow nervous and edgy, worrying that this new thought could lead to another, and another, like nuclear fission.

I was ending a homily about the need to live up to our baptism and my very last line came out:

> All of us need to have the courage to live up to the decision we
> made at baptism... or the decision that someone else made for us.

The last clause was unplanned and introduced a whole new thought. I wanted to clarify it with something like, "Of course, those of us who were baptized as infants have ratified that decision in our confirmation, and also each time we receive the Eucharist." But for once in my life I resisted the temptation, decided not to try to correct one mistake with another, and just let it be, wishing I had never said it in the first place.

5. Try to Avoid Ending with "AND SO...."

It's often a code phrase for "Here comes the repetition." It also can signal a slow, gradual ending, which we want to avoid as much as a slow, gradual beginning.

6. One of the Surest Ways to End Is with a Short Quote.

The nice thing about a good quote is that it doesn't need any follow-up words. It's the last word. Quotes make for clean, crisp, colorful endings.[2]

7. Don't End by Forcing an Application on the People.

I was quite taken by a comment from one of the folks:

> Tell them that once they've given us the gift of a good thought they shouldn't wrap the gift. Let us use our own wrapping paper, which is to say, let us wrap it in the circumstances of our own life.

The goal of a homily is to get something going in the people—to give them food for thought, not a blueprint for action. One of the best things we can do is to give them an open-ended thought as Jesus did so often with his parables.[3]

8. Since the Homily Is Part of the Liturgy (Rather than a Talk During a Break in the Liturgy), It Should Lead into What Follows.

Just as a plane taking off is not a good image for beginnings, a plane landing isn't a good one for endings. The "landing" is the Dismissal Rite. Our homily is an earlier stage in a "flight" that continues after the homily.

Father Jerry Broccolo always stressed that a homily should "lead into praise prayer." Father John Melloh puts it another way, saying that the homily must always leave the people with "a eucharistic attitude," which means that it flows naturally into the liturgy of the gifts. Our homily should ultimately be cause for thanksgiving to God. Even if our homily is a hard-hitting challenge to conversion, it should include the good news that God gives us grace to change, to see it through.

More can go wrong with the ending than any other single part of the homily. You can take this one to the bank: "Don't ever begin to preach a homily unless you know what the final two sentences are going to be."

---

[2] If we do use a quote, it should be brief. We'll talk more about that in Chapter Twenty-Six.

[3] The great short-story writers (e.g., Somerset Maugham) have crisp, sometimes abrupt endings that seem unfinished and leave you pondering. Homilies that end like that can lead nicely into the rest of the mass and also give us something to take home and think on during the week.

CHAPTER SIX

Preparing a Homily:
Some Preliminary Thoughts

It's harder to build a ship in a bottle than to build a garage.

Homily preparation is difficult to critique for two reasons: First, there isn't one way to prepare a homily. Second, nobody is (usually) there when we do it.

Still, some basics appear to be keys to success, and we'll take a look at them in this and the following five chapters.[1]

Feedback from the Folks

The feedback from the folks repeatedly expressed their sense that homily preparation, or the lack of it, shows up in the homily.

- "I like homilies well prepared, but still fresh, natural."
- "I like it when they've studied and worked hard on it, but don't give us everything they came upon."
- "I prefer some type of orderly sequence."
- "Oh, to have a homilist who doesn't ramble!"

---

[1]A golfer trying to putt can be a parallel here. The pros might look quite similar when swinging the driver, but they are very different when stroking the putter. Even the shapes of the putters differ radically. Still, pros would say that there are some basics that have to be part of any putting method.

- "You can tell when they're ad-libbing, and it's no treat to sit through it."
- "Too often, I find homilies ill prepared and lacking in structure."
- "He has something to say and says it, without drowning it in pointless verbiage."

A Method?

What's the best way to prepare a homily? Excellent suggestions are available in the literature, and I don't intend in these chapters to present a survey or try to blend them all into one. There are countless variations, and each of us has to find the one that works. The important thing is to have a method. All great artists have one.

Experience indicates that somehow the following five steps have to be incorporated into whatever method we use. (We'll talk about each of them in succeeding chapters.)

1. Study the scripture texts (which means more than reading them over).
2. Discern a core thought.
3. Do *some* writing.
4. Do some editing.
5. Get control of your finished product.

Some (Preliminary) Tips

1. <u>Get Started as Early in the Week as Possible.</u>

This has two advantages: First, it gives our thoughts a chance to brew, marinate, and percolate during the week; second, if we start early, much of the research comes to us along the way.

We look at life with the homily in mind. Everything we do—and ministry is full of life's most interesting things—is a catalyst for new insights and fresh thoughts. Great material is all around us.

We can also talk to people about some of our ideas. We may not be part of a homily preparation group, but it's not hard to bounce thoughts off people even in casual conversation. It beats talking about the weather, and people are happy, even honored to be involved in this.

2. <u>Reconcile Yourself to the Fact That It Takes a Long Time to Prepare a Homily.</u>

I've read various time estimates of how long a good homilist needs to spend in preparation. Some are overstated.[2] Six to 8 hours (spread out over the week) sounds reasonable and realistic. Still, in the busy life of most of us, that's a major commitment.

3. Cultivate a Professional Attitude–That of a Scholar, Writer, Artist, and Spiritual Leader.

Too often, we sell ourselves short: "What, me a scholar, professional writer, artist, spiritual leader?" Well, we are, and we ought to live up to it in our homilies. Don't settle for high mediocrity. At some point in our development as a homilist, we need to turn a corner and have the expectation that every homily we prepare will be first rate. Too often we approach a homily with the unconscious objective: What can I put together that will get me through this? We need to raise our sights.

4. Picture the Homily as Small.

There are thousands of people who finished all their doctoral studies but could never get started on their dissertation because it was larger than anything they'd ever written. The very thought of its magnitude paralyzed them.

When it comes to homilies (especially homilies for major events), we tend to imagine something large. Homilies are important, but they aren't large: They're a small part of this large, grand event called the liturgy.

I like to describe a thought with depth as a *pearl*. It conveys the image of something small and valuable. Looking at it this way can have a tremendous psychological effect. During preparation, we're not trying to build a colossus. We're looking for a gem that we can carefully polish and put into a setting.

When I think of the homily as something small, everything changes. I don't rush around to collect things. I search for the pearl of great price, and when I find it, I work with it. It's such a relief to approach it this way, instead of saying, "Well now I've found one thought, and I have to hurry and find a lot more." No I don't. All I have to do is go to the depth of the pearl. A good thought has plenty of richness. Generally, it unfolds into a full-fledged homily of 7 or 8 minutes, (3 minutes is okay too).

With these background thoughts in mind, let's now look at some of the specifics.

---

[2] A homilist was quoted in a Catholic periodical as saying that he spent 60 hours on each homily! That's the sort of thing that makes the rest of us think we can't be great homilists.

CHAPTER SEVEN

Preparing a Homily:
The Scripture Readings

"Whoever preaches, let it be with the word of God." (1 Peter 4:11)

Let's start with another "absolute": To prepare a homily, we have to do some *serious exegetical study* of the scripture readings.

We're talking here about study. That doesn't mean original exegesis, but it does mean going directly to the best exegetical sources. It also means informed theological reflection.

This is a different level than simply reading what someone says *about* what is in the commentaries. Read the experts' commentaries themselves *before* you look at the material provided by a homily service (if you use one). Otherwise, your view is tilted from the start.

Remember: The homilist discerns what the Lord is saying through these graced texts and helps to illumine this for the assembly. We can't do this unless we know what the texts say. We might be able to look the texts over, even pray them, and come up with some of our own thoughts, but that is not what a homily is. Every homily is to some extent an interpretation, but the interpretation must flow from the objective sense of the text itself. In this, it differs from the free association and allegorical meanings often part of our personal prayer.[1]

---

[1] The PBC 1993 document was emphatic on the need for sound exegesis: "The Bible, in effect, does not present itself as a direct revelation of timeless truths but as the written testimony to a

The Epistle of James uses an interesting metaphor for the word of God: Just as a mirror enables us to see what needs to be corrected in our appearance (tousled hair, clothing), so the word of God lets us see ourselves as we are in the eyes of God (Jas 1:23–25). We homilists must take that very seriously: It is critical that we hold before the people the Word of God, not "my reflections on life according to thoughts that came to me while reading scripture." The people need be measured by God's Word, not mine. In the mirror metaphor, the homilist is a light that helps them see what the *Word of God* is conveying.

The Catholic Theological Union in Chicago recently studied 88 homilies given by homilists whose training was post-Vatican II and who agreed to send in a taped homily of their own choosing.[2] They found that a high percentage of homilists tended to "connect" the homily with the scriptures and then do some of their own moralizing...which differs considerably from breaking open the scriptures. Among their conclusions:

> For the most part, homilists used the biblical texts to support or illustrate a preconceived theme or idea of their own....While some homilists did try to engage the text theologically, their efforts reflected a lack of a real understanding of the theological perspectives in the text.

> Almost three-fourths of the homilies that we heard did not reflect sound exegetical preparation and informed theological reflection.

Engaging the text takes work: yet, it has its own reward, a built-in golden opportunity to do something we in pastoral work find so elusive: ongoing study. Many in full-time ministry are unable to set regular time aside to study theology and scripture. The terrain is so vast that we

---

series of interventions in which God reveals himself in human history.... It follows that the biblical writings cannot be correctly understood without an examination of the historical circumstances that shaped them.... To attempt to by-pass [biblical exegesis] when seeking to understand the Bible would be to create an illusion and display lack of respect for the inspired Scripture." (PBC, Conclusion). Also, Fitzmyer makes it clear that actualization and inculturation presuppose a correct exegesis of the text: "One cannot, however, arbitrarily attribute to a biblical text any meaning whatsoever, especially a sense heterogeneous to its expressed wording or content." (Fitzmyer, *America*, Nov. 27, 1993, p. 13; also cf. Louvain Studies 20 [1995] pp. 134–46.)

[2]This study is directed by Leslie Hoppe, O.F.M., and Barbara Reid, O.P. One of its aims is to "develop suggestions for revising the biblical studies curriculum or the curricular objectives of biblical studies courses to facilitate the responsible and creative use of the Bible in preaching." The project is not yet completed or published.

hardly know where to start. We need to have an ongoing project of manageable size with a specific focus.

Writing homilies is an ongoing project of manageable size with a specific focus. Here is an opportunity to develop a consistent, rewarding, and enjoyable pattern of study that provides the continuing education we need to enhance our sense of self worth as professionals.[3]

"Settle In" with the Scriptures

Our time with the scriptures includes study, but it is more than that: We need to settle in, unhurried, and make room for study, prayer, and scribbling.

My guess, based on my own experience and conversations with others, is that this frequently doesn't happen. Our tendency is to scan the readings (they are, after all, familiar texts), trying to get an idea for our homily. As soon as we get one, we're finished with the texts. That would be like quickly scanning a great work of art and then walking away with only the impressions that already fit our pre-conceived perspectives.

Whoa! Not so fast! Settle in with these readings, and open yourself to some fresh thoughts. Light a candle, get out the books and some blank paper, and settle in to enjoy a combination of exegesis, prayer, and scribbling.[4]

Take your time with each text (including the psalm). Use the Bible (not the lectionary) so that you can grasp the surrounding context.[5] Scribble notes along the way. They don't have to be connected or organized; we're not yet settled on a core thought. We're just settling in with the scriptures. Don't pass up the prayer that happens here

---

[3] Every homilist should have a basic library to turn to during this time of preparation. A *minimum* would include:

a fine commentary on *each* of the gospels
gospel parallels
a standard commentary on the whole Bible
a Bible dictionary
a concordance

[4] Besides the professional benefits of this regular study, we should not overlook the place of homily preparation in our own spiritual formation. Careful preparation of homilies places us constantly on the receiving end of the always-fresh, graced Word of God. It gradually has major effects on us and can become one of the most formative elements of our own spirituality.

[5] For example, the reading from Acts on the 6th Sunday of Easter B Cycle is about Peter and the Cornelius event. This event takes in all of Chapter 10 and part of Chapter 11, a total of 67 verses. The lectionary reading has only nine verses, excerpted from three different places. One would never see the whole picture without the full text.

and there. There's no rush (again, the advantage of starting early in the week).[6]

All during this time, the question on our mind is this: In the light of the event of this liturgy, what is the Lord saying to us?[7]

Some Tips

1. Don't Neglect the First Two Readings or the Psalm.

Having listened to countless taped homilies (including my own), I can say with some assurance that preaching on the Old Testament is a rare occurrence. We should take a good look at this. The Old Testament texts describe God interacting with us in wonderfully understandable and human terms. They provide opportunities to connect with feelings that are universal, part of the human condition—fear, anger, disappointment, delight, doubt about whether God cares at all. Philosophical approaches (God as all-knowing, all-powerful, unchangeable) are not the only windows through which we come to know and relate to our God.

Raymond Brown points out another major reason for drawing upon the Old Testament: After their exodus from slavery to liberation, and then centuries later from exile to their homeland, the Hebrews did not enjoy unmixed blessings. There were ups and downs, and some of the "downs" were very long.

> In other words, they lived through *beforehand* what has often been the Christian experience in the centuries *after* Jesus. Both Jews and Christians have needed faith in order to see God's realities in and through a long history where at times God seems to be absent. The New Testament alone covers too short a period of time and is too filled with success to give Christians such lessons.[8]

---

[6]In spending time with the scripture passages, we are not looking to see how they could all fit together. Although that can happen, it doesn't *have* to happen, and we shouldn't force it. We're simply looking at the scripture texts to understand them better and, through them, to discern the answer to the key question: What is God saying to us in this event?

[7]Graham Greene once said that although readers mistakenly think that novelists choose the subject, for the great ones it is the other way around: the subject chooses them. There may be something analogous here for what we're about.

[8]Raymond Brown, *An Introduction to the New Testament* (New York: Doubleday, 1997, p. 328 [emphasis added]).

In practice, homilies usually leave out the second reading too. The failure to look seriously at the second reading during our preparation is a failure to open ourselves fully to what God is saying to us.[9]

The truth is that focusing on the first or second reading (or the psalm) will usually require much more study and therefore much more time. That may be one of the reasons why we seldom do it. I confess that there have been times when I didn't do a stitch of exegesis or reflection on anything but the gospel.

I am not suggesting that homilists should regularly try to *comment* on all the readings. The forced inclusion of all three readings is a mistake. I am simply saying that the process of determining our core thought should include more than the gospel.

2. Don't Avoid Difficult Scripture Passages.

There is an advantage to having the readings assigned rather than choosing our favorites. Assigned readings force us to face texts that we would not otherwise have chosen—either because they are difficult to understand or because they seem offensive (e.g., "If anyone comes to me without hating his father and mother, wife and children...." [Lk 14:26])

In somewhat the same vein, Saint Benedict stressed the need in *lectio divina* to choose a book and to pray through it from beginning to end, not selectively. Abbot Michael Casey, in his excellent book on *lectio divina*, points out that the gift of salvation often runs counter to our own expectations and requires a willingness to transcend our own limited vision and to open ourselves to the action of grace. We have to stop trying to control the process and take the risk of reading what is before us.

> Sacred reading is not merely a form of pious entertainment. Its aim is to confront us with the truth of our own existence, and to accomplish this it has to break down all the barriers that we interpose between our awareness and the truth. We have to move to a level that is different from the one on which we operate in everyday life.[10]

---

[9]As a result of our homily groups, I have been much more attentive to the first and second readings, and now and then make them the focus of the homily. It is refreshing, almost like discovering a new text to preach from.

[10]Michael Casey, *Sacred Reading* (Liguori, Missouri: Triumph Books, 1995, pp. 8–9). One of the times we might be more likely to preach on the first or second reading is the occasion where the gospel is a difficult one. For example, during the latter Sundays of the Easter season, we have those

Fulfilled in Your Hearing also speaks of the wider horizon that difficult texts might bring to us:

> A passage may make no sense to us. It may even scandalize us. We may want to ignore it, but it will not go away. The more we wrestle with it, the more troublesome it becomes.... When this happens we have one of the best signs that we are on to something vital. The Word of God may in fact be challenging our faith, calling us to conversion, to a new vision of the world.[11]

Settling in with the scriptures is a golden opportunity that should not be missed.

---

complex passages from John. We all can identify with the homilist who looks at the gospel and says, "Well, I think I'll preach on the passage from Colossians." That kind of decision is not exactly what is meant by discerning what God is saying to us through these scriptures and this event.

[11]*Fulfilled in Your Hearing*, pp. 32–33.

CHAPTER EIGHT

Preparing a Homily:
Just One Pearl...but of Great Price

There's no sense saying more if it means they'll hear less.

"Too many thoughts" is the most frequently voiced complaint about homilies, a runaway for first place. We need to talk about it.

Homilists are sometimes taught that a homily should have three points. I don't think that this is a normative model, but it presents no problem *if* the three points are the development of one core thought. It becomes a problem when, instead of one core thought with three points, it turns out to be one broad theme with three different thoughts.

Gradually, as we look over our scattered scribblings, think, and pray, we need to focus on just one core thought and stay with it. I refer to it as a "pearl" that I describe as a core thought with depth, a valuable insight to be treasured.

A Pearl

The image of a precious jewel conveys the nature of a homily as distinct from a lesson. Homilies have to do with the rich mysteries of our faith and the word *pearl* catches this.

A pearl is something worth listening to. It doesn't have to be sensational or clever or cute—the clever and cute things are often oversimplifications anyway, like most bumper stickers. A pearl need not contain something new or extraordinary; it simply conveys a profound truth in a way that we all *realize* it with a clarity we didn't have before.

Pearl also expresses compactness, compression, unity. We're not talking about a string of pearls; we're talking about one pearl. *Main thought*, on the other hand, connotes something quite broad and general, like the topic of a long lecture.

Pearl also has a symbolic quality to it, more right-brained I suppose; it evokes the heart. *Main thought* seems logical and discursive and evokes the head. If we ask a homilist, "What is your main thought?" we'll probably receive an intellectual statement. If we ask, "What is your pearl?" we tend to receive something quite different.[1]

The Difference Between One Pearl and One Theme

When talking to someone about a homily, I like to ask: What's your pearl? The ability to respond to this will surface two things: (1) whether the homilist has a thought with richness and depth (thus a pearl) and (2) whether the homilist has just one thought versus a string of flat statements.

There's a difference between one theme and one core thought (pearl): If a homily is united simply by a common *theme*, it usually moves horizontally at a surface level from one thought to another and results in too many thoughts and little depth; if a homily revolves around a pearl, it goes vertically into the depth of one thought.[2]

If asked for the core thought of the homily, the person with many thoughts will state a theme. The person with one good thought can give the pearl. Let's take as an example the gospel passage that says, "You are the light of the world.... Your light must shine before others that they may see your good deeds and glorify your heavenly Father."

---

[1] Sometimes, after a homily, one can ask "What *was* your pearl," and the homilist will give an answer that is quite different from what we heard in the homily. It can make us wish we had asked the question beforehand so that the homilist could have recognized the problem.

[2] Confusing one core thought with one theme happens frequently at funeral homilies. The theme is "the person's life," and the homily is filled with undeveloped and unrelated anecdotes that all fit under this theme. It is not uncommon to have 10 thoughts in a funeral homily. Such remembrances are appropriate at the wake, but they do not comprise a core-thought homily.

If asked what they were going to preach about, a homilist with only a *theme* might say something like:

> I'm going to talk about how we are called to give witness to our faith. We need to stand up for our faith whether we're at home, at work, at school, with our friends. Peter and Paul were willing to do that—they both died as martyrs—and people down through the centuries have done the same. There are martyrs today too. Too often we take our faith for granted and don't realize that we are often out of step with the world around us. We need to give witness to that. [Note: Working within a broad theme like that can result in a homily that has no focus and repeats bromides that we've heard a hundred times.]

On the other hand, a person with a *pearl* might say something like:

> I'm going to use the image of daytime running lights on cars. Their purpose is so *others* can see the car rather than vice versa. People have "running lights" too, from the moment they get out of bed in the morning. Others see our "running lights" whether we intend it or not. We need to take a good look at what they see. [Note: This is an insight that holds great promise for development.]

Feedback from the Folks

Failure to stay with one thought is by far the most common complaint about homilies. Let's hear from the folks. (Usually, they said just about the same thing in different words: stick with one thought.)

- "Make just one point, and let us think about it."
- "She starts out giving a good homily, but then goes on and tries to say too much."
- "Don't forget that there will be other Sundays. You'll get a chance to say more."
- "You don't follow scotch with gin and then have some bourbon. They might all be the very best, but one ruins the other."
- "He wanders from one idea to another—no one central point that you can take home."
- "He gets his point across and then starts repeating it and bringing in all kinds of other things."

• "After listening to these tapes for a couple of years, my major complaint would be: wandering all over the place. Stick to one point."

A Practical Lesson

I'll never forget a great lesson I learned from a veteran newspaperman. It took about 2 minutes. He picked up *Time* magazine and opened to a two-page ad: "Do you know how much an ad like this costs?" I didn't. He said it was something like $50,000 (and that was a long time ago!).

"Now if you're going to spend that much money on two full pages, you try to get in as much information as possible. Right? Wrong. Take a look at this ad."

It was a Ford ad. (I still have it.) Bill Cosby was plugging together a connection in the wiring system. Printed in large letters at the top was "SNAP!" Then beneath the picture:

When you own a Ford, a Mercury, or a Lincoln car with snap connectors, you shouldn't have to worry about these electrical connections.

It's simple. Ford wants to be your car company.

That was it. Two full pages.

Holding the ad in front of me, he said, "If the board of directors had written this, they'd have tried to use up all that extra space with 15 other engineering features. But the advertising pros won't let them. Why? If you filled the pages with print, no one would read anything. So they do it one point at a time. They'll have another one next week. You preachers ought to learn that. There's no sense saying more if it means they'll hear less."

That was the end of my lesson. It was a good one. A homily is not an ad, but some of the principles apply.

I'm convinced: One core thought developed well is far better than two or three.

Some Tips

1. <u>Avoid the Easy Road of Touching Lightly on Several Thoughts Rather Than Going Deeply into One Thought.</u>

For my money, this is the main reason why we fail to limit ourselves to one thought. It's easier to move on to other thoughts than to go deeply into one of them. It's easier to go laterally than vertically. It's like glad-handing at a cocktail party—clever conversations one after another, none of them with depth.

2. <u>Don't Worry About How Brief the Homily Might Be with Only One Thought.</u>

The evening network news has to fill a half-hour of air time; the homily doesn't. If now and then our homily is shorter than usual, we leave no empty space unfilled (as there was when Dan Rather walked off the set during the CBS evening news).

In writing this book, I was concerned about the brevity of a chapter here and there and was tempted to add material. Then I realized that there's nothing wrong with short chapters; readers rarely mind them.

The truth is that if we follow one thought into its depths, we usually find that it's not as brief as we feared.

3. <u>Don't Be Afraid to Cut Some Great Material in Order to Stay Focused on One Thought.</u>

I was recently at a mass where the homilist, a fine, well-prepared speaker, nicely developed a thought drawn from the scriptures. It was excellent. When he finished this (it took about 5 or 6 minutes), he paused and then said, "Now there is another aspect that deserves attention too." He then went on to another excellent thought drawn from the scripture readings.

When I realized that he was starting a second thought, I took particular notice of the effect on the people: more body movement; gradual loss of 100 percent attention; eyes looking downward. They were still thinking about the first thought while trying to listen to the second, and it was hard to hang on to both.

It would have been so, so much better if he had ended after the first thought.

4. <u>Don't Become Trapped into the "I-Only-Get-Them-Once-a-Week" Mentality.</u>

Most parishioners don't come to programs. The weekend mass is our only chance to reach 90 percent of them, so we try to include as much material as possible. But the veteran journalist with the Ford ad was right: "There's no sense saying more if it means that they'll hear less."

It's not easy, this one-thought business. I believe in it, but still it's something I have to fight constantly. Even when I have just one core thought, I have to fight off opportunities along the way to plug in briefly some other thoughts I'd like to include. These tangents, even when small, distract from or dull the point of the core thought.

Staying with one thought is as difficult as biting your lip and not interrupting someone who needs to be listened to.

But overall I'm convinced—and the folks seem convinced: If we want to give effective homilies in the parish setting, the key is one-core thought.[3]

Once we've spent a long time with the scripture readings and discerned the core thought of the homily, we're only halfway home. Now we have to start to think about how to express it.

Sometimes, we're so relieved to have a pearl that we don't give enough attention to the important task of crafting our thought. We harbor the illusion that if we can think the thought, we can express it. Not true. There are many bridges to cross in the presentation. We owe it to our listeners to do this beforehand, not in front of them.

---

[3]There can be exceptions; for example, in a retreat or a monastic setting, the assembly might be disposed to take in a mélange of meditative thoughts on the readings. There are other assemblies that would welcome it too.

CHAPTER NINE

Preparing a Homily: Writing

"Writing is something you can never do as well as it can be done. It is a perpetual challenge and it is more difficult than anything else that I have ever done." (Hemingway)

Writing brings definition to our attempt to express the joy, hope, grief, and anxiety of real life. It's a lot easier to think a good thought than to express it. It's a lot easier to savor the smell of a flower than to describe the experience. Writing brings a homily from existence inside our mind to existence outside our mind—quite a bridge to cross.

Once we've decided on a core thought, we have to figure out how we're going to express it. Writing is the best way to do that.

Doing *Some* Writing When Preparing a Homily

We generally have to do *some* writing to produce a good homily. It may be the whole thing; it may be detailed notes; it may be particular sections. But a lot of writing is essential for most of us. Here are four reasons why:

1. Writing forces clarity.
Through writing, consciousness becomes thought and thought becomes the spoken word. We never really know what we know until

we've written or spoken it.[1] If we simply think about how we'd say it, we may have the illusion that our words are concrete, our transitions smooth, our distinctions clear, and our development coherent. But this all exists vaguely in our minds. When we try to set it down in writing, the vagueness shows.[2]

2. Writing helps to surface fresh thoughts.

Through writing, we find ourselves considering something that we hadn't thought of, a slant that may change our approach or even change the pearl. William Strunk's classic *The Elements of Style* observes that: "...writing is one way to go about thinking."[3]

3. Writing frees us to go beyond the repetitive phrases we customarily use in conversation.

Writing liberates us from the confines of our own habits of speech: "Those who preach only from notes or an outline must constantly fall back on a limited stock of words, phrases, and expressions to state their case. Writing frees the preacher from the tyranny of his own cliches."[4]

4. Writing enables us to edit.

Only with the written word can we do some serious editing, and rarely does a homily have a shot at high quality without some heavy-duty editing. (We'll talk about editing in the next chapter.)

We Are Writers

We need to recognize that while all writers aren't homilists, all homilists are writers. To someone who asks, "What do you do?" we ought to be able to respond, "Among other things, I'm a writer." That sounds quite nice, even classy. Well, it's true, and we homilists should

---

[1] It's one thing to picture in our minds what we are going to say; it's another to select the words and to craft the pieces together. Imagine the person who makes violins. It's one thing to picture what the violin will look like; it's another to select and cut the pieces of wood and craft them together.

[2] Raymond Brown wonders why, because priests are well trained theologically, they don't regularly communicate more-nuanced biblical views in their preaching: "Probably a major factor is that to communicate nuanced biblical views in a way that people will find constructive (rather than puzzling or disturbing) requires more effort and imagination than many preachers are willing to expend. The bland is often effortless ...." (Raymond Brown, *An Introduction to New Testament Christology* [New York: Paulist Press, 1994, pp. 11–12, footnote #14])

[3] William Strunk, *The Elements of Style* (New York: Macmillan, 1979, p. 70.)

[4] John J. Hughes, *Proclaiming the Good News* (Huntington, Ind.: Our Sunday Visitor, Vol. I, pp. 12–13); I have some further comments on this in Chapter Seventeen on "Jargon."

be more conscious of developing our writing skills. No writer (or any other artist) is ever satisfied to stand pat.

It's fascinating to read what some of the great writers say about their art. For one thing, they seem always to be struggling to meet deadlines. It's hard enough to finish the manuscript of their current book—which often enough is behind schedule. They are simultaneously writing articles, book reviews, and shorter pieces that have even more-urgent deadlines. The pressures seem not all that different from those on the homilist who preaches every weekend.

For another thing, it was hard work for them. When Evelyn Waugh began to write *Brideshead Revisited,* he recorded this of a day's work:

> Up at 8:30...and at work before 10. I found my mind stiff and my diction stilted but by dinnertime I had finished 1,300 words, all of which were written twice, and many three times before I got the time sequence and the transitions satisfactory.[5]

Waugh's writings give the illusion of words and sentences flowing easily from his pen. The truth is he worked hard at it: "...He rewrote obsessively, cutting and rephrasing, testing the weight of each significant word and clause."[6]

The simplicity and depth of Cardinal Newman's writings have given him a place in history as one of the greatest English prose stylists. It did not come easily.

> I write, I write again: I write a third time in the course of six months. Then I take the third: I literally fill the paper with corrections, so that another person could not read it. I then write it out fair for the printer. I put it by; I take it up; I begin to correct again: it will not do. Alterations multiply, pages are rewritten, little lines sneak in and crawl about. The whole page is disfigured; I write again; I cannot count how many times this process is repeated.[7]

Most of us probably stopped working on our writing skills a long time ago. We've learned to write adequately—homilies, bulletin articles—and

---

[5]Quoted in Selina Hastings, *Evelyn Waugh* (Boston: Houghton Mifflin, 1994, p. 457).
[6]Op. cit., p. 458.
[7]Quoted in Brian Martin, *John Henry Newman* (New York: Paulist Press, 1982, p. 143).

that seems enough. We've reached a certain level of competence...and stayed there.[8]

I'm not saying that to give good homilies, we should take advanced courses in writing (although that might not be a bad idea now and then). Short of specialized courses, we can consciously work at honing our writing skills and ask people with writing know-how to critique us.

Why don't we? Because we don't think of ourselves as writers. (I notice that writing is hardly ever part of workshops and programs designed for people in pastoral ministry.)

Sketching

An additional thought: For some, it might help to do some preliminary "sketching" before writing. Take a large sheet of paper, and write scattered phrases and thoughts here and there on the sheet, like painting on a canvas; or put down something that may be a key thought, and then surround it with ideas that "radiate" from it by association. Sketching has some advantages:

- When we sketch, we give our imagination free rein and tend to be more spontaneous.
- We are more likely to avoid the fatal error of "beginning with the beginning." When sketching we can begin anywhere with any thought we want. There isn't any A, B, C because we're doing random sketches of thoughts. We don't yet have to think about where this or that is going to fit in or whether it's going to fit in at all. We can simply sketch a thought here and a thought there with a wonderful sense of freedom.[9]
- We more easily throw things out or change directions. In a more sequential framework, we want to maintain whatever line of development we've begun.
- In "sketching," we're more inclined to try something new, to change our style, to break through to something else.

---

[8]It's something like Henry Kissinger who learned English a long time ago and reached a point where he could get along quite well. He stopped there, and that's why this bright, intelligent man still speaks English with a heavy accent.

[9]Another problem with a formal outline is that I tend to want to give each point equal time. Not so when sketching scattered thoughts and phrases.

Whatever our method, we have to do some writing. It forces us to work through all the snafus that can happen when translating thought into speech. We owe it to our listeners to do this in advance, not in front of them.

CHAPTER TEN

Preparing a Homily: Editing

*Many a mediocre homily was one step
away from greatness: editing.*

The purpose of *writing* is to build a bridge from thought to words. The purpose of *editing* is to inspect the results and make some adjustments. And sometimes major adjustments are needed for structural, not simply cosmetic, purposes.

Almost everybody says that their second homily on a weekend is better than the first. Sometimes, the third is best of all. Why? Two reasons: (1) we have better control of our material; (2) we do some major editing before giving the next homily.[1]

Most of us don't realize how much editing professional writers do *after* they've "completed" their article or book, nor do we realize how much their final product is edited after they've sent it in. If you write for a newspaper, your work will be edited. Write an article for a magazine, and your work will be edited. Write a script for a movie or play, and your work will be edited. In the world of writing, there's much editing going on.

---

[1] It seems that no matter how hard I rework a homily beforehand, once I give it, I recognize glaring editing problems. What can we do to gain that clarity *before* we give it the first time? I've tried giving it aloud in my room, even recording it and pretending it was live, all with no success. The only thing I've found that comes close is actually speaking the homily to another person, sometimes on the phone.

A good percentage of the homilies I've dealt with (including many of my own) ended up as good next-to-last drafts, one step away from being great homilies.

Earlier I explained how a journalist in our Saginaw groups edits homilies during each session. For most homilists, this is a new experience. It is also an eye-opener. We discover that editing (sometimes heavy-duty editing) is an important part of preparing a homily.[2]

Rearranging the Sections of a Homily

Rearranging, rewriting, and cutting whole sections are major parts of editing; it is the kind of editing that applies to everyone, whether we write out our homily word for word or use only the barest outline.[3]

Our first go at arranging blocks of material in a homily is not necessarily the best—it would be surprising if our first go were *ever* the best—we have to take a second look not only at individual words but at whole sections. Moving blocks of material around can be a giant step toward improving a homily.

When I listen to taped homilies in preparation for our groups, I usually listen to each homily twice. Most are much clearer the second time because, having heard it all the way through, I now know in advance where they are going, and I see better how the sections connect.

When writing and giving a homily, the homilist always has foreknowledge of how the whole thing is meant to fit together, but the listeners don't know in advance where it's going. They only know what they've heard so far. Many connections that seem so explicit to us are (at best) implicit to the listeners.[4]

---

[2]As I have become increasingly aware of the value—indeed, the necessity—of editing, I am more aware of how often we in church work fail to do it. I am presented with "final copies" of proposed brochures, chancery letters, blurbs, bulletin inserts, only to find out that, although much hard work went into the project being promoted, the *written* piece was simply drafted, given a once-over cleanup, and now is ready to be printed and sent out. That is not how good writing happens. If ever there were texts that needed editing, some of the major candidates are the written materials produced at the local, diocesan, or national level, including some of our NCCB documents.

[3]It is my opinion that those who don't write out a homily should at least sketch its development in writing so that they can look it over and edit the arrangement of or the value of the individual sections. We need to write a sentence or a phrase that captures the essence of each section. We can then look at the whole thing, imagine ourselves giving it, and do some serious editing.

[4]This is an example of the value of having someone listen to my homily beforehand. A lot of obscurities can be cleaned up. Having someone read my written text is not as helpful—the reader

A good exercise when preparing any homily is to try to come up with a short title for each section (the way captions are sometimes used in published articles). By doing this, we quickly discover editing problems:

1. Having a hard time coming up with a concrete caption for a particular section probably indicates that the section doesn't have a clear focus.

2. Once the captions are in place, we have a better sense of the overall structure and flow of the homily. We become more aware of the transitions or lack of transitions.

3. We are more likely to rearrange whole sections, which can be a very creative part of editing. (In our groups, we often note major rearrangements that would have greatly improved the homily.)

Editing: The Pain of Cutting

In *Death in the Afternoon* Hemingway has one of his characters say something that all authors should keep in mind:

> No matter how good a phrase or a simile he may have, if he puts it in where it is not absolutely necessary and irreplaceable he is spoiling his work for egotism. Prose is architecture, not interior decoration, and the Baroque is over.[5]

Hemingway was true to his word and is said to have cut nearly 100,000 words from *To Have and Have Not.*[6]

Using the scalpel is the most painful part of editing. Once we put a phrase or sentence down on paper, it takes on a life of its own, and we hate to scrap it. To cast into oblivion something we created goes against our protective instincts, so we talk ourselves into keeping it, sometimes by putting it somewhere else in the homily.[7]

I have recently come upon a (nearly) painless way to cut material from something I've written...if I've written it on a computer. When

---

has the advantage of seeing the paragraphs or of rereading a section. Better for the person to hear it as would someone in the assembly.

[5]Ernest Hemingway's, *Death in the Afternoon* (in Larry Phillips, *Ernest Hemingway on Writing,* New York: Scribner, 1984, p. 72).

[6]Ibid., p. 78. To put this in perspective, the whole book you are now reading has approximately 43,000 words.

[7]Actually, some cuts can be saved for a future life and become the kernel of a future homily or used in a talk or article. There's nothing wrong with that as long as our filing system is up to it.

finished with everything but the editing, I leave the piece in its entirety in the existing file and then put the whole thing into a different file; this second file is the one I use for editing. I can now edit with abandon. I have the security of knowing that, whatever I do here, the original is sitting safe and sound and untouched in the other file. So I rewrite parts with total freedom, ruthlessly cut out anything I think is only mediocre, move sections around, and so forth.

I find that I do much more editing, and I do it faster—and it works! The truth is that I rarely go back to the original to retrieve something I've cut. Too bad I have to trick myself to pull it off.

Eleventh-hour Cuts

In filming the movie *Deliverance* the scene in which Burt Reynolds had a dramatic soliloquy trying to make Jon Voight get hold of himself and find the inner strength to carry on went extremely well.

When the movie was finished, in a private showing for the cast and celebrities, the soliloquy was a showstopper, and when Reynolds finished that scene, the group broke into spontaneous applause. Reynolds felt that it was the best dramatic acting he'd ever done.

Weeks later, just before the picture was to be released, the director met with Reynolds and said that he had some bad news: The scene had to be cut. The problem wasn't quality—it was a terrific scene; length was no problem either. The problem was simply that it didn't fit the story line. In the character development, Jon Voight was supposed to find his strength from within himself. This powerful speech had the effect of making it seem that he was drawing his strength from Reynolds. It had to be cut.

And it was.

Some of the best cuts in homilies come at the eleventh hour, when everything is finished and we've got it the way we want it. We notice some things that we didn't notice before. We begin to feel uneasy that the homily would be better if we cut a whole section, sometimes a major section, a good section. The homily would be better without it.

These eleventh-hour cuts are the most difficult ones to make, and, they're often the ones that improve the homily most. It's never too late, not even if it's 2 minutes before mass.

Cutting Unnecessary Words

Least painful of all (but still painful) is cutting unnecessary words. Edwin Newman some years ago wrote an article about the unnecessary words that creep into our phrasing.[8] Here are some of his examples:

- Instead of a *famine* there are *famine conditions*.
- There are not kinds of this or that. There are *different kinds*.
- *Urban crisis* is not enough. There is an *urban crisis situation*.
- Was it a surprise? No. It was an *unexpected surprise*.
- Are these people in the mainstream? No. They're in the *centrist mainstream*.
- A person said that he had a deeply profound religious experience. Newman wondered how *deep* and *profound* differ.

These are tiny examples. Most of us use a barrelful of unnecessary words in homilies. We don't notice it, and no one calls us to account. An editor would.

Discovering a Better Homily While Editing

Sometimes, a moment comes both wonderful and fearful. We've completed the draft of our homily and are editing it. Something strikes us, and we see the possibility of a whole new direction for our homily. It would in effect be a different homily and a better one.

This is not a rare occurrence. After all, for days we've been thinking about these texts, gathering ideas, and working them into a homily. It should surprise no one that all this could give birth to a new insight, born from the combination of all of the above. (Some of the great dramatists made *major* changes during final rehearsals, that gave the play a significantly different direction, and even eliminated or added one of the characters.)

I know well the feeling, the hesitation, the twinge of fear, the restrained surge of excitement, the thought of all the work it will take, the "go/no" decision we have to make. This is the moment when we need the dedication of a true artist. If our intuition tells us that this new direction would produce a better homily, we get out a new "canvas."

---

[8] I read this in a magazine on an airplane many years ago and only have some notes I took, not the reference.

But to let go of all we've written and to start to craft something new is so hard. One consolation is that developing the new inspiration usually goes faster; we don't start from scratch. It is more like the vine grower pruning the vine so that it bears more fruit.

Some of the best pearls come at a late stage of preparation. I have a feeling that many are lost for lack of nerve. I've heard and read many a homily that was only fair but contained a small thought that could have been the "shoot from the stump of Jesse" that blossomed into a great homily.[9]

It strikes me that the parable of the buried treasure can be adapted as an allegory for this experience. We've been working and plowing, and we accidentally come upon this great treasure, so we sell all we have and buy it.

---

[9] A common mistake is to stay rigidly with the pearl we initially chose. It causes us to put aside (or fail to notice) some of the finest pearls that come our way in the course of developing the original one. A worse mistake is simply to add on the new thought; we then end up with the bane of homilies: too many thoughts.

CHAPTER ELEVEN

Preparing a Homily:
Take Control of Your Material

Good piano players don't play the notes.
They play the song.

After all of the above, we may think we've finished our preparation. Not true. There's one more critical step: taking control of our material.

Failure to take hold of our material and have it well in hand would be like sculpting a great art work and then shipping it without proper packing. The whole thing arrives, but damaged.

This step is a sleeper, and we don't hear much about it. I'd rate it as one of the most important parts of preparation, and the one most overlooked.

- Just because we've written a homily doesn't mean that we have control of it.
- Just because we can get through a homily without leaving anything out doesn't mean that we have control of it.
- Just because we have all the words memorized doesn't mean that we have control of it.
- Just because we have notes or even the full text in front of us doesn't mean that we have control of it.

Taking control of our material means being fully at home with it so that we can speak personally and with a certain amount of freedom. It means having the *whole* so well in hand that we don't have to be pre-occupied with scattered *parts*. We could say what we want to say six different ways.

Imagine if you right now were asked to tell the story of the Good Samaritan—not recite it word for word, just tell the story in your own words. You could do it at the drop of a hat. If asked to do it again a week from now, some of the words might be different, but the heart of the story would be the same. That's what it means to have control of your material. Frank Sinatra once said that movie-acting wasn't difficult at all. You simply had to know your lines like you knew your name. (That would also be a very good tip for lectors.)

A major reason why our homily at the second mass is often better is because we have control of our material.[1] Too bad we don't have it that well in hand before the first mass.

We can tell whether we have control of our material if, after preparing it:

- without the text or notes, we can easily give an abbreviated version of it to someone (an excellent exercise, by the way).
- we know for sure what parts are core and what parts are not.
- we are ready to go out there with full confidence of being able to leave some things out, rearrange sections, or extemporize enhancements, without going off on a tangent.

How Do We Take Control of Our Material?

Methods of taking control of our material will vary, depending on whether we preach with a text in front of us or preach with nothing in front of us. But for everyone, even those who use the full text, taking control of the material involves more than going over it a couple of times.

One good method of taking control of the material is this:

- Once you have the final product, list on a blank sheet of paper a short sentence (or phrase) for each of the major sections, skipping a couple of lines between each. This is not an outline (you leave out a

---

[1] This is probably why homilies at special events (e.g., the installation of a bishop, anniversaries, ordinations, big funerals) are often not so good—these are one-time homilies. Presumably, if we had a chance to preach it a second time, we'd have a better sense of and control of our material, and we'd make major changes.

lot of things that would be in an outline). You should end up with only three or four (not many more) sentences/phrases.

- Go over these until they are *completely* clear in your mind. Above all, get a sense of how they flow from one to the other. Work with them until you have the conviction that it would be impossible to forget these kernels.

- "Let go" of the rest. You don't scuttle it; you simply decide that you are going to focus on the pillars of your development and talk about them from the heart. You're not going to worry about the exact words for each.[2] [Note that this doesn't mean that all the effort we spent writing the whole thing was wasted time. The primary purpose of writing in preparation for a homily is not to produce a great text; it is to think through a *thought* that will become a great homily and to work through ways of expressing and organizing this thought. Too many homilists mistakenly worry more about the words and phrases than the core thought. Take hold of the thought and you take hold of your homily.]

Now you're ready to go out and preach from the heart.[3]

The Ego...Plus the Risk

What's difficult about this is letting go of all those things we worked so hard to craft, especially clever turns of phrase or one-liners. (We're not necessarily going to lose any or all of them, but we might.)

It's the subtle temptation of the ego—wanting the hearers to admire the homily more than the thought—or it's a lack of nerve. We're afraid that if we don't keep track of all the parts, we might go out there in front of the people with nothing to say.

So instead of coming before the people with the core of our thought well in hand, we fill our minds with all the pieces and details that we put together. We become more preoccupied with the text than the message. This preoccupation dulls the live sense of a heart-to-heart talk:

---

[2]For those who regularly use the full text or detailed notes, letting go does not mean that you leave these behind. It simply means that you are not tied to each word or phrase.

[3]Interesting that this is probably very close to what we do in preparing to give a weekday homily...and another reason why these are often better.

Our timing isn't as good, the creative edge isn't there, and we don't make those on-the-spot adjustments (and cuts) that are needed.[4]

A Musical Analogy

Some excellent musicians play with the musical text in front of them, and some without it. Regardless, what separates a mediocre musician from a good one is the extent to which the musician has control of the music. Some are busy trying to play the *notes*. The good ones are playing the *song*.

A musician might have the music in front of him or her and play it note for note but play it woodenly. Another might have memorized it and be able to play without the music...and still play it woodenly.

The opposite can be true: A musician with the music and another without the music can both play the song wonderfully.

Some musicians can improvise and play a given melody any number of ways. The melody will be the same, but some of the notes, chords, and rhythms might be different each time. Such a musician has full control of the music.

There are obvious parallels among those who preach.

––––––––––––

In the last stages of preparing a homily, with the deadline drawing near, if we don't have the material well in hand, it would be better to make some major cuts, get to the core, and stay with what we can concentrate on and feel confident with. Better to eliminate a whole chunk of material if it helps us to control the heart of what we have to say. Having control of the material is that important. It really is.

––––––––––––

[4]On 90 percent of the occasions when I wrote out a homily word for word—*and then memorized it word for word*—the homily didn't turn out to be very good.

CHAPTER TWELVE

Depth

"He's a good speaker. It's just that he's got nothing to say."[1]

Depth will make up for many things, but nothing will make up for a lack of depth. Preaching techniques won't do it, length won't do it, nor, for that matter, will brevity do it. (With shallow material, brevity is simply more merciful than length.)

Kansas City, Missouri, is the world headquarters of Hallmark Cards. While there in 1997 for the NCCB meeting, I happened to meet a Hallmark executive. Fascinated by his line of work, I asked many questions, one of which was: "In a greeting card, which is more important—the text or the design?" He didn't have to give it a second thought. "It's the text by a mile."

Artwork can't make up for the lack of something to say. The same is true in homilies.

Homilists frequently wonder: How can we reach all the different people in the congregation—young and old; folks with mixed understandings of the faith, varied levels of education, such a wide range of joys and sorrows? The answer is depth.

No homilist, whether married, single, man, woman, rich, or poor can

---

[1]Comment from one of the folks about a young homilist.

hit upon all the varied circumstances of people's lives. What we can do is to reach a certain level of truth that connects with everyone. The greater the depth, the more it connects.

The Depth of Our Life

The truth is that unless we have depth in our lives, we can't have depth in our homilies. Whether we intend it or not, the inner quality of our lives will show in our homilies.[2] If we don't have depth, our homilies won't either. They'll be like weak coffee, and no amount of sugar or cream will make up for the missing strength.

As I listen to homilies, I think that I can tell whose world is large and whose is small. I can guess who reads and who doesn't, who continues to learn and who doesn't. The quality of one's life is as important to a homilist as leg strength to an Olympic hurdler.

Fulfilled in Your Hearing speaks about this:

> Regular and sustained contact with the world's greatest literature or with its painting, sculpture, and musical achievements can rightfully be regarded by preachers not simply as a leisure time activity but as part of their ongoing professional development. The same can be said of attention to modern entertainment media....[3]

Feedback from the Folks

Depth was another of those concerns high on the list:

- "What he says is a rehash of what I've heard a hundred times. It's predictable stuff, nothing to take home and think about."
- "I expect so much more from a highly educated person."
- "Too much banality."
- "I want the homily to have some meaning, something you remember afterward."
- "I like it when homilies help us see something in a new way."

---

[2]"Every writer, by the way he uses the language, reveals something of his spirit, his habits, his capacities, his bias.... All writing is communication; creative writing is communication through revelation—it is the Self escaping into the open. No writer long remains incognito." (William Strunk, *The Elements of Style* [New York: Macmillan, 1979, pp. 66–67].)

[3] *Fulfilled in Your Hearing*, p. 13.

- "Usually, it's the same things I've heard over and over. Nothing new, interesting."
- "I like to get beyond the eighth-grade catechism."
- "Homilies should give me an insight, expand my vision."
- "She has a way of calling us to live the gospel at a deeper level."
- "I find homilies themeless and meaningless."
- "He always has a 'jewel' to give us."
- "I hate filler, drivel, low-grade material anyone could throw together."

Pearls Are Everywhere

Jewelers' pearls result from a grain of sand in a clam. Homilists' pearls result from the Word of God in real life. These pearls are all around us, and they're plentiful. The trouble is that until they're polished and placed in a setting, they don't look like pearls and are often passed by. Many a time, we've heard them passed over in a homily, and we say to ourselves, "They should've taken hold of *that* thought and worked with it instead of all that other stuff."[4]

Depth takes hard work. The most common escape route? Instead of digging straight down to the depth of one thought, we skim along the surface of three or four thoughts; then we're back to what the folks cited as the chief fault of most homilies: too many thoughts. An interesting exercise in many a homily would be to take any part of it where there was some substance and ask what would happen if the homilist went straight down from there, that is, went into its depth, stayed with that thought, tried to make it clearer, tried to make sure the people caught it and took it inside themselves, and so on.

Discovering and working on a thought that has depth brings a sense of exhilaration, like a prospector striking gold. Our hearts, minds, and souls were made for this. We know that we have something to say and we can't wait to say it, not because it's clever, but because it's true.

When I think about the times I've chosen glitz instead of depth in my homilies, the fig tree in Mark becomes a metaphor that haunts me:

---

[4]From the world of arts and sports, examples abound of great pearls being missed: great songs, paintings, manuscripts, and athletes initially rejected.

Seeing from a distance a fig tree in leaf, [Jesus] went over to see if
he could find anything on it. When he reached it he found nothing
but leaves. (Mk 11:13)

That can easily apply to homilies. I know how to put together an
impressive homily—or at least one that will get me through the occasion
with respect—but is more performance than substance. Down deep, I
know that I have not drawn from the depth of the word, or of my spirit,
nor have I reached out to touch the inward depths of the people. In my
heart, I know the difference...and the words in Mark's Gospel haunt me:
"nothing but leaves."

CHAPTER THIRTEEN

Connect with Real Life

"Some homilists are good with God, and some are good with real life...and to find one who's good with both is really something."[1]

Aside from "stay with one thought," the folks' most frequent comment about homilies had to do with our ability to connect with real life. When we do, the people catch it, like suddenly hearing words of their own language in a foreign country.

Feedback from the Folks

Here is a sample of comments about homilists connecting with life (the folks had a lot to say—this is a small sample):

- "Tell it like it is."
- "I like it when the homilist connects with things that happened during the week...real people, real events."
- "It has to tie in to what's going on today."
- "Somehow or other, the homily has to enter the door of the real life I live."
- "He talks about the things we all face, and I feel not so alone in this."

---

[1] Comment from one of the folks.

- "Homilies leave off just where they could get interesting."
- "I want the homily to 'get into my system.'"
- "The homilist has to do more than repeat the creed in general terms."
- "I'm sure he believes in what he's saying, but it all comes off as bromides, truisms, platitudes...with no clue that he ever wrestled with them."
- "I feel included in what he's talking about."
- "I always ask how this will affect me in the coming week; give me something I can use in everyday life."

Here's another of those absolutes: Every homily has to have some perceptible connection with what is going on in the joys, hopes, grief, and anxieties of the people listening.[2] The purpose of this is not to establish our credentials as someone who knows what's going on; it is to get the wheels turning in the listeners.

As long as I'm throwing around absolutes, here's another one: Unless we start the wheels turning in the listeners, no matter how clear our logic or well-rounded our phrases, nothing happens. They may be impressed, but nothing *happens*.

In reviewing a homily draft, some helpful questions might be: Where in this homily will the wheels start to turn in the listeners (which is different from asking where they will be most fascinated, taken with our thought, entertained)? Does the whole homily have the ring of real life? Is it spoken from inside or from outside the real world?[3]

---

[2] I know a priest who was taught that every homily had to have a "life reference;" he felt it was the most helpful thing he ever learned about preaching. I lived at his rectory for a while, and as he was preparing a homily, he'd sometimes stop by my room and say, "I still don't have my life reference." Later when he found it, it was a "Eureka" moment. I think there's something to that. Where is the life reference in this homily? Where does it "plug in" to the people's lives?

[3] To quote Hemingway: "If a writer of prose knows enough about what he is writing about he may omit things that he knows and the reader, if the writer is writing truly enough, will have a feeling of those things as strongly as though the writer had stated them. The dignity of movement of an iceberg is due to only one-eighth of it being above water. A writer who omits things *because he does not know them* only makes hollow places in his writing." (Ernest Hemingway, *Death in the Afternoon* [in Larry Phillips, *Ernest Hemingway On Writing*, (New York: Scribner, 1984, p. 77)]) (emphasis added). I also remember the analogy of someone who studies anatomy in preparation for sculpting a clothed figure.

Cross Over the Bridge

Truisms tumble easily off our lips in homilies. To the people, they sound like filler—oft-repeated things every preacher is expected to say, and things we've all heard a hundred times.

The regular complaint is that we homilists too often stop short at the bridge that crosses into real life. We develop a point and stop just where things could become interesting. We speak principles that are true and make general applications, but we don't get into the fray. There is no indication that we are part of the struggle beneath the words.

For example, Jesus tells the rich man to sell what he has, to give to the poor, and to follow him. One can easily imagine a homilist speaking in generalities about this: "We're too attached to our possessions, and we have too many of them anyway, so we have to learn to let go of them. And we neglect the poor except on Thanksgiving and Christmas. Well how about all year round? If we are true followers of Jesus, we have to take seriously what he says. How much time do we give to the Lord in one week?" And so on.

That's no help. None at all. General statements. Bromides. What *does* a middle-class person with family responsibilities do with this gospel?

Now imagine standing in the backyard trying to light the barbecue with your brother-in-law. He mentions that when he hears the gospel passage about selling what you have and giving to the poor, it always sets him wondering how it applies to someone who is raising a family. What do you say to him about how this applies to his life—which also involves your sister and your nieces and nephews? That's the bridge that is often left uncrossed because it's a hard one to cross. But *that's* why we have homilies.

An Example

One of the homilists in our sessions talked about winning the "gold medal" of life (it was during the Olympics) and toward the end asked a number of questions:

> During our lifetime, did we learn to love one another? Did we learn to forgive one another? During our lifetime, did we learn to help the needy? During our lifetime, did we learn to encourage each other? During our lifetime, did we learn to walk that second mile?

Did we learn to turn the other cheek? Did we learn to become more committed?

We applauded the effort but noted that, speaking of going the extra mile, it didn't. It stayed with generalities that hovered just above the fray. Here is a rewrite using the same material, thought by thought:

> During our lifetime, did we manage to bite our tongue when we wanted to swear at the driver who didn't signal a left turn? When we had a falling out with our in-law or "out-law" or anyone, did we let it fester, or did we let go of it and try to mend the fence? Did we try to put ourselves in the shoes of poor people, think about them, help them, even defend them when people made sweeping statements about "welfare cheats"? In conversations, were we the ones with the positive words or the ones with the negative words? Even when things on the job or at home didn't seem 50–50, were we willing to go the extra mile to try to make things work? If family and friends were to write our biography, which would be our trademark: to hit back or to give some slack? Granted that we can't become involved in everything, were we involved in *some* things? Think about it: What *are* we involved in beyond our own personal or family concerns?

If homilies at times don't connect with life, it's not necessarily because homilists don't know the score. Most do. It simply takes a lot more effort to go from generalities to real life, and homilists who are married, raising families, and/or working in the marketplace (e.g., permanent deacons, lay preachers) have just as much trouble doing it. It's easier to talk *about* the scriptures, make some general applications, and leave it at that.

Some Tips

1. When Writing a Homily, Picture Real People.

I often find myself picturing "people" rather than real people. The ones I picture are generic, or individuals I imagine to be already interested in what I am planning to say.

This is a great mistake. It becomes evident when I am giving the homily and realize they're not nearly as taken with these thoughts as when I pictured them.

I do better when, during preparation, I picture specific people, "regular folks"–people whose lives don't revolve around church work. I think of some of my own acquaintances who come to church fairly regularly and some who don't. I picture the people in the checkout line at the supermarket. Sometimes at an airport, I watch the people streaming off a plane and try to guess what is going on in their lives, what they are thinking and worrying about, what awaits them as they go wherever they are going. When writing a homily, I try to bring all that back to mind and see if I can find the thoughts that will click with these people.

Picture real people. You'd be surprised how much this helps.

2. When Writing a Homily, Have Some Newspapers Handy.

We already know what's in the newspapers. Yet, to mix the newspapers and the scriptures together at the same time has an effect. Scan the newspaper from time to time while thinking and writing–not to get particular examples or to cut and paste, but rather to get a feel for the scriptures intersecting with today's world.

This can have a greater effect than we might think.

3. Call People Who Are Not Involved in Church Work, and Run Your Homily Thoughts by Them, Inviting Their Ideas and Examples.

We ought to have a couple of people whom we can call now and then when we're writing a homily, people who will give us their honest reactions. Run the core thought by them. Run a key section by them. Ask them for some ideas, examples. It's easy, painless; they're happy to do it, and the real-life quality of the homily usually takes a geometric leap forward.

A Caveat

Keep in mind that the connection with life has to flow from the scripture text. When we preach, we are trying to help all of us discover what the *scriptures* have to say to our lives today.

The mistake is to use something in the scriptures as the *occasion* to say something about real life, but without any serious engagement of the text. We use the text as a peg, a thought-starter, and then go on with our own development.

One of the conclusions of the study done by the Catholic Theological Union in Chicago is this:

The congregation sometimes judges the homily to be successful insofar as the homilist is able to relate the biblical text to the Christian life today. Our participants are aware of that since almost all made an effort in their homilies to do that. Most, however, made superficial connections that had the effect of trivializing the concern of the text.[4]

If in our homilies we talk about real-life situations concretely and effectively, we will surely receive very positive feedback from our listeners, even if our insights aren't really drawn from the scriptures. Most people will be (understandably) so happy to hear a message that connects with their lives that they won't know what they're missing...and what they're missing is the power of God's Word.

We homilists generally will have to call ourselves to account on this one, and it is something we have to take seriously.

Picture these two scenes.

SCENE ONE: After the last weekend mass, you and some of the liturgical ministers and parish ministers are having coffee in the rectory. The conversation easily turns to the liturgy, sometimes to the homily. Nothing wrong with that.

SCENE TWO: After the last weekend mass, you and some unexpected visiting friends who happened to be at mass are having coffee in the rectory. The conversation is different: They talk about things that are happening in their lives—their jobs, their families' health, a trip they're planning, their children. That doesn't mean that the liturgy or the homily was a failure; it simply reminds us that their reference point from the time they walk into church to the time they walk out of church is not the liturgy as such. It's their life.

---

[4]p. 16. Study directed by Leslie Hoppe, O.F.M., and Barbara Reid, O.P. One of its aims is to "develop suggestions for revising the biblical studies curriculum or the curricular objectives of biblical studies courses to facilitate the responsible and creative use of the Bible in preaching." As of the publishing of *this* book, the project is not yet completed or published.

CHAPTER FOURTEEN

Stories

Everyone Loves a Story.

People will listen with interest to almost any story we tell. But in homilies, all stories are not equal. Just because a story is interesting doesn't mean it ministers the word.

There are three kinds of stories and it is an immense help to recognize the difference between them.

1. A story primarily to entertain, loosen everyone up, and get their attention.

This is a story that is connected only artificially to the core thought of our homily. Nothing would be lacking to our thought if we left out the story.

I once heard a homilist on Stewardship Sunday begin this way:

> Let me tell you a story about a fellow who was placed in charge of a door-to-door fund-raising program in his parish. His name was Pat, and he wanted to do a first-rate job, so he asked the pastor to give him the name of the hardest nut to crack. The pastor told him about Mike, who never contributed to anything.
>
> So, Pat drove over to Mike's house and knocked on the door, and Mike answered. Pat told Mike that he was there to get a pledge

from him for the parish drive, and he presented three or four good reasons why Mike should give.

Mike responded, "You're asking *me* for a contribution? Look: my mother has been an invalid for 23 years. My brother had a serious accident 10 years ago and needs round-the-clock care. My wife is crippled with arthritis. My daughter needs a kidney transplant."

"Pat was embarrassed and was trying to think of how he could politely leave, when Mike added, "I don't give money to any of them, so why should I give to you!" [loud laughter from the assembly]

Well, I'm sure we don't have that kind of problem with any of our parishioners here, and I want to invite you to think about some of the reasons why we all need to get behind this pledge drive. You see....

A clever story, and entertaining. But entertainment is not the purpose of a homily, and as for getting their attention, the homilist had it before he began.

Tempting as such stories are, they generally don't belong in homilies. Placed at the beginning, they interrupt the flow of the liturgy of the Word and use up peak attention that might better have focused on something substantial. Placed anywhere, they are more diversion than enlightenment.[1]

2. A story to illustrate the message.

This is a story that lights up our core thought, puts flesh and blood on it, and connects it with real life. If we left it out, some of the clarity and force of our core thought would be lacking.

It was a wedding. The homilist took out a newspaper, turned to the sports section, and said:

There are some interesting things here. Fred Couples shot a 78 yesterday, 7 over par. Imagine. Fred Couples 7 over par. Do you know what batting average is leading the American League? Imagine: 348. That means 65 percent of the time he *didn't* get a hit.

Sampras was eliminated from the U.S. Open early in the first round. I guess the great ones don't win every tournament they enter.

These are the best in the world, but their golf swing, or their

---

[1] In the earlier chapter on beginnings, I pointed out in a footnote that there are times when the assembly seems "dead" or distanced and that we need to do something to get some chemistry going. It may require a quip or a few sentences at the beginning but not a full-fledged story, and it should be the exception.

baseball swing, or their tennis stroke isn't perfect. Their key to success is that they've found ways to make an imperfect swing work very well over the long haul.

Peter [the gospel reading had been about Jesus asking Peter three times "Do you love me?"] learned the hard way that his love wasn't perfect. But he also learned, with God's help, to make his imperfect love work well for the rest of his life...even to martyrdom.

The love of any couple, however true, is imperfect. What they're saying in the sacrament of marriage is: "With God's help, we're going to find ways to make our imperfect love work for a whole lifetime."

The story illuminated the message.

Always the key question is: What of the *message* would be missing if the story were left out? That's the difference between this kind of story and the first example.

3. A story that *is* the message.

In this case, the story doesn't just illustrate the message; it is *itself* the message and needs no further development. The best examples are some of Jesus' parables, for example, the Good Samaritan. When he finished, there was no more to say except; "Go and do likewise."

These stories are difficult to write and take considerable skill. They can be very effective.

Here is an unusual example of a "live story" that was in itself a homily.

It was the Memorial Day weekend, and I celebrated the Sunday afternoon mass at the cathedral. The gospel passage included Jesus' prayer "that they all may be one."

I had prepared a homily suggesting that Jesus was like an elderly mother or father praying that the family would get along and stay together. I was going to apply this to the way God feels when we go to war.

I began by asking if anyone had lost a family member in a war. A woman raised her hand and said she had lost a brother in World War II. I asked where he was killed, and she said it was in France during the advance against the German army. Then a woman on the other side (the seats were arranged choir style) raised her hand and said that she had lost a brother in World War II. I asked where. She paused and said slowly with a slight accent, "He vas in der German army."

You could have heard a pin drop. Here were these two elderly women facing each other, the altar between them.

The thing to do, of course, was to pitch my homily and simply say, "Let's all take a few minutes of quiet and think about war, including the 'wars' in our own lives."

What, pitch my homily? I had some good material! So I gave it. To this day, I shake my head and say, "How could anyone be so dumb."

There are some homilists who are creative enough to write a story that is in itself the message, and it can be very effective.

Any time we use a story or a lengthy illustration in a homily, we should make sure we know which of the above three it is.

Some Tips

1. <u>Don't Belabor the Story.</u>

As much as we love stories, remember how you feel when someone starts to tell a joke that you know is going to be long and detailed. You don't feel good.

The best stories are brief and to the point (a little longer if the story IS the homily). Almost all the stories used in homilies in our groups needed major editing; they had way too many details.[2]

I recall a homilist who on Father's Day invited all of us to think of things that bring back memories of our parents. He brought out his father's toolbox, took out a pair of pliers, and talked about memories associated with it. Then he took out another tool and did the same thing. Then another. Then another.

It was a fine story, but the listeners got the point early on. They were thinking of their own parental treasures and tuned out the rest of the story—even though he was enjoying it thoroughly. (An editor would have caught this and done considerable cutting.)

Some of the best-known parables in the gospels are surprisingly terse. In workshops, I've invited people to try to write the parable of the Lost Sheep as best they remembered it. Almost all of them were at least a third longer than the actual text (which has only 72 words).

---

[2]*Too long* doesn't necessarily mean "long"; it just means longer than necessary.

2. Try to Use Stories That Are Part of Everyone's Life.

The best story or example is one that everyone can identify with. Unusual stories that are far removed from our common experiences may hold people's interest, but they don't accomplish one of the main purposes of a homily, which is to start the wheels turning in the listeners.

People remember the stories, so whenever we use a story, we have to ask ourselves if *this* is what we want them to remember. Do we want them to remember something funny, dramatic, or clever or to remember a pearl that they will find helpful in living their lives?

CHAPTER FIFTEEN

Length

No matter how well a homily (or any talk) is going, don't think they're enjoying it as much as you are.

Length is relative. Some short homilies can seem long, and some long homilies can seem short.

The wind-chill factor is instructive here: The stronger the wind the more we feel the chill. In homilies, there is something analogous that could be called the quality-quantity factor: The lower the quality the more we feel the quantity.

When I first began to ask people for feedback I was sure their biggest concern would be length. It wasn't. Length didn't even come in second or third.[1]

Not that they remained entirely silent about length: Here are some of their comments.[2]

---

[1] As mentioned in Chapter eight, the chief plea from the people was that we stay with one thought. The question of length is closely related to the problem of too many thoughts. When we give a good thought and go on to another, the people are still thinking about what we've just said. They want to chew on it. The wheels are turning. What they need is the silence that is supposed to follow the homily, not another thought. When we go on we're interrupting the best result any homily could have, like a waiter interrupting a fine meal: Even if we go on to say something good, it isn't doing any good; it's working against all the good food we've already served.

[2] The general feedback from the folks indicates that a bad homily is one of two things that can have an oppressive effect on the whole mass; the other is bad music. Although the homily and the

Feedback from the Folks

- "Our pastor knows how to say a lot in a short time."
- "She takes forever to say something."
- "Long or short, I like a concise homily. It has a sharper point to it."
- "If only he would limit himself to 10 minutes."
- "What's important is not how much he says: It's how much I end up taking home."
- "Most homilies are too dragged out."
- "You can talk as long as you want, as long as you're talking about my life."

How Long Should a Homily Be?

There really is no set length for a homily. It's not like the fixed space of a TV show that would have several minutes of a blank screen if we didn't have enough to fill it or would run into the 11:00 news if we had too much.[3] If now and then our homily is shorter or longer than usual, we leave no space unfilled or overflowing. If in a particular case the homily should be shorter or longer than usual, we should have a sense of freedom to vary our length in accord with our content and the circumstances.

Of course, any homily, short or long, that has too many thoughts or lacks depth is not a good homily.

That does *not* mean that length isn't an important factor: Homilists have to take length into account. At the funeral liturgy for someone who has suffered a tragic death, a 2-minute homily might be inappropriate; funeral homilies are meant to help us move through grief to hope, and there are some things you just can't do in 2 minutes. On the other hand, at a Sunday liturgy where there are 6 baptisms, a 15-minute homily would probably be of inappropriate length.

There is also the question of proportion relative to the whole liturgy. Even a homily that is well written and stays with one thought can be too long. A homily is usually one of the longest single parts of the mass. Most

---

music are not in themselves the most important parts of the mass, they are sometimes the most difficult parts for the assembly to overcome if not done well.

[3]This applies to other parts of the mass as well. The scripture readings are of no set length; some are brief, some are longer. The eucharistic prayers vary in length. The homily has no set length either: It can be 3 minutes or 10 minutes.

homilies are longer than all the scripture readings taken together, longer than the longest eucharistic prayer, and sometimes longer than the whole communion rite. If it exceeds any of them by too great a margin, it can become disproportionate, as though it was the centerpiece of the mass—which it isn't.

After attending a wedding, someone recently commented to me: "The content of the homily was as fine as I've heard at a wedding. The priest obviously was a close friend of the couple and worked hard on the homily. But it went on and on and on. He didn't repeat himself or talk drivel—the content was excellent. He just plain went on too long."

Looking at length from a practical angle, a homily becomes too long at the point where the people stop listening. A person in one of our homily groups commented to another: "Your homily was pretty good. But when you got to such and such a part, I thought you should have quit there. So I did."

That comment defines when it becomes too long. If the people feel like quitting at a certain point, they will, without any conscious decision.

We might find ourselves saying, "But the problem is that they're not conditioned to listen. They have to change and learn to settle in and stop being in such a rush." That may be true, but this will happen gradually, and we have to make our homilies so compelling that they will learn to do this. In the meantime, we can't live life in the subjunctive—what *should* happen. Homilies are communication, and what is communicated is not what is said (or written). It is what is received.

The Discipline of Brevity

I am not suggesting a fixed time limit for homilies, but the discipline of brevity can help produce a better homily (or talk).

From the point of view of the people, homilists seem often to err not by being too brief, but by being too long. That is no surprise inasmuch as, even with good material, it is easier to be long than brief. Remember the famous remark of Mark Twain when he sent a long letter to a friend: He apologized for the length and said it would have been shorter, but he didn't have time.

Our goal should be to say a lot in as brief a time as possible. There is a certain discipline to brevity: It forces depth, focus, clarity. We have to go to the heart of our topic and stay there. We are not seeking brevity in itself, but brevity as a way of forcing us to produce a better homily. It forces us to pare our homily down to the "A-grade" material, and never to use "B grade" to give it a respectable length. Aiming for brevity can force us to stick only with the best, which inevitably produces a better homily.

I recently promised a 4-minute tape on why Catholics oppose assisted suicide. My first draft was about 7 minutes long. When I finally got it down to 4, it was not only within the time limit; it was much improved.

Some Tips

1. Have Someone Time Your Homily Now and Then.

For the speaker, time usually moves more quickly: When someone says, "I'll talk for 2 minutes," it usually ends up closer to 5; when they say 5 minutes, expect 10 to 15. It doesn't seem that long to the speaker, but it does to the listeners.[4]

Because the homilies in our Saginaw groups are taped, it is easy to time them. When homilists first hear the actual time, they are usually surprised: They think their homily is shorter.

2. There Really Is Nothing Wrong with a Short Homily.

Realizing that there is no allotted time for a homily and no set amount of space in the mass to fill should free us from the fear of being inappropriately brief. Sometimes less is more.

When I'm having a tough time with a homily and the deadline is near, I've found that two things can help remarkably: (1) Cut it to the core; (2) take a good hold of the core. (The first focuses me on the best material; the second enables me to speak it with ease.)

Here's something you may want to try now and then: When you've finished preparing a usual-length homily, cut it in half (which takes some minor rewriting). It's not difficult, just painful. What's left is the very best material.

---

[4]At a banquet, I was to give the main talk. I knew that with all the other things going on, main talks at banquets are best done concisely. Before dinner, I asked one of the people who was to receive an award how long his thank-you was; he said it would be about 2 minutes. I timed it: 5½ minutes. My talk, which was the keynote, was 8½ minutes. He probably thought mine was 20 and his was 2. When inviting people who are not experienced in public speaking to "say a few words," I find it best to give them not a *time* limit but a *space* limit, for example, "Write out something that fits onto half of an 8½ x 11 sheet of paper." Space is something they can understand; not being used to public speaking, they don't have a feel for time.

I remember listening to the tapes of a conference in which the speaker gave four lectures, each about 50 minutes long. I listened to the first and had a hard time getting the substance, although it was good material. At the beginning of the second lecture, the speaker said he was aware that some of those present had arrived late and missed the first one, so he gave a 10-minute summary of his first talk. It was excellent, and I got much more from this 10-minute summary than from the original 50-minute version.

3. The Bigger the Event, the Shorter the Homily.

Our brain tells us exactly the opposite: This is a big event so I need a great homily. The trouble is that *great* usually translates into size. One thinks of parish centennials, the installation of bishops, the feasts of Christmas and Easter, large funerals. Homilies on these occasions are often long and unremembered.

It never crosses our mind to think smaller. Everything about the event is bigger, so the homily should be too. It seems almost wrong to be brief.

The reason for this the-bigger-the-event-the-shorter-the-homily principle is not because we're in a hurry; it's because major-size events really don't require a major-size homily. The rituals and components of the event do their own share of preaching, and all we need to do is help the flow.

It's difficult to convince ourselves of this. People expect the homily to be larger, and we feel we must live up to their expectations. (Note that *expecting* it to be larger is to be distinguished from *wanting* it to be larger.)

Another reason is that we want to do well on these occasions; Many important people plus some friends will be there. Bigger seems better, more impressive, so we try to do a large masterpiece. Enter, again, the ego.

The truth is that we don't need to be more erudite, more clever, to preach a great homily. All we need is depth.

4. No Matter How Well a Homily (or Any Talk) Is Going, Don't Think They're Enjoying It as Much as You Are.

We've all been on the receiving end of an ad-libbed talk that failed to recognize this time-proven principle. The speaker is nervous, overcomes it, begins to enjoy the experience, and inflicts his or her joy on the rest of us. Experienced speakers should know better.

I once heard someone say, "Speak only for so long as your speaking is an improvement on silence." That is a good measure of the length of a homily. We don't easily improve on silence before the great mysteries we are celebrating in the Eucharist. Furthermore, silence is scarce these days, so we mustn't think that spoken words are automatically a benefit.[5]

---

[5]Preparing for a homily at a university baccalaureate mass, I came up with something I thought was good, but it was brief (it turned out to be $4^1/_2$ minutes). I called the president and told him that I wanted to give a brief homily but didn't want to be inappropriately brief. There was a pause at the other end (he was savoring the thought of a short baccalaureate homily). Then he said, "It's hard to imagine being *inappropriately* brief."

CHAPTER SIXTEEN

Sidebars

"It was an interesting thought. Too bad it got in the way of everything else you were saying."[1]

I learned from our journalist what a *sidebar* is: a newspaper term for something related to a story and put alongside it, often in a box.

Sidebars are like asides, footnotes, or ramblings: In newspaper stories, sidebars are usually made up of material that was *taken out* of the main story.

Newspapers use them all the time. Alongside a story about floods in the Northwest are several maps showing the hardest-hit areas. Another sidebar might be a chart of this century's 10 heaviest rainfalls.

A story about a papal trip to Cuba might be accompanied by a sidebar that profiles the Castro years in Cuba. We can read the story and look at the sidebar afterward or go back and forth as we read along.

Sidebars contain interesting information, but if they are put into the main story, they divert readers from the flow of the story or tax their attention span.

---

[1] A layperson's comment about part of one of my homilies.

Stories with Sidebars

A good example of things that *ought* to be sidebars (i.e., eliminated) frequently occurs when someone is telling a story. We experience this often. The wife wants to tell a hilarious thing that happened on an elevator. She begins by telling why she went downtown in the first place. It has nothing to do with what happened on the elevator, but we learn the interesting detail that the CEO of the corporation is her cousin and that she went to try to get a job for her nephew. The husband interrupts and says, "No, that was the year before. You went to see cousin Ralph that day because he had promised to take you to lunch in the executive dining room." She disagrees and says she remembers that it was about her nephew because it was late afternoon, not lunchtime. The husband holds his ground, they keep arguing about it, and the rest of us say to ourselves "Who cares *why* you went to the building? WHAT HAPPENED ON THE ELEVATOR?!"

Think of the sidebars that some storytellers could include if they were writing the parable of the Good Samaritan. They might start out like this:

> There was a man who lived in Jerusalem who regularly traveled the 7-mile stretch from Jerusalem to Jericho. He had a brother in Jericho who sold jewelry. He'd take orders from his friends in Jerusalem, and every couple of months, he'd make the trip. He usually had quite a bit of money on him.
>
> It was a risky trip because the road was such a desolate one. Bandits had taken advantage of this for centuries, and it was often called "Robbers Road," but it was the only route from Jerusalem to Jericho. He always tried to link up with a group along the way, but when he had no luck, he went anyway. We warned him against traveling alone, but he wouldn't listen.
>
> Well, one day it happened. He was about 3 miles from Jericho. Travel was especially light that day—he hadn't seen anyone for nearly an hour. As he came to that big curve in the road where there are those huge boulders, he heard some footsteps behind him; when he turned around, there were three robbers closing in on him. He tried to run but had no chance. They had clubs and began to hit him until he was unconscious.

Compare the actual text of the gospel:

> A man fell victim to robbers as he went down from Jerusalem to Jericho.

That's just 14 words. The version with all the potential sidebars took 215 words just to get just that far into the parable.

In the gospel, the entire parable took only 153 words. That includes the robbers assaulting the man, the priest passing him by, the Levite doing the same, and the Samaritan tending to him, going to the inn, and the next day making the arrangements with the innkeeper.

If we apply the same ratio, the imaginary story with the sidebars would have used more than 2,300 words to tell this 153-word story.

Watch for sidebars in homilies, and take them out. The trouble is that while newspapers can use them in a box alongside, we have nowhere to put them. That's why it's so painful to eliminate them. They are so interesting, so instructive, so directly related to our core thought, and so enjoyable to tell.

But they have to go because they are in the way of our message. A person told me about something in my homily that was really a sidebar: "It was an interesting thought. Too bad it got in the way of everything else you were saying."

A sidebar is something like a footnote, except that sidebars are usually more interesting. Still the principle is the same: The reason why footnotes are not in the text is because they would interrupt the flow and/or be distracting; sidebars have to be taken out for the same reasons.

We talked earlier about editing and the pain of cutting interesting material: Sidebars are among the main victims. Once we recognize what a sidebar is, we recognize the need for the scalpel. The trouble is, we don't have novocaine to take away the pain. Dedicated writers must acquire the grit to do what has to be done.

CHAPTER SEVENTEEN

Jargon

"I'm 'signing' for the deaf today. Keep me in mind when you're up there preaching."[1]

I use *jargon* in a broad sense to mean words that are abstract, overused, or "church-speak." We know well enough not to use technical words such as eschaton, soteriology, and teleological. That's not the problem.

The problem has to do mainly with our failure to use picture language, sensual words—words we can see, feel, smell, hear, taste. We think we do, but often we don't, or we use overworked words and phrases that become trite.

In one group, I went through the transcript of a homily and underlined in green all the words that were not image words and in red all those that were. It was another eye-opener. There was a sea of green ink, with only four or five words underlined in red.

Abstract Words

Just before mass, a woman came up to me and said, "I'm 'signing' for the deaf today. Keep me in mind when you're up there preaching." If I'd

---

[1] Comment to me before mass by a person who was "signing" for the deaf.

pretend she was doing this for every homily, my words would be more concrete; I'd remember that she has a harder time with *mutuality* than *work together.*

This is a critique of one of the homilies in our groups:

> One of the things you have to be particularly attentive to is avoiding abstract words. These are not necessarily large words, or technical words, or even words whose meaning people don't understand. They are simply words that do not have the concrete character of kitchen-table talk. They're not the words Shakespeare or Steinbeck use. Examples from your homily would be: tangible, interactions, sensitive, encounter, approachability, and accessible.

This is a common problem in homilies, and usually the homilist is unaware of it.

On the other hand, here are two excerpts from homilies that instantly connected with real life:

> 1. Moral conversion is a change in the way we behave. A person might say, "I've been a couch potato for the last 10 years and, by gosh, I'm going to get up off my couch and take the talents God gave me and do some good in this world."

> 2. A number of people in my life have been able to calm the storm. They were always there at the right time. My dad was one of those people. He would turn on the light if you were afraid of the dark. If you messed up the big play in the ball game, he'd remind you that a game never depends on just one play. If you broke something, he'd help fix it or tell you it could be replaced.

Here is a small sample (taken from actual homilies) of words or phrases commonly used by church people that fit the "abstract" category:

faith commitment	lived reality
empowerment	parameter
faith journey	problematic
mutuality	receptive
spirit-led	faith community
spirit-filled	

Most *-ize* words are candidates for the abstract category. Some samples:

concretize	strategize
conscienticize	sensitize
marginalize	prioritize
actualize	theologize
interiorize	

The parables in the Gospels are not abstract. They're full of concrete, real-life, descriptive words. Here are two examples.

1. From the parable of the sower:

...birds came and ate it up...rocky ground...sprang up at once...when the sun rose, it was scorched and it withered for lack of roots...some seed fell among thorns and the thorns grew up and choked it and it produced no grain. (Mk 3:4 ff)

2. From the parable of the owner of the vineyard who sent servants and finally his son for the produce:

...planted a vineyard, put a hedge around it, dug a wine press, and built a tower...they seized him, beat him, and sent him away empty-handed...that one they beat over the head and treated shamefully...some they beat, others they killed. (Mk 12:1 ff)

Overused Words

Some words should be deleted simply because they are overused. In the following list (taken from actual homilies), many are also abstract.

journey	prophetic	interaction
exciting	relevant	fantastic
commitment	significant	module
relevant	time line	outreach
dynamic	credibility	framework
pragmatic	sharing	praxis
operative	innovative	thrust

Obviously, this cannot be an absolute. But if we catch ourselves using such words, a red flag should go up to make us think twice.

Here are some overworked phrases:

where you're coming from	bottom line
zero in on	blows my mind
a theology of...(anything)	really get into it
get in touch with	consciousness-raising
deal with	the system
that's what it's all about	in our heart of hearts
mind-boggling	

Lest we think these are foibles limited to homilists, here are samples from various notices in Catholic publications for workshops:

We must image Christ with creativity as a reconciler, wisdom in hearing many things and drawing them together, synthesizing, resiliency, truth telling, community building.

Structures—social, economic, Church and others—have a way of marginalizing people, but the marginalized have much to offer. This workshop will deal with how the marginalized can survive, and while surviving, can strategize to change structures and make them more human, more responsible, more creative, and more supportive to life.

A new excitement and integrity in our common task has resulted from the use of case materials and methods due to the integral relationship of affective and cognitive learning inherent in this approach.

Here's one from outside the church sphere. An Associated Press story told of the parent of a high school student who received the following communiqué from the principal about a special meeting on a proposed program:

Our school's cross-graded, multi-ethnic, individualized learning program is designed to enhance the concept of an open-ended learning program with emphasis on a continuum of multi-ethnic, academically enriched learning using the identified intellectually gifted child as the agent or director of his own learning.

The parent wrote back:

I have a college degree, speak two foreign languages and four Indian dialects, have been to a number of county fairs and three goat ropings, but I haven't the faintest idea as to what the hell you are talking about.

Artificial "Public-Speaking Phrases"

We move on to another category, a strange one, maybe a new one. For some reason, when we speak publicly, certain phrases we never otherwise use tumble off our lips. Most everyone, homilist or not, does this. Here are some samples:

so to speak	suffice it to say
if you will	without further ado
as it were	just to name a few
every fiber of my being	it is my privilege
any way, shape, or form	it is an honor and a privilege
first and foremost	the all too familiar
to name but a few	call to mind
we embark upon	go forth
each and every	would venture to say
part and parcel	it is my distinct pleasure
hopes and aspirations	

Why do we do this? Why do we say *call to mind* instead of *remember,* *embark upon* rather than *start?* Something happens when we speak publicly: We take on a certain style, assume a certain mode, and use stilted phrases almost as though we're supposed to. We unconsciously mimic those we've heard and pass it on from generation to generation.

No big thing, in one sense, but it does lend an artificial tone to our homily.

Feedback from the Folks

- "It should be practical, not just philosophical."
- "Make it down-to-earth."
- "Not over our heads; on our level."
- "On a level even the young people can understand...but the adults don't feel that they are treated like children."
- "Too theological."
- "Down-to-earth; relates to life."

- "Use the language you'd use at the kitchen table."
- "People really don't understand terms like *faith life* or *faith community*. Be concrete. Don't give us pious concepts. Give us meat and potatoes."

Some Tips

1. <u>Make a Written Transcript of Your Homily Now and Then, and Go Over It with Felt Markers, Using One Color for Picture Words and Another for Those That Aren't.</u>

Only when I saw the transcripts of my own homilies was I convinced that so many words were not concrete.

2. <u>Enjoy Reading Excellent Authors, and Have an Eye to Their Use of Words.</u>

I refer here to works of fiction, biography, and history rather than theological and pastoral materials. Those of us in the ministry of writing and speaking should always have a good book going. The best writers read one another.

3. <u>Practice, Practice, Practice.</u>

We do a lot of writing, more than just homilies. Be attentive, even in writing letters or E-mail messages, to the use of just the right word in the right place. *Kitchen-table language* doesn't mean the limited vocabulary of most conversations; it means words that we *could* use in a conversation over a cup of coffee, words everyone understands but seldom makes the effort to use. These are not strange or unusual words. They are words with a freshness to them.

Some aspects of writing (i.e., sentence structure, phrasing) are hard to change, but the choice of words is not. It's doable. All it takes is some attentiveness. Do it.

CHAPTER EIGHTEEN

Personal...but Not Self-Centered

"When he talks about God, it sounds second-hand. Come to think of it, the same is true when he talks about sin."[1]

The folks consistently called for homilists to be "personal." This covers a wide range: It has to do with our bearing, style, delivery, and content. They want the homily to come from the heart, not just the head. They want to have a sense that we are "with" them, not above them, that we have a real life and share some of their experiences. They want to know that we're speaking from the depths of our souls, not just saying things we're supposed to say.

I had been a priest for 12 years and had ministered to hundreds of people at times of death. Then my father died (the first death in my family). When people came up to me at the funeral home, I could tell whether they had experienced death close up; I could tell if "they knew." It wasn't because of what they said—often they said less than others; it was because I knew that they knew. It made a great difference, and I think it comes close to what people mean when they say that they want the homily to be personal. They want to be able to see and feel that "we know."

---

[1] Comment from one of the folks.

Feedback from the Folks

- "I appreciate it when they share the scripture out of their own life, and have tried to live it...not just teach it or act it."
- "He acts like he's above us."
- "What our pastor says comes off as honest and personal, not canned."
- "It helps me when the homilists risk their own faith struggle, but do so to help us, not to ventilate or feel better themselves."
- "Her sincerity shows through."
- "Homilists should be personal, but not overdone, and not self-centered."
- "We have two priests. One uses personal ideas and examples too often; the other writes an 'essay' and practically reads it."
- "I like it when he doesn't use the pulpit and comes out to us."
- "If they can do it, it's better if they can look at us rather than always looking down at notes."
- "She has a 'pulpit tone'—maybe call it a teacher's tone or telephone tone. Whatever it is, it isn't personal."
- "I'd like more spontaneity, relaxed, one to one."
- "Sometimes it seems so spiritless. Where's the enthusiasm, liveliness?"
- "When he preaches, he uses different words and even a different voice than when he normally speaks. He should just be himself."
- "It's easy for us to say, and it might be hard to do in front of a crowd, but show some of your feelings."
- "Seems like a chore he has to do."
- "We know the creed. We want to hear *your* faith."
- "With my pastor, a homily is always a heart-to-heart talk. We like it."

But Not Self-Centered

A large number of folks added a caution: They want the homily to be personal, but they don't want it to revolve around the homilist. It is illusory to think that our life is as interesting to others as it is to us, or that our life is the best touchstone for most of the great questions of life.

In an article entitled "Reflections on Preaching the Word of God," Catherine Mowry LaCugna offered five principles. One was that the homilist should never be the focus of a homily:

The homilist's feelings, religious insights, habits or hobbies—in short, the *persona* of the homilist—should not dominate the homily.... This does not mean that a homily cannot be highly personal; even without intending to, the preacher will convey a great deal of his persona just by the way he preaches.[2]

It can be appropriate to use our own experiences as examples *if* these experiences are the kind everyone can identify with and *if* we don't overdo using ourselves as an example. As someone put it, "I'm tired of hearing about his family, his dog, his last trip, and his golf game."[3]

The criterion for using an example from my own life (or for that matter from anyone's life) is this: Does it help these scriptures flow into the lives of the regular folks?

Some Tips

1. Check to See if the *You's* Should Be *We's.*

Preaching is not a doctor-patient relationship or even a teacher-student relationship. We need to include ourselves in the assembly that is receiving the word. (This should take no mental gymnastics. The truth is that we *are* part of the assembly and we *are* on the receiving end of the word.)

On the other hand, one must be careful about using *we* when it would falsely imply that everyone shares *my* point of view, for example, "We would all agree that..." or "As we all know...." There are times when that would not be a fair statement.

2. Preaching Is Always Sinner to Sinner.

I have often said that I have been helped more by the acknowledged struggles and failures of good people than by the paraded virtues of the righteous.

People don't want us to recite our sins; they simply want to sense that we know that we're sinners too. A genuine awareness of our own sinfulness is something we can't posture or fake. The people can tell.

---

[2] *America*, March 19, 1994, p. 4.

[3] On the other hand, some may like these homey anecdotes and tell us so. Perhaps it's because they like dogs or golf or whatever. Their feedback shouldn't delude us into thinking that the majority are of the same opinion.

3. <u>Consider Preaching "Out Among the People," That Is, Not Behind the Lectern.</u>

This is not an absolute. There may be good reasons why some should *not* do this.[4]

When I began to gather comments from the folks, I discovered early that most preferred the homilist to be "out there" with them, but I also found that they well understood why some might not do this. They were simply expressing a preference. What they want most of all is a good homily, and if someone preaches better with something in front of them, fine.[5]

4. <u>Love the People to Whom You Preach.</u>

Well, of course we love them. We love everyone..."theologically."

I'm talking here about affection, caring for them, identifying with them. When I'm with people in pastoral ministry, I notice how they talk about their parishioners, and I watch for signs of genuine affection. Usually it's there, sometimes beneath the surface—but not always—or at least not always manifest.

In his letters, Paul cared enough about his people to speak his feelings, even angry ones. He could also tell them that he loved them:

> For out of much affliction and anguish of heart I wrote to you with many tears, not that you might be pained but that you might know the abundant love I have for you. (2 Cor 2:4)

> By the truth of Christ in me, this boast of mine shall not be silenced.... And why? Because I do not love you? God knows I do! (2 Cor 11:10–11)

If we love (more than abstractly) the people to whom we preach, we're more apt to be personal in our homilies. But don't be too quick to say, "Of course I love them." It deserves some serious thought.

---

[4]Examples that come to mind are: We wouldn't be seen as well by some of the people; we preach better with notes; we are much more comfortable in a pulpit; the portable microphone doesn't work well. (Also, cf. Chapter eleven on the need to have control of our material.)

[5]I usually ask the people their thoughts about homilists' use of notes or even a full text. The clear consensus was that this isn't a problem as long as it doesn't interfere with the personal tone of the homily. Some said, "When they use notes, we know they're prepared, and that's a good feeling." As for a full text, they had no problem as long as the homilist doesn't read *at* them and is able to be lively, engaging, personal.

5. Consider Informal Conversation with the Assembly Before the Entrance Rite.

Some informal conversation with the congregation (in addition to greeting them individually as they arrive) has a good effect. Once the entrance procession begins, we are in a ritual relationship, and casual informalities are less appropriate. But 2 or 3 minutes before mass is scheduled (I prefer this to beginning late), we can do any number of things to improve the "chemistry."[6]

The entrance procession (especially at major liturgies) can be done in a way that works against what the introductory rites are supposed to accomplish. The presider sometimes isn't seen by the people until he emerges in the procession. One has the impression of the entrance of the stars, something akin to the opening parade of the Olympic athletes, or of Jay Leno coming onstage or of a bride coming up the aisle.

The General Instruction of the Sacramentary says about the introductory rites:

> The purpose of these rites is that *the faithful coming together take on the form of a community* and prepare themselves to listen to God's word and celebrate the Eucharist properly. (#24, emphasis added)

Of the entrance song itself, the text says:

> The purpose of this song is to open the celebration, *intensify the unity of the gathered people,* lead their thoughts to the mystery of the season or feast, and accompany the procession of priest and ministers. (#25, emphasis added)

We who preside and preach are part of this "unity of the gathered people." Some back-and-forth with the people *before* the entrance rite can help achieve what the General Instruction describes and can give the homily a more-personal character.

---

[6] I find this particularly helpful at weddings and funerals because the assembly is usually made up of people who don't know each other and/or are of different faiths. Something needs to be done to break the ice.

CHAPTER NINETEEN

Good Feedback Is Priceless Because It's Hard to Get

They remember...and the memory helps.

Good feedback on a specific homily is hard to get. We don't have professional critics as in drama, music, and literature. We receive immediate reactions ("Nice homily"), but those can mean no more than "Have a nice day."

When I taught homiletics at St. John's Seminary, the students gave weekday homilies at nearby parishes. The congregation received an evaluation form with 14 criteria that they were to rate A, B, C, or D. Some of the criteria were:

- The homily presented one point and stayed with it.
- The language was simple and concrete.
- The length was just about right.
- The voice was clear and expressive.

The last question was: "All in all, how would you rate the homily?" Frequently, they would give high marks on the specifics and answer the last question "D."

I discovered that evaluating homilies is tricky business.

Immediate Feedback

Immediate positive reactions usually mean the homily was interesting, lively, entertaining, enjoyable, and well spoken. We still don't know if it struck a chord down deep where beats the heart of human life.[1]

Feedback after mass is usually not helpful and generally should not be taken too seriously. It is mixed in with other things:

- *Politeness:* People want to be friendly, so on the way out, they compliment us on our homily. It's not insincere; it's more like noticing someone with a new outfit and complimenting them. It's a kind thing to do, but it isn't a careful critique. (The tipoff on this is given when someone else gives the homily and parishioners say to us on the way out, "Appreciated your homily.")
- *Affection:* Much like the above. They like us and what we do in our ministry. Thanking us for our homily is a way of affirming our whole ministry.
- *Enjoyment:* They're thankful for a homily that was interesting, even entertaining. They laughed and were taken with our stories. Such reactions are sincere but tell us nothing about whether we ministered the word of God.[2]

Delayed Feedback

The best feedback is the kind that comes days, weeks, months later. Great homilies don't always look great up close. They're not sensational. They're too close to real life.

In the movie *Amadeus,* people initially liked Salieri's music much more than Mozart's. Whose music lasted? Years later, Salieri spoke of "my music growing fainter and fainter.... I am the patron saint of mediocrity."

I have concluded that there are two ultimate criteria for a good homily: (1) The people remember, and (2) the memory helps.

---

[1]This is true of the whole liturgy. I once heard it well said that if we want immediacy of response, we don't want liturgy. Liturgy is the long haul: It touches the depths of our being. An immediate response is not always telling.

[2]This is often true of specialized preachers with a canned message. They can be dramatic, bring tales from around the world, mesmerize with stunning stories, and everyone is taken with it. But even if the people remember, will the memory help?

It's a good sign if, months later, people still remember something from our homilies, but the other criterion has to be there: The memory helps. People might remember something because it was humorous, bizarre, fascinating, interesting, and well put together. This may not be helpful in living life on this planet, but if the memory helps, it indicates that the homily was something "for us and for our salvation."

If our homilies are good, we'll receive delayed feedback. People will say something like, "You know, your homilies mean a lot to me. They give me something to chew on and help me get through the week."

The key is not simply whether they like our homilies, find them interesting, admire the craftsmanship—all that is fine—but the real key is how our homilies affect their lives. There is a difference between admiring an art piece, a poem, or a song and being affected by it.

The best homilies engage the reflective process of the listeners, a process that continues for days, weeks. Someone wrote these thoughts to me about this:

> I love to hear a good preacher, not for this or that thought, but because over the long haul it stretches my own reflections in a personally helpful way. When the homily is a bad one, I tend to consider my own thoughts more interesting and stay with them. A good homilist is able to cause new reflection that continues over a long time. That is how true conversion happens.

There is also our own feedback to consider. Do *we* in fact remember our homilies, and does the memory help? This is more than being able to recount the gist of what we said: It is the kind of remembering that stays with us without our having to think back, like the refrain of a song. If our own homilies stay with us, make us think, urge us to reform, and sometimes haunt us, it's an indication we're on the right track.

What about people who thank us for saying something we didn't really say (a phenomenon we've all experienced)? It simply means that something we said triggered something else by association, or that they were thinking about other things during the homily, or that God had something else in mind for them and used our words to evoke it. It tells us nothing about the quality of our homily. It shouldn't lull us into thinking that it really doesn't matter what we say because God will turn it to something good.

Some Tips

1. The "Fidget Level" Can Serve as Helpful, Immediate Feedback.
Homilies generally start out with zero fidget level. A good homily will retain this from beginning to end.[3]

If the fidget level starts to rise above zero, even if it doesn't go past medium, we can be sure there is a homily problem—too long, too abstract, too many thoughts, not connected with life, no depth, and so on. A reasonable expectation of every homily should be zero fidget level from beginning to end. If now and then we fail to sustain that stillness, so be it; if often, we need to take a good look at our preaching.

2. Now and Then We Should Tape Our Homily, Wait Three or Four Days, and Then Listen to It.
This is a way to get some good feedback, namely, our own. One of the most beneficial parts of the Saginaw program is listening to our own tapes. Most of us rarely do that.

When I later listen to a tape of one of my homilies that I thought was pretty good, it usually turns out to be not as good as I thought it was. It seemed so clear to me while I was giving it because I knew exactly what I intended to say, but after several days, the whole thing isn't as fresh in my mind, and I hear it somewhat as the people did. I discover that the development left much to be desired. It may have been a good homily, but it was not as good as I thought. I've learned a lot from listening to my own homilies, disappointing as it might be at times.

It can also be helpful to do a written transcript of our homily now and then. The transcript should be word for word, with the half-sentences and the dangling phrases. When we read it, we notice patterns that we weren't aware of and that we want to change...and can change.

Indeed, good feedback is priceless...and hard to get.

---

[3] I do not include here the sounds of crying or cranky children: This is not the place to address this problem, but it is a problem. The lay people to whom I send tapes from our homily groups have observed how frequently such sounds interrupt the homily and make listening difficult. Even more serious is the way it interferes with the assembly's reception of the readings, the eucharistic prayer, or the precious times of silence in the mass. I'm not talking about the occasional cry or shout of a little one. It becomes a problem only when it goes on and on. This problem shows up in about 25 percent of the tapes. It needs to be addressed...but not here.

CHAPTER TWENTY

Learn from Weekday Homilies

*"If only they would preach on Sundays the
way they do on weekdays."*[1]

A weekday homily is a different species, just as a weekday mass is different from a Sunday mass. The preparation process suggested earlier would be impossible every day of the week.

On the other hand, perhaps we do some things intuitively in preparing and giving weekday homilies that give us a clue to what we should do on Sundays.[2]

A frequent comment from the folks is that we would do better if we preached on Sundays as we do on weekdays. I was surprised how consistently this surfaced.

Intrigued by this, I pursued it with some of the folks. Was it the brevity of the weekday homily? They said no, observing that some weekday homilies are as long as Sunday homilies, for example, a school mass when the homily has some give-and-take with the youngsters.[3]

---

[1]Comment from one of the folks.

[2]Golfers know that their swing at the driving range is often better than their swing on the golf course. It's more natural, fluid, relaxed. Something analogous may apply to the difference between weekday homilies and Sunday homilies.

[3]A related comment is that people say that they get more out of our homilies when we preach to youngsters.

After much thought, more questions put to the folks, and discussions with homilists, I have come up with the following:

- Weekday homilies almost always stay with one thought.
- In preparing a weekday homily, we think small rather than imagining a large space to fill. This produces a more-focused homily.
- Weekday homilies tend to come right out of the readings.
- Our faith shows through more easily in weekday homilies. We are more reflective and more personal, probably because the small, familiar weekday mass group provides a more homey setting.
- On weekdays, we are willing to take a risk, be creative, try something new (e.g., a prop). We know and trust the people who are there.[4]
- In weekday homilies, we are more apt now and then to involve the assembly in the homily.
- Beginnings and endings are better. We get right into it, without a long beginning, and we more-easily end it, without repeating, reviewing.
- (I think this is a big one.) On weekdays, we're not as concerned with "looking good." On Sundays, even more on big feasts or big events, the ego enters in. I want people to be impressed by a good homily, and by trying to make it so, the homily usually becomes less heart-to-heart. The truth is that in weekday homilies, we are less concerned about form. We are less concerned about what people will think of the homily. Our only concern is the thought we want to convey.

If all or most of that is true, why don't we do on Sundays what we do on weekdays? Maybe it's nerve. I don't know. But I think we should know.

---

[4] It's not as though we're always experimenting, but now and then we have to try something new, break new ground, as do writers, musicians—all artists. I would guess that most poor homilists have preached pretty much the same way from the very beginning: They have never seen the need to change or thought that they could change.

CHAPTER TWENTY-ONE

Using Props

A picture is worth a thousand words.

People like it when a homilist uses a "prop"–something visual.

I know a priest who uses a prop in every Sunday homily. Before mass, he comes out and places a paper bag (with the prop in it) by the lectern, and everyone's curiosity is piqued, especially the youngsters'.

I asked his parishioners if they thought that a prop every Sunday was too often: Does it wear thin? Not at all, they said; it makes the homily more interesting and easier to remember. If homilists can use props well, the parishioners would recommend doing it frequently.

Not every homilist should use a prop regularly, but some might find it effective now and then.

A Guiding Principle

One could apply to props the same criteria as stories (see Chapter Fourteen). Props shouldn't simply be entertainment or attention getters: Their sole purpose is to illuminate the core thought of the homily.

A measure of this is whether, after unveiling the prop, we would be able to hold it until the homily is finished. If not, it may indicate that we used it as a gimmick or that we had more than one core thought, which eventually made the prop no longer useful.

This happened in one of our homily groups. The gospel told of Jesus saying, "And you shall be my witnesses." At the beginning, the homilist held a fishing pole and talked about the time he was caught fishing without a license. When the game-warden's boat approached, the homilist tried to hide the fishing pole and to claim he wasn't fishing. This, he pointed out, wasn't exactly giving witness to our beliefs about truth. He then went on to talk about how difficult it can be in everyday life to live up to "and you will be my witnesses." So far so good.

But then he put the fishing pole down and went on to some other thoughts. The gospel included the story of the risen Lord asking the disciples if they had anything to eat. This, the homilist thought, was a good opportunity to develop some reflections about the significance of eating together (for example on Thanksgiving Day) and how the Lord is with us at such times, and so on. It was a different thought and should have been left out. We kidded him by saying, "You would have looked awfully funny holding that fishing pole when you were talking about Thanksgiving dinner."

Advantages of a Prop

The use of a prop has several advantages:

- It focuses the attention of the people.
- It "forces" the homilist to stay with one thought.
- The people are more likely to remember the pearl that was illustrated by the prop.
- We tend to be more creative and concrete in preparing the homily.
- We tend to be more natural, more connected with the assembly in delivering the homily.

An Example

Another of the priests in our groups had a pineapple upside-down cake as a prop. First, he held it up and invited the youngsters (it was a regular Sunday liturgy) to tell him what it was. This produced some excellent interaction: They first identified it as a cake; he asked what kind of cake and they guessed a fruit cake, coffee cake, and several others before someone finally guessed "pineapple upside-down cake."

Then, still interacting with the youngsters, he determined that all the "good stuff" (the brown sugar, the cherries, the pineapple) is on the bottom. To get to the good stuff, you have to turn the cake upside down.

The gospel reading was the passage where Jesus says, "You have heard that it was said, 'An eye for an eye and a tooth for a tooth.' But I say to you...." The homilist talked about how Jesus turned our world upside down, and he developed it well. His closing line was, "The next time you see a pineapple upside-down cake, remember that we are all meant to turn this sinful world upside down to reveal God's glory to all people."

It was an excellent use of a prop.

CHAPTER TWENTY-TWO

Don't Try to Make the Homily Do Everything That Needs to Be Done

"Sometimes the homily seems more like a grocery list."[1]

One of the greatest mistakes is to try to make the homily say everything that needs to be said at a given liturgy. Picture this scenario:

- It's the last sign-up Sunday for the religious education program, and the response has been low.
- You learned in midweek that there was to be a special collection for famine victims.
- It is also the Sunday when the second reading begins with "Wives should be subordinate to their husbands."
- Yesterday, a youngster in the parish was killed by a drunk driver.

These are all things that need to be dealt with. Some, instead of preaching a homily, would use that time to deal with these pastoral concerns; others would try to preach a homily that would somehow stretch wide enough to include them.

Neither option is necessary. If we look at the whole event of the mass, there are opportunities other than the homily to address these concerns, and the homily can still be a homily.

Here is how it could be handled.

---

[1] Comment from one of the folks.

Just Before Mass

The gathering rite begins long before the entrance procession: It begins when people start to gather. There is an opportunity here.

Two or 3 minutes before the entrance procession would be an excellent time to come out and talk to the people about the child's death. It is on everyone's mind, needs to be dealt with, and seems best dealt with right from the beginning. Some words about the anger, shock, and grief everyone feels and some consoling and supporting words directed to the family—this is how a good pastor gathers the flock and helps bring all of this flow into the liturgy.[2]

Some might wonder if this would be better after the opening greeting of the mass. I think not. The purpose of comments after the greeting is to "very briefly introduce the mass of the day."[3] Dealing with the child's death, in my opinion, needs a bit more time (2 or 3 minutes), needs a different setting, and is best done when the people are seated, not standing.[4]

After the Gathering Prayer

When the gathering prayer is finished, we have one of those natural breaks in the mass. The gathering rite has ended, the people are comfortably seated, and we are about to begin the Liturgy of the Word. If some background about the forthcoming scriptures is in order, this is a fine time to do it—succinctly.[5]

Here's a sample of one that could be used on our "imaginary Sunday" with the reading about wives and husbands:

> The last part of the Letter to the Ephesians, which deals with family relationships, is conditioned by the household structure of the

---

[2]Apart from occasions when all these things converge, it can still be helpful to talk to the people before the entrance procession. It changes the chemistry, creates a closeness, breaks down barriers. We can do any number of things depending on their appropriateness: welcome visitors, welcome home college youngsters who are present, ask who is having a birthday or anniversary this day or during the week, bring up something that is "in the air" and make comments on it. All of this is part of "gathering."

[3]Rubric of the Roman Missal.

[4]I think that in many cases, the introduction to the mass after the initial greeting is becoming too wordy, too preachy. It is meant to be brief.

[5]Even if the readings don't present an unusual problem, I believe that, at least for a generation or

time—slaves, children, wives—with the husband as "patriarch" over all. Today's excerpt talks about husbands and wives. Later, the epistle will talk about children and parents, slaves and masters. What we learn is not that we should re-create the primitive social structures of the time. We learn the timeless truth that Christ's love for us should affect the way we love one another.

After the Prayer of the Faithful

The shift from the Liturgy of the Word to the Liturgy of the Gifts is another break in the mass. Again, the people are seated. Normally I wouldn't suggest any remarks at this time (the people need some quiet time after the Liturgy of the Word), but this imaginary Sunday is not a normal one. Some carefully prepared informative comments about the famine collection could be given in less than 30 seconds.

At the End of the Communion Rite

The shift from the communion rite to the dismissal rite is the last of those natural breaks in the mass.[6]

The rubric says that, upon completion of the prayer after communion, "If there are any brief announcements, they are made at this time." It would seem appropriate to take about 2 minutes (not 5 minutes) for some well-prepared remarks (not meandering thoughts) about the religious education program.

---

two, it would be helpful to give some background on the first two readings; they appear to come out of nowhere, and the people need help to understand the context. But the background would have to be brief (no more than 30 seconds per reading), truly be background (set up their receptivity to the reading without telling them the content), and above all must not be a homilette.

[6]Keep in mind that the prayer after communion is not part of the dismissal rite. Because it is the ending of the communion rite, its content hearkens back to communion, not ahead to the sending forth. The General Instruction of the Missal says: "In the prayer after communion, the priest petitions for the effects of the mystery just celebrated..." (#56). Some celebrants remain seated for this prayer, which means that the people do too. Thus the prayer more easily flows from the time of silence after communion. Also, it eliminates having the people stand and then sit right back down for the announcements.

The upshot of all this is that all four pastoral matters are dealt with, the mass is extended by less than 4 minutes, and the homily is a homily, not a potpourri. We do everyone a favor, including ourselves, when we don't try to use the homily to say everything that has to be said.[7]

A Closing Thought

There are already too many words in most liturgies, and we should be looking for ways to economize not expand. Remember: This is an unusual Sunday, an exception, not the rule. The only other options would be to do nothing about these pastoral needs or to jettison the homily and deal with them at that time. I don't think those are good options.

On the other hand, I would not want to appear to suggest that we should take every opportunity during the mass to teach, explain, or give a homilette. Sometimes, we presiders use too many words in those ritual introductions that we're permitted to ad-lib—the initial greeting, the introduction to the Lord's Prayer, and so on. Generally speaking, a laconic presider is a most welcome one.

Also, there is a risk in each of the above that the celebrant will be too wordy. Remember: "I'm just going to talk for about 2 minutes" easily becomes 5 minutes. Speaking briefly on four different and important topics takes great discipline and much preparation, but it is worth the time spent crafting these comments—the good work of pastors shepherding their people.

---

[7]When I've had to deal in reality with such an imaginary Sunday, I have used this approach and it seemed to work.

CHAPTER TWENTY-THREE

Assembly Participation

"All we get to do is say 'Amen' or go to the bathroom."[1]

Most of the talk during mass is one-way (*at* the assembly), and most of the movement is restricted to the ministers. There is something refreshing about now and then getting things going the other way.

We forget how seldom people get to say or do something at the eucharistic liturgy. They can sing, of course, but during most of the liturgy, someone else does the talking and the moving around. A person in the pew once said to me, "All we get to do is say 'Amen' or go to the bathroom."[2]

Dialogue Homilies??

Dialogue homilies were an attempt to reverse this, but they seem to be on the wane, at least the open-ended kind in which anyone who

---

[1] Comment by a lay person in a group discussing ways to involve the assembly more in the liturgy.

[2] I once watched the video of a good Sunday liturgy with a stopwatch in hand and added up the amount of time the people spoke. I counted everything—every "Amen," every "And also with you." I was astounded to discover that the final total in this hour-long liturgy was 92 seconds, and that most of this was consumed in the Creed and the Our Father. I hope someday we can take a good look at this and revise the structure of the liturgy. But even in its current form, some participation of the people in the homily can make a big difference.

wanted to could speak. These tended to go on and on, as the fidget level of the assembly rose higher and higher.[3]

The dialogue homily can still work in small groups—if the group is small enough (which means very small) and if the homilist avoids the implicit expectation that everyone should say something.

Other Approaches

Still, in the regular Sunday homily, there is something to be said for interaction now and then. It can have a positive effect on the dynamics of the whole celebration. Even if only a few people actually respond, the whole assembly feels the flow coming from "their side of the altar."

The key to its success is a homilist who is comfortable with this and knows how to do it (as with props, which we spoke about earlier). It has to fit the style and personality of the homilist. Most can probably do it well, and now and then it can be helpful. It is probably done most frequently at children's liturgies, and it may be one reason why people often comment that most homilists are at their best with children.

One way of obtaining participation is inviting people to comment on something. Unlike the dialogue homily, this is not open ended, nor does it go on and on. We simply ask for a few comments to start the wheels turning.

Another easy way to obtain interaction is to invite the assembly to respond in survey fashion (by raising their hands). It's surprising how even this limited interaction can change the chemistry and give everyone a sense of being part of what's taking place.

Here is an example of the use of both of the above in one homily. Preaching on the gospel passage where Jesus says that the whole law and the prophets come down simply to loving God and loving our neighbor, the homilist wondered aloud which of those two was harder and said he wanted to do a survey.

"How many think loving God is harder?" (A small number of people raised their hands.)

---

[3]A key to any form of assembly participation is a homilist who has the skill to handle it. The dialogue homily requires more skill than most other forms. An analogous situation (not a homily) is the wake service when people are invited to share remembrances of the deceased. These work well and serve a good purpose, but unless the leader knows what he or she is doing, it can go on too long.

"How many think loving our neighbor is harder?" (The majority raised their hands.)

He told them to give both sides of the question some thought because the truth is that sometimes it's hard to love God. He then invited them to give examples of times when loving God is difficult. They came up with four or five examples that *everyone* could identify with. The homilist then gave some reflections on how we can love God even more fully when we honestly face up to this. The whole assembly felt part of the homily and came away with a pearl to take home.

Even that minimal kind of interaction makes a difference. Also, there's a better chance that they might talk to one another about it later, wondering how the other person "voted" in the survey.

There's something to be said for assembly participation when it can be done appropriately.

CHAPTER TWENTY-FOUR

There's a Time for Consolation

*"Remind them that for a lot of us, coming to mass
is the only 'retreat' we have."*[1]

The people were strong in their feedback about the need to hear more positive, uplifting homilies. I wasn't expecting the frequency with which they voiced this plea. Here are some of their comments.

Feedback from the Folks

- "When I leave, I want to feel better about myself than when I came in, even if the homily challenged me."
- "I wish homilies were more positive and uplifting."
- "When she preaches, I always leave feeling inspired."
- "People should feel lightened, not burdened."
- "Emphasize the positive now and then, not just the negative."
- "I don't like someone who is harsh, always blaming, repeating rules."
- "Homilies often have the same mood we get from radio, TV, and newspapers. They're always knocking things. That's easy to do. Give us something uplifting."
- "I don't like it when they use the pulpit to harangue."

---

[1]Feedback from a layperson.

- "When I read the gospels I feel consoled. When I hear his homilies I feel like I got 'bad marks' in class."
- "Our pastor talks to us as a friend who wants to help us."

Preaching Consoling Homilies

There is a time to settle in with the sorrowful mysteries, but there is also a time to settle in with the joyful and glorious mysteries. We might ask ourselves: When is the last time I faithfully went with the flow of the scriptures and gave a homily that was clearly uplifting, inspiring, and filled with the good news of salvation?[2]

The feedback from the people indicates that in their opinion this isn't done frequently enough.

The purpose of a consoling homily isn't to give the people a break from the things they really need to hear. The purpose is to preach the full gospel, and consolation is part of it.[3]

Experiences of lightness and joy are necessary for spiritual progress and for perseverance. We need an inner conviction that through God's grace we are worthwhile; life is worthwhile. We are more likely to respond to reform if we believe we are reformable.[4]

One of the comments from the folks affected me more than I can say. It came from a divorced woman whom I knew well and who had a tough life. I told her I was working with homilists and asked her if she had any suggestions. She thought for a moment and then said with a certain sadness something like this:

---

[2]There may be some relationship here to the fact that we seem to be having a hard time catching on to mystagogia.

[3]In Mark's Gospel, Jesus sends out the 12 Apostles, and "they went off and preached *repentance*." (6:2) In his commentary, D.E. Nineham says that it could be that the content of their preaching at this preresurrection stage ("repentance") is deliberately distinguished from the full Christian gospel to which the word *preach* normally refers and which they would preach after the resurrection. If this is true, he says, then the preaching of the 12 Apostles at this stage is similar to the preaching of John the Baptist. They are only able to preach a mission of repentance. Not until after the passion, death, and resurrection when their eyes were opened did their preaching become the good news of salvation.

[4]In its 1993 document, the Pontifical Biblical Commission includes a surprisingly strong statement on this:

"Preachers should certainly avoid insisting in a one-sided way on the obligations incumbent upon believers. The biblical message must preserve its principal characteristic of being the good news of salvation freely offered by God. Preaching will perform a task more useful and more conformed to the Bible if it helps the faithful above all to 'know the gift of God' (Jn 4:10) as it has been revealed in Scripture; they will then understand in a positive light the obligations that flow from it." (IV 3)

Tell them that you priests get to have days of prayer and retreats, and I'm glad you do. But I'm trying to raise five children alone. Coming to mass is the only "retreat" I have. Just once I'd like to sit there and be consoled...told that God loves me, and not have extra burdens put on my head. Just now and then, let me feel good.

As she spoke I thought about how many people hope for this from our homilies, and I felt not so good. Not every homily must be consoling from beginning to end, but some ought to be.

Consider, for example, the gospel passage, "You are the salt of the earth. But if salt loses its taste, with what can it be seasoned? It is no longer good for anything but to be thrown out and trampled underfoot." (Mt 5:13) Homilists are generally inclined to pick up on the last two sentences and preach about the need to live up to these expectations.

But might there be a time when we would simply focus on the first sentence and take consolation from the fact that the Lord thinks so much of us? I heard a homilist do that one time. He said something like:

Now, remember whom Jesus was speaking to. These were just regular folks from the small towns up north trying to eke out a living. Imagine what they must have thought when Jesus said to them, "YOU are the salt of the earth." They looked at one another and said, "Hey. What's going on here? He must have pulled out the wrong speech. *Us* the salt of the earth? You've gotta be kidding. We're not the ones who spend hours every day studying the law. We can't even read. Somebody get up there and tell him who we are."

The homilist then went on to talk about how Jesus knew exactly to whom he was speaking. His message was different, startling. We are all daughters and sons of God. No matter who we are—rich or poor, healthy or lame, clean or unclean—we are made in the image and likeness of God. We have greatness within us and we're the ones Jesus came for. We're all "important people" in his eyes. The starting point for any disciple of Jesus is not how much we love God. It's how much God loves us.

It was good news, and we need to preach it more often.

We can take a cue from the second verse of the great spiritual "There Is a Balm in Gilead":

If you cannot preach like Peter,
If you cannot pray like Paul,
You can tell the love of Jesus,
And say, "He died for all."

CHAPTER TWENTY-FIVE

Preaching About Sin

We're a "full gospel" church.

The good news is sometimes hard news, and if we are true to the proclaimed scriptures, there are times when we must preach a hard message about sin.

Strangely, the feedback from the folks over the years didn't include much on this. Perhaps that is a reaction to so many moralizing homilies in the past that harped on sin.

Occasionally, I hear people speak positively about a particular homily that addressed thoughtfully but strongly the sinfulness that we tend to gloss over these days. I'd have to admit that I don't hear about such homilies often. (I'd also have to admit that I don't give them often.) But when they are done well, the feedback is very positive.[1]

In the last chapter, we talked about homilies that mainly console. There is also a time for homilies that mainly challenge. Preaching from assigned readings is an advantage that shouldn't be overlooked. We preach the full Word of God, not our own favorite texts. We are guided by the scriptures, not our own temperament or leanings.

---

[1] I'm not referring here to social-justice homilies. We have increased the frequency of these. Here I am speaking particularly of the sins (often referred to by the misnomer "personal sins") that are within our immediate power to face up to and resolve.

The Good News Is Sometimes Hard News

All of scripture is ultimately good news. The Old Testament, for example, has within it an unbounded optimism that Yahweh will somehow, someday, set all things right; the New Testament, which is centered around the death-resurrection-ascension, is good news.

On the other hand, scripture does not teach that anything goes or that sin does not have consequences. God offers sinners the gift of salvation, but the disposition that enables us to receive this gift is a willingness to change. Scripture challenges us to repent and reform. God is infinitely merciful, not infinitely permissive.

Someone once pointed out to me that the Lord holds his arms wide in mercy. He was willing to forgive anyone: tax collectors, a woman taken in adultery, even his executioners.[2] But he also holds his arms wide in his demands. He asked for everything: leave your boats, nets, father, mother.

There is a clue here for homilists: We have to preach the full gospel and make sure we neglect neither the consolation nor the challenge. To preach that the Lord forgives everything but makes no demands misses the gospel. The opposite is also a failure—to portray the Lord as demanding everything but limiting forgiveness.

The church struggles with this. Fifty years ago, our arms were wide in demanding everything and not so wide in expressing God's forgiveness (we wouldn't bury someone who committed suicide). Today, our arms are wide in mercy, but I wonder if we adequately stress the demands of discipleship. We have to do both.

Preaching the Hard News

In her article giving advice to homilists, theologian Catherine Mowry LaCugna had something to say about addressing sin and repentance.

> [Finally]—and this is a matter of great delicacy—the homily, precisely because it is a means of encounter with the word of God, is an occasion to call us to repentance of our sin. And sin must always be

---

[2] Luke's words of Jesus from the cross ("Father, forgive them...") are missing from some early manuscripts. Contemporary scholarship leans toward their authenticity and attributes the deletions to a reluctance to portray Christ as modeling such lavish and wide-sweeping mercy. (Cf. Raymond Brown, *The Death of the Messiah* [New York: Doubleday, 1994, Vol. II, pp. 971–81].)

named in relation to grace. Sin is certainly not a popular subject, and much in our culture would prefer us to feel good about ourselves, so good, in fact, that we see nothing wrong with anything about us or our choices. There is no doubt that, in the past, sin was rather narrowly understood, and too much negativity about the human being, especially in matters of sexuality, flowed from our pulpits. But we seem to have gone in the opposite direction, so that the profound tensions between sin and grace are rarely mentioned. Certainly we do believe mightily that God loves us, and loves us just as we are, and there are many Christians who cannot hear this enough. But this must be joined with the equally important belief that, compared with the holiness and pure love of God, we are indeed sinners. The word of God being proclaimed, precisely because it is *God's* word, is the only reliable barometer of the truthfulness, integrity and holiness, or self-deception and selfishness, of our lives.[3]

This may be the key: "the profound tensions between sin and grace are rarely mentioned." If we are clear about grace but not clear about sin, there is no tension, and if we dilute them in a mix, the result is a homily that appears to be half-hearted about both. We neither challenge nor console and end up with a lukewarm message.

Guilt is a reality in everyone's life—real guilt that causes anxiety. If this is easily dismissed, then what we say is hollow, doesn't connect, and comes off as cheap sin and cheap grace.

We have to stop and think about this and ask ourselves: When is the last time I faithfully went with the flow of the scriptures and preached the hard news of repentance and reform?

I am not speaking simply of a sweeping message about the sins of today's society or of "the world" in general; I am speaking also of the sins that are part of our lives close at hand.[4]

The caution, of course, is to make sure that we do this sinner to sinner. We are ministers, not messiahs, and true ministry is lateral, not vertical.

Remember too that the homily flows into the rest of the liturgy and should prepare us for the praise and thanksgiving of the eucharistic prayer. Sin must be dealt with but always in relation to grace.

---

[3] *America*, March 19, 1994, p. 5

[4] I do remember giving a homily about how our language has deteriorated so that we casually throw God's name around to express anger or amusement plus vulgar expressions that are disrespectful of others. Actually, the reactions were quite positive, and people said in various ways, "We need to hear more of that." But I haven't really done much of that—even this one was more on a "peccadillo" than the down-deep sins that need to be addressed.

CHAPTER TWENTY-SIX

Ten Demons

This chapter contains cautions that came up consistently in the responses from the folks or discussions in our homily groups. Each does not require a whole chapter. I simply list them here as demons to avoid.

Demon #1: Retelling the Gospel

I was surprised not only by the frequency with which this came up, but also how livid people become about this and how little retelling it takes to trigger their reaction. They become downright belligerent.

The following is from a Thanksgiving Day homily. The gospel was the story of the 10 lepers. In this excerpt from the homily, the parts that retell the gospel are italicized.

> *Jesus encountered a group of 10 of them,* a pathetic colony of suffering. *From the prescribed distance, they called out, "Jesus, have mercy!"* My guess is that they were asking for money for food. What follows is fascinating. *Jesus sends them off to see a priest. On the way, they are cleansed. One of the 10 returns to find Jesus and falls on his face, thanking him.* Jesus sounds like my mother when *he wonders out loud about the other nine and then says to the man, "Get up and go your way; your faith has made you well."*

This is a "mild" case of retelling the gospel, and I cite it to emphasize that even this relatively small dose would irk a lot of people. After all, this is one of the best-known passages in the gospels.

We can refer to something in the gospel, but we have to find ways of calling it to mind without retelling it. For example, imagine preaching about the mustard seed. We say that the parable was partly a response to the puzzlement of the disciples about the unspectacular and outwardly insignificant ministry of Jesus. Then we refer to the parable itself by saying:

> So Jesus asked the question, "What is the kingdom of God like?" He answered by comparing it to the mustard seed. Now the mustard seed is the tiniest of all the seeds, but after it is sown, it grows to become a large plant with big branches, big enough so that even the birds can come and dwell in those branches.

As brief as this is, it retells too much. It would have been better to say:

> So he told them the story of the mustard seed that seemed so tiny but was the seed of something great.

Speaking of tiny mustard seeds, this may seem too small a difference to matter, but in the eyes of the people it is a much greater concern.[1]

Interestingly, *quotes* from the gospel are fine, provided they are brief. People don't mind it when we cite a short excerpt from the text to reenforce it: We are giving them the very words. What gets their goat is when we retell in our own words the same thing they just heard.

Demon #2: A "Pulpit Tone"

Some homilists speak in a different tone when they preach. The pitch of their voice and their inflections are different, not natural. This is usually evident to everyone except the homilist.

In the Saginaw groups, our attempts to help with this have usually been only moderately successful, even when homilists, after listening to their own tapes, began to notice it themselves. We're not skilled in adjusting speech patterns—most of us simply "speak."

One suggestion is to practice giving the homily to one individual. It will almost always become more conversational and natural. *Feeling*

---

[1] I suspect that some readers will be skeptical about this one, but the feedback over the years has made me a believer, and when I showed a draft of this book to various lay people, this was one of the items frequently picked out as something that should be emphasized strongly.

that difference can help. Beyond that, all I can suggest is the consultation of an expert.

This is more than a minor matter. A pulpit tone is perceived by the listeners as artificial and can get in the way of a good homily.

Demon #3: Warming Up Old Homilies in the Microwave

I disagree with the old axiom that when a person moves to a new parish, every old homily becomes a new one. If a homily is the ministry of the living Word of God to *these* people at *this* time, then old homilies will not do. The readings might appear to be the same, but they aren't the same. They are always living water, the fresh bread of life. The world has changed since these readings were proclaimed three years ago; the community has changed; I have changed.

Furthermore, microwaving old homilies has a bad effect on us. We lose our creative edge.

I am uncomfortable when I hear someone refer to "my wedding homily" or "my funeral homily" or "my confirmation homily." I am uncomfortable when homilists use a canned homily linked artificially to the readings of the day.

This doesn't mean that some of our excellent past homilies are of no use at all; insights from them and parts of them can emerge later in different ways and become a new homily. What we should avoid is reheating the whole old homily with no fresh discernment.

Demon #4: Repetition

People hate repetition in homilies: This ranked near the top in their feedback. They find it boring, pointless, aggravating, and an insult to their intelligence.

Why do we repeat ourselves? Sometimes to fill space, sometimes because we're treading water while figuring out what we're going to say next, sometimes because we're not sure we said it right the first time.

Whatever the cause, repetition—except when skillfully done for purposes of emphasis—always works against us.

Demon #5: Cut-and-Paste Homilies

By *cut-and-paste homilies,* I mean homilies that are almost entirely constructed out of materials that are not our own, for example, homily helps and stories we've collected.

There's nothing wrong with borrowing good material for homilies. One of the faculty members we respected most in the seminary told us that to be a good preacher, we have to swallow hard and use good material that is not our own. Our task, he said, is to serve good food to the people, no matter where we get it.

What I refer to here is a homily that is made up of collected pieces that we cut and paste together without taking them inside ourselves.[2]

There are two pitfalls in cut-and-paste homilies. First, too many thoughts: We glue together stories, examples, and applications that fill the space, but they really aren't connected except on the surface. Instead of going deeply into a particular thought, we paste in another and then another. We skim along the surface from thought to thought.

The second pitfall is the loss of the personal character of the homily. We may be sharing good material, but our faith doesn't show through. Not that we don't believe what we're saying—it's simply that we haven't wrestled with and worked through it in our own lives. People can tell the difference. They know, for example, when we use a story borrowed from a homily aid and tell it in the first person as though it happened to us.

A cut-and-paste homily with interesting pieces beats a drab homily, but one would hope that most homilists could do better.

Demon #6: Long Quotes, Too Many Quotes

Quotes from a book or a poem almost always mean more to me than to the listeners. For one thing, I already like it—that's why I chose it. For another, I know the larger context from which it was taken, and most or all of the people do not.

Using quotes in a written article and using quotes in a homily are quite different things. In a written article, readers can take their time, reread the quote, and think about it. In a homily, they have none of these options.

When I read a quote aloud in a homily, it always seems longer than it seemed when I was preparing the homily. Nothing surprising there. We read faster than we speak. (When I use a quote of more than two or three sentences, I often end up shortening or eliminating it in the homily at the next mass. It was too long and didn't have the effect I thought it would.)

---

[2]Homily helps can stir the imagination, and trigger something inside of us; that is fine. But they cannot replace careful study, reflection, and prayer, nor can they connect with the actual people to whom we are going to preach.

Quotes can be effective, but keep in mind three things:

- First, it has to be *great* stuff to be worthwhile. That it fits the topic isn't enough; it has to be great or it comes off as filler.
- Second, it has to be something that has wide appeal. Because a poem is special to me doesn't mean it will be cherished by the majority of the assembly. It may be special to some who are of the same temperament, but that's not enough; it's got to click with most everyone.
- Third—and I'm not sure just how to put this—we shouldn't make some of the people feel inferior because they're not familiar with an author we quote. Everyone has heard of Plato, Milton, Shakespeare, even if they're not reading them regularly. People don't feel second class when such authors are cited. But citing authors many have never heard of can come off as elitist.

Quoting a passage from scripture, even one from the scriptures just heard, can be very effective, especially as an ending. (Quoting from a passage we just heard is perceived quite differently than retelling it.) However, I usually find that rereading too many scriptural passages or a few long ones is not as effective as I thought it would be.[3]

Demon #7: Leaving Out Singles

The most frequent examples used in homilies have to do with married life, and the shortest phase of married life at that: parents raising young children. The result is that many people can feel left out of a lot of homilies:

adult families
single people
elderly people who live alone
divorced people who have not remarried

More than one-fourth of the nation's households are occupied by people who live alone, and their numbers have doubled in the past 25 years. They are among those most often left out in our examples because the examples that spring most naturally to mind are those about households with two parents and young children.

When this omission was first pointed out to me, I recognized it

---

[3]People seem less enthused about homilies that consist mainly in citing a scriptural quote from the readings, commenting on it, citing another, and so forth. They want *an insight* into the readings, not a rundown on all three readings, or even a complete rundown on one of them.

immediately in my own homilies; then I began to notice it in others. Correcting it is easy.

The ones most left out are single people who have never married and have no children. Here's an example, my critique of a homily given by a religious woman in one of our groups:

> The image of responding to God's "invitation" was excellent. One point about that. When talking about invitations, you used the example of wedding invitations, and invitations to your own religious profession, and you even mentioned ordination invitations. Lay single people were left out. Now I don't want to make too much of that because it was one brief example. I mention it because single people are so often left out. Sometimes, I think we need to be as sensitive to this as we are to inclusive language.

There is nothing at all wrong with using examples about family life as long as we also use examples that include those who never married and never had a family. All they ask is a word now and then to feel included.

An interesting sidelight is that the gospels have few examples from family life and plenty from elsewhere. Jesus talked about:

the sower	weeds among the wheat
a lamp in the house	yeast in the dough
the mustard seed	a buried treasure
salt	patches on clothing
the fig tree	new wine in old wineskins
tenants in the vineyard	the lost sheep
the poor widow	workers in the marketplace
a house built on rock or sand	a king giving a wedding feast
a tree and its fruit	a thief in the night

It's worth some thought.

Demon #8: Picking Out Scripture Readings
That Say What We Want Them to Say

We are a "full gospel" church. We don't pick and choose readings that we happen to like or want to preach on. Assigned scriptures are set before us week after week, and we must let them speak to us. (It's worth noting that scripture interprets life, not vice versa.)

We're faithful to the Sunday readings, but at other liturgies the readings are changed at the drop of a hat. Now there can be good reasons—for example, children's liturgies. A special event (e.g., 25th wedding anniversary) might also be an appropriate time to change the scriptures of the day.[4]

However, it can be done too easily and too often. The presumption ought to favor the readings already there. It may be appropriate to change them, but we ought at least to take a good look at them before making that decision. I'm thinking of masses at conferences, religious jubilees, priest jubilees, gatherings of teachers, and such.

If it is pastorally wise to change the readings (or if it is a celebration that warrants special readings, e.g., weddings or funerals), the selection ought to be done with awareness of the purpose of the scriptures at liturgy—to open up to us the mystery of redemption and salvation, to nourish our spirit.[5]

In my experience, this is not always the guiding principle; instead, scriptures are chosen to support a preexisting message, or they are chosen simply as a garnish to the event.

Demon #9: Lousy PA Systems

I have an axiom: "The bigger the event, the more likely something will go wrong with the sound system."

I don't know what to do about that, and it isn't my concern in citing this demon. I'm talking about sound systems that are inadequate and/or function poorly *all the time.*

There was more feedback on this than I expected. People expressed frustration about having to strain Sunday after Sunday to hear what is being said.

There's not much to say about this, except that it is a basic necessity for the people and that we ought to take it as seriously as we would if the air conditioner at home wasn't working in July.[6]

---

[4]On the other hand: A couple was celebrating their 50th wedding anniversary at the Saturday evening mass. Relatives came from near and far. The assigned gospel was the passage when Jesus says, "If anyone comes to me without hating his father and mother, wife and children, brothers and sisters...they cannot be my disciple." Because it was a parish liturgy, I stayed with the readings, and it forced some good thoughts about the meaning of this passage and the meaning of marriage.

[5]General Instruction of the Roman Missal, #33.

[6]Someone recently told me that dioceses should conduct a "sound audit" of their parishes: "If the word of God is as important as you say it is, then it's important to have a decent sound system," he said, "as it is to have balanced books." An interesting thought.

Demon #10: Unnecessary Qualifiers

This is another of those things I never noticed until I started listening to so many taped homilies. We tend to use, almost unconsciously, words and phrases that mute the message. I'm not sure why; all I know is that we all do it and that it gets in the way.

Here's a sample of the unnecessary qualifiers (italicized) found in just one homily:

- "I *probably only* got halfway through reading it and..."
- "The main focus, *it seemed* was that..."
- "I had *kind of* forgotten all about that periodical because I didn't *really* want..."
- "We have enough evil, *sometimes,* in our world..."
- "I *kind of* forgot about it, until..."
- "It's *just* so predominant..."
- "I *think* the Lord loves us enough to..."
- "To cleanse ourselves *maybe* of any interior prejudice..."
- "That's the gift *I think* we have..."

For some reason, these unnecessary qualifiers turn up frequently in our homilies. We use words and phrases such as *it seems to me, I think maybe, somewhat, perhaps, kind of, just sort of,* and *I just kind of want to set the tone....*

There are times when it is appropriate, even necessary, to qualify something as a conjecture. It was our experience, however, that most were not for precision but simply symptoms of sloppy speech habits.

CHAPTER TWENTY-SEVEN

A Homily to Homilists

At a Chicago Theological Union gathering of biblical scholars and homily scholars, I was invited to preside and preach at the Eucharist.

What follows is not a transcript of the homily; none exists. Rather it is what, looking back afterward, I wanted to say. In these pages, I have said several times that when we give a homily twice, we have more control of our material the second time; this, in effect, is my homily "the second time."

The readings were the call of Jeremiah (Jer 1:4 ff), Paul on the primacy of love (1 Cor 12:31 ff), and the reaction of the people in the synagogue at Nazareth to Jesus' words (Lk 4:21–30). Here is the homily:

The combination of these readings and this event force upon me a reflection that I'd rather not make, but it's nearly inescapable. It's also hard to put into words.

You see, it involves a *very subtle* temptation that sneaks up on all who minister the word, especially those who can do it well. I'll try to describe how it plays out in my life, and you can ponder if and how it plays out in your life.

I am quite capable of doing a homily that is well written, well presented, interesting, even entertaining. It will be connected both with the scriptures and with real life. It will convey some good thoughts. People will like it, even be helped by it–and they will like me.

But sometimes it is more a piece I produce than a ministry to help illumine what God is doing. It is more "See what I'm doing" rather than "See what God is doing." I act more like a chef than a waiter.

Funny. I never do that with the Bread of Life that is the Eucharist. When I minister communion, I easily and rightly accept my role as the waiter. As I hold the Bread of Life before someone and say, "The Body of Christ," the focus is never me. With considerable wonder and awe, I think, "The Body of Christ." Never do I think, "Look at what I am doing." After mass, I don't ever think about whether people will compliment me about the way I "did" communion.

Why isn't it the same with the Bread of Life that is the Word? Why does this subtle temptation worm its way into that part of my ministry?

There is a difference–and deep down I can tell the difference– between aiming to *do a good homily,* rather than *doing something good* through my preaching.

I can tell the difference between being taken with my homily, rather than being taken with the Spirit at work in the word.

I can tell the difference between thinking about what I am achieving in my homily, rather than what *God* is doing in this liturgical event.

I can tell the difference between "giving a talk" and really "talking to them"...between "making a good presentation to them," and "presenting something that is good for all of us to think about."

Does all this strike any chords within you? Perhaps it will help if I tell you about some of signs that are sure symptoms. I can tell, when I am honest with myself, that I have been taken by this temptation...

- if when writing the homily, I think about how some people in the assembly will admire it.
- if when giving the homily, I spend more energy trying to remember the words I worked so hard on—especially clever phrases—than trying to speak from the heart.
- if, after mass, I am beaming, expectant of praise.

It's so damned subtle–and so clear.

When I listen to the word of God in today's liturgy, I am ashamed of those times. I listen to Luke's account of Jesus speaking in his hometown synagogue, so consciously aware of the influence of the Spirit upon him, and conscious of little else.

I listen to Jeremiah realizing that he has been called by God in this time and this place for these people, to do, as God says, "the things that *I* command you."

I listen to Paul speak of love—not abstract or theological love, but love that is genuine. This is the point when it hits home...when he speaks of a love that is not inflated, does not seek its own interests. He doesn't let up. "If I speak in angelic tongues,...comprehend all mysteries and all knowledge, but do not have love, *I am nothing.*"

Now, you must understand: The problem we're talking about here isn't a case of being a charlatan. Even when I succumb to this temptation, I am sincere in the message that I am trying to convey so skillfully. I really believe what I'm saying, and I want the hearers to get it and be affected by it, all to the betterment of their lives. No, the problem is not hypocrisy; it would be easier to identify if it were.

But it's more as if I am doing a painting with which people will become taken, rather than doing a ministry that helps to draw out the artistry of God's living Word.

The difference is so damned subtle—except that I *know* the difference.

I don't do it with the Bread of Life that is the Eucharist. I have to stop doing it with the Bread of Life that is the Word.

Perhaps it would help if, when preparing a homily, I said an adapted form of the prayer we say when the gifts are brought to the altar to become the eucharistic Bread of Life. It would fit. I think I'll do that. I'll look at the Word of God, remember that this too is the Bread of Life, the "real presence," and say:

> *Blessed are you God of all creation. Through your goodness we have this bread to offer...which you have given, and which human hands have shaped. May it become for us the bread of life.*

THE
BEST
AMERICAN
POETRY
2001

◇　◇　◇

Robert Hass, Editor

David Lehman, Series Editor

SCRIBNER POETRY

NEW YORK　LONDON　TORONTO　SYDNEY　SINGAPORE

SCRIBNER POETRY
1230 Avenue of the Americas
New York, NY 10020

SCRIBNER POETRY and design are trademarks
of Macmillan Library Reference USA, Inc., used under license
by Simon & Schuster, the publisher of this work.

For information regarding special discounts for bulk purchases,
please contact Simon & Schuster Special Sales at 1-800-456-6798 or
business@simonandschuster.com

Manufactured in the United States of America

1   3   5   7   9   10   8   6   4   2

ISBN 0-7432-0383-6
0-7432-0384-4 (Pbk)
ISSN 1040-5763

CONTENTS

David Lehman was born in New York City in 1948. He is the author of five poetry books, including *The Daily Mirror: A Journal in Poetry* (2000) and *The Evening Sun* (forthcoming in 2002), both from Scribner. Among his nonfiction books are *The Last Avant-Garde: The Making of the New York School of Poets* (Anchor, 1999) and *The Perfect Murder* (Michigan, 2000). With Star Black he is coeditor of *The KGB Bar Book of Poems* (HarperCollins, 2000). He has received a Guggenheim Fellowship in poetry, an Academy Award in Literature from the American Academy of Arts and Letters, and a three-year writer's award from the Lila Wallace–Reader's Digest Fund. He is on the core faculty of the graduate writing programs at Bennington College and the New School for Social Research, and teaches "Great Poems" in the undergraduate honors program at NYU. He directs the University of Michigan Press's Poets on Poetry Series. He initiated *The Best American Poetry* in 1988.

FOREWORD

by David Lehman

◊   ◊   ◊

A curious thing has happened. While American poetry continues to
flourish, this has occurred in an inverse relationship to the prestige of
high culture as traditionally understood and measured. High culture has
taken a beating. At regular intervals journalists announce the demise of
the "public intellectual." Stories circulate about dysfunctional English
departments (Duke, Columbia). Outrageous hoaxes bamboozle the
faculty's talking heads, whose peculiar patois and preference for theory
over practice provoke savage indignation in some corners and satirical
merriment in others. A respected professor at a major university told me
that the only thing unifying the warring factions in the English department there is "a common hatred of literature." In the twenty-fifth
anniversary issue of *Parnassus: Poetry in Review,* the journal's editor, Her-
bert Leibowitz, laments the dwindling of "the audience for belletristic
criticism—as opposed to the jargon-riddled academic variety." Leibowitz regards poetry criticism as an art, an art in crisis because of bad
academic habits on the one side and the timidity of poets on the other
("the reluctance of poets to write honestly about their peers"). He
surely has a point and is in an excellent position to know. Yet what is
equally noteworthy is that the virus afflicting poetry criticism has left
poetry itself uncontaminated.

In the last decade the audience for poetry has grown; enthusiasts keep
turning up in unexpected quarters, and the media are paying attention
and magnifying the effect. Poetry readings, fairs, and festivals have pro-
liferated. National Poetry Month has raised April sales (without lowering those of other months). Initiatives ranging from "Poetry in Motion"
posters in buses and subways to Robert Pinsky's "favorite poem project"
have helped bridge the gap between poetry and the ordinary citizen. The
radio voice of Garrison Keillor reads a Shakespeare sonnet in drive
time, and on the *News Hour* with Jim Lehrer that evening a retired Air

Force officer tearfully recites Yusef Komunyakaa's poem about the Vietnam Memorial, "Facing It." Are these things causes or effects of the poetry boom? Probably both, as are Bill Moyers's PBS documentaries, *The Language of Life* in 1995 and *Fooling with Words* four years later. Moyers's efforts have met with highbrow derision, but that is true of many efforts to popularize a cultural phenomenon with a reputation for difficulty. One critic has called Moyers the "Bob Costas of the American poetry world," the "ultimate fan," which may be one of those left-handed insults that conveys something of a compliment despite its contemptuous intent. Quarrel with Moyers's taste and judgment all you want; there is no denying the value of his TV programs in building an audience for the poets lucky enough to get air time.

More popular than ever, creative writing programs have helped make up for the neglect of literature elsewhere on campus. It is an argument for the health and vitality of contemporary poetry that so many talented young people devote two graduate years to its study despite knowing that "there's nothing in it" (as Ezra Pound's Mr. Nixon warns in "Hugh Selwyn Mauberley"). It is, of course, easy to mock the locutions of the universal workshop, though I find not only humor but a sort of charm in them. One day in a workshop last February, somebody said, "I had issues with the pronouns in the other lines, too," and off went that little mental explosion that tells me a poem, in the case at hand a villanelle, was on the way. I called it "Issues":

I had issues with the pronouns in the other lines, too.
It started to kick in for me with the part about the war.
Did what I say make sense to you?

I wondered whether what "you" said was true,
Which may have been what "you" were aiming for.
I had issues with the pronouns in the other lines, too,

And not just the pronouns but the branding ("Mountain Dew").
I like the imagery especially "in the forest there's a door."
Did what I say make sense to you?

But I wish the poem didn't dodge the repercussions of "Jew,"
And I winced at "hoodlums and whores."
I had issues with the pronouns in the other lines, too,

But in the other lines what comes through is you,
What I hear is your voice, a kind of quiet roar.
Did what I say make sense to you?

Don't get me wrong, I like the second-person point of view,
But it raises issues. Like what. Like gender.
I had issues with the pronouns in the other lines, too.
Did what I say make sense to you?

As one who teaches workshops I recognize their structural defects. I sometimes wonder how certain great poems would fare in a workshop. I can well imagine that after the class got through with Wallace Stevens's "Of Mere Being" the amazing last line of that poem ("The bird's fire-fangled feathers dangle down") would not survive intact. Nevertheless I'm convinced that the study of poetry, fiction, and serious literature depends more and more on creative writing programs on all levels. This may seem a supreme irony to anyone who remembers the combination of condescension and skepticism that English department regulars directed at their creative writing colleagues twenty-five years ago. Creative writing is sometimes denigrated on the grounds that few workshop-trained poets will go on to write poems as great as those of Wallace Stevens, who studied law, not poetry or creative writing. But few poets, workshop-trained or not, will write great poems. Our mission is to nurture talent and keep the love of poetry at its liveliest, most receptive, and most creative state, and if the student publishes few poems but becomes an avid reader we will have done a job that others have relinquished.

A good deal of creativity has gone into the teaching of creative writing. Low residency MFA programs, such as the ones at Bennington in Vermont and Warren Wilson in North Carolina, which convene for short periods twice a year and do the rest of their work by correspondence between student and faculty, enable grown-ups with families, spouses, jobs to give sustained attention to their writing. Given demographic trends, it is easy to predict the growth of such programs as well as the spread of summer writing conferences lasting anywhere from a weekend to several weeks in picturesque locales. Already the ambitious initiate of whatever age can take instruction at Bread Loaf, Sewanee, Squaw Valley, Saratoga Springs, Provincetown, the Napa Valley, and numerous other desirable sites including the European cities of Prague, St. Petersburg,

Dublin, and Paris. I can hear the retort of the scandalized idealist who associates the creative writing workshop with the decline of civilization: "In the baby boom generation, no one will retire. Instead they will write poetry." Well, maybe, and all of us must sometimes secretly fear that everyone wants to write the stuff and no one wants to read it. At such moments we would do well to recall that Seamus Heaney's verse translation of *Beowulf,* not your conventional potboiler, sold two hundred thousand copies in hardcover and occupied a slot on the *New York Times* bestseller list for ten weeks last year. Readers do exist, more than you might have thought. The trick remains how to reach them.

On the "everyone wants to write the stuff" front, New York Mets' reliever Turk Wendell, he of the animal-claw necklace, writes it ("Life Is Like a Baseball"). Monica Lewinsky moved to New York and came out in favor of "The Love Song of J. Alfred Prufrock," which she imitated (loosely) in a Valentine's Day poem commissioned by a British magazine. Paul McCartney is writing a book of poems. Julia Roberts has written poems for years and particularly loves Neruda. Ashley Judd, who memorizes a poem for each birthday, chose Wordsworth's "Daffodils" last year and is leaning this year toward Rudyard Kipling's "If." Kim Cattrall, who plays Samantha in the HBO hit *Sex and the City,* likes reciting Rupert Brooke while her boyfriend plays the string bass. Helen Hunt says she is "obsessed with Rilke." Her favorite "is an untitled one in a collection that Robert Bly translated," which she proceeds to paraphrase: "I want to unfold because where I am closed I am false; I want to be with those who know secret things or else alone." David Duchovny, who studied with Harold Bloom at Yale, has never made a secret of his admiration of John Ashbery's "Self-Portrait in a Convex Mirror." Asked by a *Movieline* reporter to analyze the poem, the star of *The X-Files* gladly obliged: "It's about a man who's painting his self-portrait, but he's looking into a mirrored ball, and the closer he gets to it, the further away his image seems to be going." Duchovny then drew a parallel between the poem's posture and his own style as an actor: "I'm trying to protect what I advertise. That's my stance on any kind of self-expression."

I have a cultivated interest in the unusual ways people use poetry in their public or professional lives. Last year did not disappoint. Dona Nieto, a California performance artist who calls herself La Tigresa, bared her breasts and declaimed "goddess-based, nude Buddhist guerilla poetry" at timber sites north of San Francisco to protest the logging of ancient redwoods. Anonymous cyber-scribes adapted familiar lines by

Longfellow, Poe, Whitman, Ogden Nash, Joyce Kilmer, Alfred Noyes, and Clement Moore to satirize the post-election stalemate in Florida. Salman Rushdie in the *Guardian* versified the electoral results in the manner of Dr. Seuss. (Aided by "the great Legal Grinches, / and Grinches of Spin," the Grinch exhorts his cohorts to "Grinch / This election!") On TV, a contestant on *Who Wants to Be a Millionaire?* won $2,000 for shrewdly relying on the audience to know that the number of lines in a couplet is two. In one episode of the TV drama *Bull,* a ruthless tycoon quotes Yeats ("But one man loved the pilgrim soul in you, / And loved the sorrows of your changing face"), while in a different scene a bearded financial shark tosses off an allusion to Edna St. Vincent Millay ("My candle burns at both ends") to ridicule a Smith College alumna during a game of "humiliate the host." In HBO's hit series *The Sopranos,* Anthony, Jr., listens as his older sister, Meadow, a Columbia freshman, knowingly explains the symbolism of the snow in Frost's "Stopping by Woods on a Snowy Evening." "That's fucked up," her brother replies. If you get a chance to see Melissa Palmer's movie *Wildflowers,* you'll note that the guest editor of this year's *Best American Poetry* plays a poet named Robert who gets to recite his poems and court the character played by Daryl Hannah.

After the Los Angeles Lakers won the NBA championship in June 2000, Shaquille O'Neal quoted Shakespeare's "Some are born great, some achieve greatness, and some have greatness thrust upon them" at a victory celebration. While the Lakers' center left it unstated how these lines applied to the situation at hand, none could deny their grandeur. A few months earlier coach Phil Jackson had made a gift to O'Neal of Nietzsche's selected writings. "He was ahead of his time," O'Neal said. "Everybody else was analog and Nietzsche was digital." As the stock market swooned, Charles Millard, the former head of Internet investment banking at Prudential Securities, turned to Keats to explain the inevitable discrepancy between actual and anticipated profits. "Heard melodies are sweet, but those unheard / Are sweeter," Millard quoted, adding: "That reality is now hitting people right in the face." When a jail sentence smacked Dana C. Giacchetto, formerly Leonardo di Caprio's financial advisor, he took up poetry. Sample line: "At the nexus where art meets justice, a chemistry dancing like angels sweating with peace, yet, halfway asleep." Now there's a man who could benefit from a poetry writing workshop.

The Best American Poetry is committed to the notion that excellence in poetry is not incompatible with the pursuit of a general audience. Robert Hass, who succeeded Rita Dove as U. S. poet laureate and now succeeds her as the guest editor of this anthology, has dedicated himself to this project with the zeal that has characterized his efforts over the years to promote literature and literacy on the widest level. As poet laureate Hass, a distinguished critic as well as poet, wrote a weekly column ("The Poet's Choice") for the *Washington Post* recommending poets and poems in language direct and unaffected, adjectives not usually associated with critical writing; he would print the poem in full and comment briefly on it, careful not to let the commentary eclipse the verse. (When, after 212 weeks without a break, Hass gave up the column in January 2000, it was, fittingly, Dove who took it over.) Back when I asked him if he would undertake the editing of this anthology, Hass described himself as the "Raskolnikov of deadlines." After working with him on *The Best American Poetry 2001,* I am able to attest to the justness of this epithet—and to say that working with him was worth stretching any number of deadlines.

In the year 2000, as the IPO market crashed and one dot-com after another went under, some of us cherished all the more such "old economy" staples as books and magazines. Yet for poetry, which resists being turned into a commodity, the Internet remains a particularly friendly and potentially transformative space, offering a revolutionary means and method of publication and distribution. You can't help but admire the energy and enterprise informing electronic magazines and literary Web sites such as *Slate, Salon, The Cortland Review, Poetry Daily, Nerve, Pif, Can We Have Our Ball Back?* (its title evidently a nod to the Beatles' movie *A Hard Day's Night*), and most improbably two different 'zines named after Arthur Rimbaud's poem, "Le Bateau ivre" ("The Drunken Boat"). Both are brand-new. The one edited by Ravi Shankar (not the sitar player but a recent graduate of Columbia's MFA program) is called *Drunken Boat* (at www.drunkenboat.com) in contrast to the one edited by Rebecca Seiferle, a contributor to *The Best American Poetry 2000,* which is *The Drunken Boat* (at www.thedrunkenboat.com). It was in general an excellent year for Rimbaud, whose "Une Saison en enfer" ("A Season in Hell") is quoted by Marcia Gay Harden playing Lee Krasner in Ed Harris's movie *Pollock.*

This is the fifteenth volume in *The Best American Poetry* series. I have had many occasions to celebrate the accomplishments or recognitions of the fifteen guest editors to date. But until this year I have not had to mourn the passing of one of them. A. R. Ammons died on February 25,

2001, a week after his seventy-fifth birthday. "We're gliding," he wrote
in the concluding lines of *Sphere: The Form of a Motion.* "We

are gliding: ask the astronomer, if you don't believe it: but
motion as a summary of time and space is gliding us: for a while,
we may ride such forces: then, we must get off: but now this

beats any amusement park by the shore: our Ferris wheel, what a
wheel: our roller coaster, what mathematics of stoop and climb: sew
my name on my cap: we're clear: we're ourselves: we're sailing."

Robert Hass was born in San Francisco in 1941. He grew up in Marin County and attended St. Mary's College of California and Stanford University. *Field Guide,* his first book, was selected by Stanley Kunitz as the winner of the Yale Younger Poets competition for 1973. Three subsequent collections have appeared: *Praise* (1979), *Human Wishes* (1989), and *Sun Under Wood* (1996), all from the Ecco Press. *Sun Under Wood* won the National Book Critics Circle prize in poetry. A book of essays, *Twentieth-Century Pleasures: Prose on Poetry* (1984), had previously won the National Book Critics Circle prize in criticism. Hass, the recipient of a MacArthur Fellowship, has long collaborated with Czeslaw Milosz on the translations of his poems. He has also edited a volume of Tomas Tranströmer's selected poems and he edited and translated most of the contents of *The Essential Haiku: Versions of Basho, Buson, and Issa.* For two years starting in 1995, he served as the nation's poet laureate. Both during and after his appointment, he has worked tirelessly to promote literacy and to protect the environment. For many years he taught at St. Mary's College and is now a professor at the University of California, Berkeley.

INTRODUCTION

by Robert Hass

◇ ◇ ◇

It was August when I finally got down to the business of this anthology.
I had been reading literary magazines for months; David Lehman, the
editor of the *Best American Poetry* series, had also been reading, and
sending me quite regularly, like news bulletins, his cullings from dozens
of literary magazines, some of them hallowed and of long standing, some
of them new and completely, even intentionally, obscure. I had imagined,
when I was asked to edit this book, and I do mean *imagined,* a year that
resolved itself into a procession of quiet and orderly evenings in which
I finished dinner, did the dishes, took a short walk in the weathers as they
changed, and then sat down in a comfortable chair, in a circle of lamp-
light, and read a year's worth of the poems of my time with immense
clarity of mind.

It was my usual mistake. I had not so much agreed to undertake a
task as I had signed up to be the main character in a poem by Wallace
Stevens with a title like "The Room Was Quiet and the World Was
Calm." The room was not quiet and the world is not calm, and I was in
the poem by Emily Dickinson that I'd been in in the first place, the one
that begins: "A Day! Help! Help! Another Day!" And I don't think I was
even the main character. There are hundreds of literary magazines in
America, as well as many general interest magazines that publish poetry.
Many of them are quarterlies, so had I had my succession of nights like
days in the peaceable kingdom, I would have had the task of reading at
least one new magazine a night for three hundred and sixty-five days.
Some of those magazines—like the special summer poetry issue of the
Paris Review—contained as many as a hundred poems, whereas an envi-
ronmental journal like *Wild Earth* or a political weekly like *The Nation*
printed only two or three. One way and another, it is a lot of poetry. I
went at it mostly in fitful attacks, binges, when I found I had a few
hours, whatever the time of day. Mostly I just marked poems that I liked
well enough to return to. Some days, it seemed, I liked everything I

read. Some days I liked nothing. I had no clear sense how much of this was mood and how much the quality of the work I happened to be reading. It was not the ideal circumstance in which to read poetry, but the magazines were full of interest and, though I felt some anxiety about the final shape of the project, I liked doing the reading.

That there was so much poetry to be read I took to be a sign of cultural health. It meant a lot of people were literate and alive. You have to have some kind of interior life to make a work of art and in a world as busy and heedless as this one we need all the consciousness we can muster. Think of it this way. On my bookshelf there's an anthology of seventeenth-century American poetry. It's almost entirely the poetry of the New England colonies and it's over five hundred pages long. At least two poets from that time—Anne Bradstreet and Edward Taylor—wrote real poems, poems that can be read today for more than scholarly or antiquarian reasons. There are fifty-one poets in all published in the book and a substantial selection of anonymous poems. There were about a hundred thousand people in New England in 1700. So—if this were in any sense a sample human population: think of all the ways in which it wasn't; they had a world to build from scratch—this would imply that you might get two poets of unusual gifts and fifty or so poets in all in a population that size. If that were true, then there ought to be in the United States three hundred years later, with its three hundred million population, at least six thousand poets with some special talent and one hundred fifty thousand people or so who occasionally write poems. Of course, the gene pool doesn't seem to work in quite that way. But you take my point. There are more literate people in Kansas City today than there were in Shakespeare's London. There's no reason why every American city should not produce a writer of great interest to the rest of us.

This reflection engendered others. Anne Bradstreet produced the first book of published poetry by a North American. The book was printed in England and it was called *The Tenth Muse*. It consisted mainly of long, learned poems on themes of interest to seventeenth-century Protestants and very few people would have any interest in reading it today. The poems of hers that people do read are a few short personal poems written to her family. They have a fresh, intimate directness and simplicity and Anne Bradstreet seems to have thought them too personal for publication. They found their way into print in the middle of the nineteenth century, two hundred years after her death. Edward Taylor, who was a frontier minister, wrote very learned and bookish, but also homely and sometimes quite wild, devotional poetry. He did this apparently as a spiritual practice. He produced a couple of hundred of these poems, lines written preparatory to his receiving the Lord's Supper, bound them in a leather book of his own making, but did not publish them and asked his children not to publish them. They were discovered in the Yale University Library in the 1930s and published after that.

As everyone knows, Emily Dickinson published a handful of poems in her lifetime. When she died, her sister found a boxful of carefully composed small booklets in her hand made of thick folded paper. They contained over a thousand poems. Four hundred of them or so are among the four hundred best poems ever written in the English language. She died in 1886. Some of the poems were published in 1890. There was not a thorough scholarly collection of her work until 1955, the year before Allen Ginsberg published *Howl* as a paperback book, then a distinctly subrespectable format, issued by a small bookstore in the Italian district of San Francisco. I don't know whether "Howl" ever appeared in a magazine, but it seems unlikely that, had there been a *Best American Poetry* volume of 1956, it would have appeared there. Walt Whitman, Emily Dickinson's contemporary, and the other founding genius of American poetry, published his first book with a small press that specialized in odd Victorian versions of New Age fads: ocean bathing and reading people's characters from the bumps on their heads. It was published in 1855, the year, as everyone likes to notice, of Longfellow's "Hiawatha," which would certainly have made it into the *Best American Poetry* of 1855. As for Dickinson, her poems were not available for publication, but any imaginary and retrospective *Best American Poetry* of 1862 or 1863 would have to consist of seventy poems by Emily Dickinson (Walt Whitman did not write much in those two years) and a little room for others, out of what she liked to call "civility."

All of which is to say that, as the poems were piling up, I had no great confidence that I was going to reflect accurately the best poetry written in the past year. The present is notoriously blind to itself in the first place. And, more pertinent to my ruminations, America has this history of buried and recovered poets. I'm not clear about the reasons, but they must combine at least two facts. One is that poetry is a very private kind of art. One can generalize about the health or direction of "American Poetry" at any given moment, as if it were a corporate enterprise, but it isn't in the end a team sport. The resonances of American poetry, like the resonances of our great song lyrics, "April is the cruelest month," "After great pain a formal feeling comes," "I hate to see that evening sun go down," speak to our collective experience but they do so, almost always, in tones that come, unmistakably, from depth and silence. So that poetry not only can turn up just about anywhere, just about anywhere is where it is most likely to turn up.

The second reason is the fact of American space, the great distances between our metropolitan cultures. In Europe and in Asia, it would seem, written poetry flowered wherever the center of learning was, especially if it was also a center of commercial vitality. And each culture—even one as vast as China—seemed to have one cultural center, which was also the center of political power. Poetry in Sweden is mostly Stockholm, in Korea mostly Seoul. Boston is still the representative city of learning in America and New York the world capital, the center of publishing, of commerce, often of innovation, always of fashionable opinion. In the arts judgment has always tended to issue from critics writing in East Coast journals and from professors at eastern universities, literary reputations got made in the publishing houses and reviewing organs in New York. Chicago had its own vitality, and, in the early years of the century, its own gathering of poets and one of the world's most important literary magazines in the *Poetry* of Harriet Monroe and Ezra Pound. Briefly, in the 1950s and 1960s San Francisco became a kind of alternative staging center for the energies of a new generation of poets. And Los Angeles became the capital of the glamor of commercial entertainment, movies, and music.

The young have been heading to cities to get educated, for learning and for style and for sexiness and for jobs, probably since Theocritus left Sicily for Alexandria two thousand years ago. As soon as there was writing, and jobs to be had as scribes, the young went to cities and started making poetry. And, of course, it still happens in America and a few cities—probably just these few, Boston, New York, Chicago, Los Angeles, San Francisco—draw young artists who gather there and invent themselves into schools. But creative writing programs have changed that pattern in ways that still seem unpredictable. If Sherwood Anderson's *Winesburg, Ohio* is accurate, to be a person with an imagination in a small American town at the turn of the twentieth century meant that you would, eventually, some spring night, end up running down the street in the middle of the night naked and screaming. Now those people, growing up in all the towns and suburbs of the continent, can find their way to a local college, some place that has art studios and a music scene and a poetry or fiction writing class. Poets are likely for this reason to turn up anywhere, or not turn up, not be in the midst of making a splash on some literary scene known to the scanners that devise literary reputation as 'the state of American poetry.'

And here I was, one of those scanners, about to sit down on a bright summer morning, a cup of coffee in hand, and take out the boxes of marked-up magazines and xeroxes of poems from magazines, my own markings and the xeroxes and notations of the indefatigable David Lehman, and try to find what I was looking for. I'd read a lot of poems I liked, many poems very different from each other and of a similar quality. There are roughly three traditions in American poetry at this point: a metrical tradition that can be very nervy and that is also basically classical in impulse; a strong central tradition of free verse made out of both romanticism and modernism, split between the impulses of an inward and psychological writing and an outward and realist one, at its best fusing the two; and an experimental tradition that is usually more passionate about form than content, perception than emotion, restless with the conventions of the art, skeptical about the political underpinnings of current practice, and intent on inventing a new one, or at least undermining what seems repressive in the current formed style. Traditions, of course, are always in flux, and the best work is often being done in the interstices between them. At the moment, there are poets doing good, bad, and indifferent work in all these ranges. I had marked for rereading a couple of hundred poems and I had David's sometimes overlapping lists. I needed either to declare that my taste today was going to be definitive, or I needed a principle of selection. Reading for a while, I was aware that David had, on the whole, favored a poetry of wit and that I, on the whole, had singled out poems that were a little spiky or raw, and intellectually demanding. He was drawn to charm and I had been drawn away from it. I needed an idea. I was looking for what Ezra Pound called, as he was trying to find his way in the *Cantos,* "the rose in the steel dust."

What gave me a way in was coming across in succession some posthumously published poems by Elizabeth Bishop and one by James Schuyler. There was also one by Joseph Brodsky, written in Russian when he was in prison in the 1960s but translated into English in the last American years of his life and found among his papers. I did not in the end reprint the Brodsky poem—I ruled out translations at a certain point in the process, regretfully. Brodsky was a presence in American poetry and there are other poets like Czeslaw Milosz toweringly, and the younger Polish poet Adam Zagajewski and the Slovene Tomaž Šalamun who teach sometimes at American universities and whose work is regularly translated and published here. I would have liked to include their work; it would have said something about the life of poetry in America. I would also have liked to include some English and Irish poets—particularly Irish poets like Paul Muldoon and Seamus Heaney and Eavan Boland who teach regularly in this country. In the end, crowded for room, I was looking for reasons to exclude poets and ruled out the European poets, both the ones who wrote in English and the ones who didn't, and a couple of Latin American poets I might have included, like the Mexican Alberto Blanco, and also the Chinese poet Bei Dao. I had a glimpse, looking in that direction of what might have been done by including work in translation by American poets, especially translation of their contemporaries, so that this anthology would have had running through it like a rift of ore, Forrest Gander's translations of the Mexican poet Pura Lopez Colome, or Lyn Hejinian's translations of Russian experimental poets or Norma Coles's translations of new French poetry or John Balaban's translations from Vietnamese. The mix of poets drawn here from elsewhere—by exile, by cultural curiosity, by the salaries at American universities—and the foreign poets being studied and translated by American poets would have been one kind of portrait of the culture—I had to let it go.

But for the morning I entertained the idea of beginning the book with poems by Bishop, Schuyler, and Brodsky. There seemed something very pure about it. You want new poems. Here are new poems, new in the way that things read for the first time are new, and also in that other way, of the freshness of poetry. There was also some notion in it of the dead no longer having the fevered literary world at stake. They were in the place, it seemed, that Auden had spoken of when he said that poetry survived in the valley of its saying. Reading literary magazines for poems, one also reads the essays and reviews. Poetry may not be a team sport, but you would not know it from the magazines. Young poets school up, for support. They are also inclined to be competitive, and moralistic about it, convinced that any writing that is not doing exactly what they're doing is morally reprehensible. The shrillest, it often seems—Ezra Pound is the great counterexample—are the mediocre writers to whom only the allegiance of a school and a method gives legitimacy. It's one of the reasons why Milosz, in a moment of either impatience or conviction, called literature a tournament of hunchbacks. Many of the magazines this season had something of that tone; the polemics in literary cyberspace had even more. Poets sniping at each other not only about the purity of their literary technique but about the sources of their income. In one particularly mullahlike exchange, an eminent critic complained that a well-known poet of antirealist tendency had sold out by appearing on the same stage with an elder European poet who had a realistic aesthetic. The presence of Bishop and Schuyler, both very private poets, less than expansive, in their different ways domestic and meticulous, both writers whom, I always felt, wrote as if they had psychic wounds they needed to work around rather than confront—a tactic I did not judge; who is to tell someone else how to survive in such intimate territory?—seemed to me to give my imaginary anthology a tone I could begin to hear. It spoke to something essentially private in poetry communicated one-on-one from writer to reader, and also something about the way ego is burned off by writing absorbed in its task, and of course it touched with what felt to me a certain coolness a central mystery of art, that it is human utterance, or gesture, that sometimes survives death. I had no way of knowing if these poems would outlive their generation, but here in this book they stand for that possibility—poems about what? eros, the oddness of a sense of place.

The next thing that caught my eye, connected probably to these considerations, was that among the poems I had clipped there were a large number of poems by the poets I had grown up, or had grown into poetry, reading, that were about, in different ways, the changes of age. It's a strangeness, I suppose, that belongs to any generation that one ages watching the artists a half a generation older than oneself go from being the young ones to being the old ones. It is not easy to age in America, as many people have observed. But it is, it seems, easy enough to age in poetry. It's not downhill skiing, or mathematics for that matter which seems to use up its talents quite young. As longevity has increased, there has grown up in American poetry a considerable body of work made by older artists—the late poems of Wallace Stevens and Hilda Doolittle and William Carlos Williams and Robinson Jeffers, even the final fragmentary *Cantos* of Ezra Pound come to mind—that has solidity and strength, sometimes brilliance or wisdom. One is grateful for it in the fathers and mothers. But it is odd to see it in the older brothers and sisters, especially that rowdy generation that came of age in the 1950s and 1960s. Many of them are gone, of course. Allen Ginsberg and Frank O'Hara and Sylvia Plath and James Wright and Charles Olson and Denise Levertov and James Merrill. And just this year Gregory Corso and Gwendolyn Brooks and A. R. Ammons. There was in them a mix of impulses—they were radicals and mandarins and swells, wild ones, populists, aesthetes and isolatos, masters of the perfected or the apparently tossed-off gesture.

As a generation, they were my way into contemporary poetry— from the middle of high school, really, when the newspapers in San Francisco were full of stories about the Beat generation and the trial to keep a lewd book called *Howl* out of the innocent American mind, they were the poets I read to understand the rhythms of time in the time I was growing into. Harold Bloom remarked in an introduction to one of these anthologies that the ideal reader of poetry was a superbly educated one. Maybe so. But a person has to get there somehow, and there is something to be said for the youthful and ignorant reader. It seems to me that at a certain point in my early reading of poetry I had a kind of attention in which, as in sex, the minute became huge. Every oddness of line ending, stutter of rhythm, intricacy of music, or—think of early John Ashbery—resolute flatness of tone seemed momentous. There is, I suppose, a certain narcissism in this. One is waking to oneself and to the poetry at once. It's a time when you also begin to learn the range of ideas that can instigate a poetry. There was a time, I remember, when I first went to poetry readings and was often offended that the poets reading their own poems did not sound like they were supposed to sound, that is, did not sound as they sounded in my head. I formed the idea then that the poems were superior to the poets and that I, as their disinterested reader, was more faithful to the poems than the poets were, who had gone on to the next poem or the next stage of their lives. So it was affecting, as I went through the magazines again, to see how many poems there were about aging, or about time and change, by the writers of that generation—from Kenneth Koch's delicious and complicated ode to the Second World War to Grace Paley's wry notational lyric to the poems of Richard Howard and John Hollander and Anthony Hecht, three of the generation's formalists, to Galway Kinnell's palpably physical meditation on decomposition as a central part of the world's work.

These poems became for me the idea of a stratum or layer in this book. I thought at first of beginning with the dead poets and ending with the living older poets, and then organizing the anthology in rough chronological order by decades, so that the very young would come at the beginning. It is an interesting time for young poets. They've inherited an aesthetic or set of aesthetics in which the basic relationship to language has become the central problem and it has given their work, so far, its particular forms of playfulness and tortuousness, interest and opacity and risk. Partly they're reacting against what has come to seem effortless and therefore indulgent in a previous generation, the poem of incident in plain language, which aims at a certain sincerity of address and tone, as if life was exactly the size of the self and consisted of a set of serial epiphanies. Some of this echoes the influence of the critical tradition in European philosophy in the universities, some of it is the ground-clearing required of any oppositional art. In this case, because it's suspicious of subject matter as such, suspicious, as I've seen it described, of the "aboutness" of poetry, it's preoccupied with issues of style, with the relationship therefore between language and perception. It also goes largely on instinct and the instinct is that some right, cool, strange, or estranged ferocity of language would catch the instability of things and undo, in its utopian versions, if not the whole global economy at least the self-satisfied clichés which present that vision of power in the world as triumphant and inevitable. Any young art— think of Rembrandt's early self-portrait—has an element in it of showboating, of display, fury and display, or mockery and display, hilarity and display, or woundedness and irony and display, but it often has, ought maybe to have, the exuberance of young artists coming to the medium, and I thought that would sit interestingly against the poems of Bishop and Schuyler who were beyond that impulse, or had turned it into something else. So an idea of an anthology was coming into focus. In the end I don't think I've represented the younger poets nearly as well as I would have liked. To some extent they got crowded out when I began to read the poets of my own generation. But I hope there is enough of this work so that readers will feel the restlessness and force of what's coming.

Another truth of this kind of reading is that it was a great pleasure to revisit the poets whose work I knew well, the ones who were beginning to publish as I began to publish. I was aware that this more than anything made it difficult for me to come to anything like the objectivity—the transparent-eyeball clarity of mind—I had imagined I could bring to this process. If I mentally conjured a *Best American Poetry 1924* or *1949,* there would be, I was sure, very good poems by poets who were not the poets I had read and read, poems that were in some ways better than the poems written in those years by the artists I have most studied and lived with, but the truth is, I think, that a lesser poem by Wallace Stevens or Marianne Moore would seize my attention because I was interested in and had some feeling for the whole enterprise of their art. They may not have written their most achieved poems in some given year, but they were poets who did not fail to interest me. I knew this was the case with reading my contemporaries. I was aware that, with some poets whose work I knew only casually, I would like a poem well enough to set it aside to reread, but I lacked a sense of its context in their work. There is a way in which the poems in a literary magazine—or an anthology—can be like pieces of luggage on an airport carrel. They go by: an awful lot of them very much alike, various of them distinctive in their way, but in no relation to the others or, in an odd way, to themselves. They have specificity without character whereas a piece of luggage you recognize, your own, or a lover's, or a friend's, or a child's, seems inimitably battered or elegant or mutedly stylish or functional or eccentric. Others are going to have to make of my choices what they make of them—many readers will be reading them with a fresher eye than mine, but I found that there were a large number of poems that gave me pleasure, seemed to have inventive force, or intellectual passion or surprise. I was amused by the sudden raucous rhyming, for example, in Lyn Hejinian. I had a sense of the trajectory that brought Yusef Komunyakaa to the compact odelike song form he brought to the subject of the seven deadly sins. I'm interested in every stage of Louise Glück's art so that a quality austere and hieratic, but also summary and dryly wistful I thought I sensed in her recent work moved me. It interested me that Michael Palmer's poem—his poems are always beautifully written, they often have a quality of comic or mesmerized philosophical opacity—seemed for him unusually direct and that John Koethe's seemed so intentionally to invoke the later manner of Wallace Stevens. This part of the choosing seemed like gathering a party of friends. Some of them in fact are my friends. Others are people whom I hardly know at all and whose work I know in considerable detail. Several of the poets I admire most aren't here, for one reason or another, but the range of work in my generation is represented, I think. I would have liked to have a clear sense of common themes or common preoccupations in this layer of the work, but if they're here I don't have a feeling for them. I thought of it as the work of experienced poets who had been at it long enough to have acquired a fate and who were engaged in the process of making sense of that fate toward the end of the middle of their lives.

This was the point at which I stopped imagining that I would try to talk David Lehman and the editors at Scribner into abandoning the format of this series, which requires that the poems appear in alphabetical order by author. I thought that the generations were going to be a rhythm of this book, also some attempt given my own tastes to represent the range of styles and preoccupations within the generations. In addition to this, I had made a point of picking a certain number of poems by people whose names I didn't recognize. I think there were at least a dozen of these. I wanted long poems and short lyrics. David and I negotiated the impulse to include poems that were accessible and immediately appealing with poems that expected a good deal of readers and gave them therefore the chance to get lost, to get lost and found. It seemed the best thing once there was a map in my head to scramble it. They say that the aesthetic pleasure of cities has to do with the helter-skelter quality of their development on the one hand and the fixity of the grid pattern of streets on the other and the way that mixture of randomness and order keeps tossing up visual surprises. It began to seem to me that this would be the best principle here.

I had months more of reading to do and so did David Lehman. (I read his poems and was informed that he had ruled himself out of appearing in the series he's been shepherding.) I also began not to trust my eye and asked several young poets to reread the whole year's worth of poems and make their selection of poems—I wanted to see with some other sets of eyes. These poets were Jessica Fisher and Brian Glazer and Jennifer Scappettone and Tim Woods, and I want to thank them here. When David asked me to do this work, I think I pointed out that there were whole centuries in which there weren't seventy-five good poems. By the end I was trying to talk him into a format that included eighty-five poems, or eighty, or, my last pitch, seventy-eight, just three more, why not? what's the difference? It didn't happen. A form is a form, and what you have here is seventy-five poems which I hope will convey a sense that there are a dozen or so more poems that are clamoring at the silent wall to be let in.

It would be good if that force were felt by readers coming to this volume as an instance of the force with which human beings seem to need to represent themselves, to make symbols out of their experience, to say what it is like to be themselves, to make things that have not been made before and to bring them into the world and alter the world by doing so, to protest or celebrate the terms of existence, or at least not to go through it mute.

THE
BEST
AMERICAN
POETRY
2001

◇ ◇ ◇

Notes for a Sermon on the Mount

◇   ◇   ◇

1. Pussies are not gods. They are created beings.
2. Unlike god, they do not always exist.
3. Dignified, majestic, intelligent, we must attend to them nonetheless.
4. Like all spiritual beings, pussies cannot be seen with the human eye at just any time of day.
5. Pussies represent both the visible and the invisible, the sacred and the profane.
6. They appear to be nowhere and everywhere at once. To be personal and impersonal, human and divine.
7. In the occult story of Adam and Eve, God placed a sword-bearing angel at the entrance of the divine pussy to keep the unwary from ever returning.
8. Revelations describe them as being "robed in a cloud with a rainbow over their heads."
9. Many times a pussy has taken on the form of an actual woman and is sometimes mistakenly thought to have a human spirit.
10. One must not forget to entertain strangers, for by doing so, one might entertain a pussy without even knowing it.
11. Always remember: one must never pray to pussies. Or other golden heifers.
12. Nor should one ask God to send forth a pussy to help minister to one's soul.
13. A pussy must come of its own accord. For thus is the way of the pussy, and of the alpha and omega.

from *Another Chicago Magazine*

The Plan

◊ ◊ ◊

"Who told you
you were visible?"

God said,

meaning naked
or powerless.

★

We had planned this meeting
in advance,

how we'd address each other,

how we'd stand
or kneel.

Thus our intentions
are different

from our bodies,
something extra,

though transparent
like a negligee.

★

Though a bit sketchy,

like this palm's
impression of a tree—

flashing scales,

on the point of
retraction.

But *sweet.*
You don't understand!

Like a lariat made of scalloped bricks

circling a patch
of grass

from *American Poetry Review*

Crossroads in the Past

◇   ◇   ◇

That night the wind stirred in the forsythia bushes,
but it was a wrong one, blowing in the wrong direction.
"That's silly. How can there be a wrong direction?
'It bloweth where it listeth,' as you know, just as we do
when we make love or do something else there are no rules for."

I tell you, something went wrong there a while back.
Just don't ask me what it was. Pretend I've dropped the subject.
No, now you've got me interested, I want to know
exactly what seems wrong to you, how something could

seem wrong to you. In what way do things get to be wrong?
I'm sitting here dialing my cellphone
with one hand, digging at some obscure pebbles with my shovel
with the other. And then something like braids will stand out,

on horsehair cushions. That armchair is really too lugubrious.
We've got to change all the furniture, fumigate the house,
talk our relationship back to its beginnings. Say, you know
that's probably what's wrong—the beginnings concept, I mean.
I aver there are no beginnings, though there were perhaps some
sometime. We'd stopped, to look at the poster the movie theater

had placed freestanding on the sidewalk. The lobby cards
drew us in. It was afternoon, we found ourselves
sitting at the end of a row in the balcony; the theater was unexpectedly
crowded. That was the day we first realized we didn't fully

know our names, yours or mine, and we left quietly
amid the gray snow falling. Twilight had already set in.

from *The New York Review of Books*

Jazz

◇ ◇ ◇

I'd like to know everything
A jazz artist knows, starting with the song
"Goodbye Pork Pie Hat."

Like to make some songs myself:
"Goodbye Rickshaw,"
"Goodbye Lemondrop,"
"Goodbye Rendezvous."

Or maybe even blues:

If you fall in love with me I'll make you pancakes
All morning. If you fall in love with me
I'll make you pancakes all night.
If you don't like pancakes
We'll go to the creperie. If you don't like pancakes
We'll go to the creperie.
If you don't like to eat, handsome boy,
Don't you hang around with me.

On second thought, I'd rather find
The fanciest music I can, and hear all of it.

I'd rather love somebody
And say his name to myself every day
Until I fall apart.

from *The Nebraska Review*

Crossed-Over, Fiend-Snitched, X-ed Out

◊　◊　◊

O Sweetie, O Hon, in this weather—split sea pea,
green horizon, mended infinitude—sweet
the lips licking the honeyed, the candy-

coated, the sugared-up. O sweet
those inscrutable untruths. Let me have another
sip of nectar.

Now the wind shifts
the bees downstream; they float, wings dread-drenched.
This is pretty too. This death

set, this cool cup and saucer, clinked
in the mustachioed moment. May I have a little
more? Flutter. Flail.

A stark stake is down driven, a megalith marker
masks the lack. Wreath on the head
of whom? The child is loved

in narcissistic longing to be and to be (again).
That too is translated
onto the stage, the screen. A plane dives. O that?

That's the Twentieth Century, sputtering
its hind parts. The plurality of premises, of needle drop
chandelier tears in a ceiling rose

well over their heads. The planned dance
where one leg crosses
the other. A curtsy. A bow. O anachronym.

We are only here to help you.
We are only here
with our Tarot cards, with our wooden Egyptian

figures, an entire antiquity collection
constructed in a room recess. The outrageous dawning
of opinion—swayable, swayed. Suede

brushes against the train
as it enters the opening, a napkinish ring with a we portrait
of the wedded couple. And then it exits

and we with it. We've been. But where?
Brief picture postcard with a date firm in its intention
to detail. Head bent

over the slate at the rigorosum,
a fertilizing dew collecting at the brink of the lip.
That famous scene from the life of____

comes to mind, the reek of lilac and laburnum.

from *New American Writing*

When the Gods Put on Meter

◊　◊　◊

I cleared mother's apartment of her urine-soaked rags today, while she wept.
She wanted to keep them, you see.
She will make more so long as she lives, an hour,

      o loveliest of forms that I may behold you an hour,

      Wife of the Gaze, Husband of the Breath,
      Gleam on the round side of the tear.

★

A woman is dead in the house across the river.
River of shudders river of quivering grief.

   O hummingbirds who drank from her tower of red,
   know that the Queen of Red River is dead.

   Her pink-haired doll, ape, and pony have fled
   through the dresser mirror, as on a pickup bed,

   but stare back the while, as if it's not too late
   to see the Jean moon rise

      —o gods of the ear, is it meter you love?—

             to dazzle Fate,

the Alien doll who hauls them off, whose eyes ate
the room and frightened them, such lonely hate!

The widow Jean will never again open
a window in the Castle Ibuprofen

and float out over dress-ups of snow on
the noble firs of Foss River Grove. In

the morning she thought her husband had spoken.
Now every bone in the darkness is broken.

★

What would you regulate—
         the tiny plenitude of "spontaneous" symbols?
The arrhythmical mass writing of the rain?

                  oh loveliest of forms

Every bone in the rain is broken

★

You were born in the glade of an averted Eye,
you dressed before the mirror of a hundred arteries—
         oh, don't confuse your arm
with those hanging waters!
         Not *that* leg, the carrot
                           of the downward path!

You learned to desire from where you would never quite be,
         pressed against the flat side of the tear.

★

Where is the rescue?
Cornered children call you River Platte,
your loafshaped covered wagons in their eyes.

Where is the rescue?
Mothers run out to bring in the oxygen
   of the laundry,
shaking themselves into beauty they cannot see.

Do you pick it up, broken-headed animal
                    and blow on its snow-light fur?

I look into the rain barrel of grief
                              and see that it is raining.

★

How frail is our world:

          by day, caramel forests
          lift their green travels. At night,
          quartets of sparks
          fly down to us,
          the coals of the Offering.
          The moon is given
          and taken back,
                         as decided.

★

          you have sacrificed in my desire.

+

Under atmosphere blue as decided,
what is it that lives,
          spine-startled, thrilled by the Flutter-road
of Files-too-near?

★

Ear flushed of its privacies,
                    flushed of its silences,
drawn out to the husband, the Breath,

as Kant walked into Beauty,
forgetting why he opened the door—

"For neither the veil nor the veiled object is the beautiful,
                    but the object in its veil"—

———

Kant catches fire.

★

The rest is the hymn.
What you see despite the eye is the hymn.

This woman reeking of urine is the hymn.
Jean with her doll-crimped thin dyed hair is the hymn.

★

The moist cloud spits the star-seed.
   So begins the sacrifice.
The moon brings the white sheet.

Who accepts breath is sacrifice.
Who sings
    sings worlds frightened and dear.

from *Colorado Review*

Vague Poem

◊   ◊   ◊

The trip west
—I think I *dreamed* that trip.
They talked a lot of "rose rocks"
or maybe "rock roses"
—I'm not sure now, but someone tried to get me some.
(And two or three students had.)

She said she had some at her house.
They were by the back door, she said.
—A ramshackle house.
An Army house? No, "a *Navy* house." Yes,
that far inland.
There was nothing by the back door but dirt
or that same dry, monochrome, sepia straw I'd seen everywhere.
Oh, she said, the dog has carried them off.
(A big black dog, female, was dancing around us.)

Later, as we drank tea from mugs, she found one
"a sort of one." "This one is just beginning. See—
you can see here, it's beginning to look like a rose.
It's—well, a crystal, crystals form—
I don't know any geology myself . . ."
(Neither did I.)
Faintly, I could make out—perhaps—in the dull,
rose-red lump of (apparently) soil
a rose-like shape; faint glitters . . . Yes, perhaps
there was a secret, powerful crystal at work inside.

I *almost* saw it: turning into a rose
without any of the intervening
roots, stem, buds, and so on; just
earth to rose and back again.
Crystallography and its laws:
something I once wanted badly to study,
until I learned that it would involve a lot of arithmetic,
     that is, mathematics.

Just now, when I saw you naked again,
I thought the same words: rose-rock, rock-rose . . .
Rose, trying, working, to show itself,
forming, folding over,
unimaginable connections, unseen, shining edges.
Rose-rock, unformed, flesh beginning, crystal by crystal,
clear pink breasts and darker, crystalline nipples,
rose-rock, rose-quartz, roses, roses, roses,
exacting roses from the body,
and the even darker, accurate, rose of sex—

from *The New Yorker*

The French Generals

◇   ◇   ◇

Whenever Jesus appears at the murky well,
I am there with my five hundred husbands.
It takes Jesus all day to mention their names.

The growing soul longs for mastery, but
The small men inside pull it into misery.
It is the nature of shame to have many children.

Earth's name is "Abundance of Desires." The serpent
Sends out his split tongue and waves it
In the air scented with so many dark Napoleons.

A general ends his life in a small cottage
With damp sheets and useless French franc notes;
He keeps his plans of attack under the mattress.

I have said to the serpent: "This is your house."
I bring in newspapers to make his nest cozy.
It's the nature of wanting to have many wives.

Sturdy rafters in lifejackets are pulled down
Till their toes touch the bottom of the Rogue River.
Wherever there is water there is someone drowning.

from *The Paris Review*

Sonnet Around Stephanie

◇   ◇   ◇

What rituals are in Benares?
Our little cat's grave smells of incense, earth—
three candles, three days now, burning.
Through the window from my desk I can see

them in the dark. Beneath yellow leaves
is the earth we all pressed down, turning
it over to smell it dark with ferns.
His spirit plays in shadow, we still see

it in the halls. In my mind, your self-portrait
slowly unwraps suicidal arms to show your face.
Blessed are the small, for they shall be buried.

Blown into darkness, I could only wait
for the Gift to come around again—drawn to empty space.
Blessed are the angry, for they shall be carried.

from *Verse*

Notes About My Face

◇   ◇   ◇

1
Traces. Then things themselves are not names
not words only.

2
Hay. I am not hay.
I am not hey either.
My mother meant one of these. Or both.

3
Both moons in one month.
Both rains on Tuesday.
Both cold snows on 5.

4
Reaching for the salt:
a) she is stabbed by the father
b) she is stabbed by the father's fork
c) she is stabbed by the father's father
d) hello. she is inside

5
"I miss myself
in the earlier version"
I write to Jean.

6
"interesting"—1 of my mask words

7
she is inside:
                    "I" wrote

to literal companion of
mine in literal light
on "porch-stage" (Jean's)
of 1968, the summer the

New Yorker published a
translation by Babel's daughter
of "You Must Know Everything"
—and Jane Flory read it

aloud in the back evening
—and Sheldon Flory took
notes about my face during
this and put them in a

                    poem—
                    or so
                    it
                    seems

then—Jean Valentine's small
"porch-stage . . ."
"ghost guide . . ."
i became "I" at some pivot
in this place —> arrow
                    is the
                    face of,
face of

No rearranged rider.
No ghost behaviors.
No umbrella.

8
"too much glass" K's
translation of T reads
—one thinks of one's own
house or house past or
room as having too much
too—but one is silent

no recovery artist
no box of recovery
the boys in the basement
are shattered in the skull
and in the heart—in the
cases

9
of these two murders by
the father the heart is
equal in size to the shattered
skull and the shattered window

10
and in at least 6 other moments
on this globe this appropriate word
globe for this earth at at least
6 other moments there are equal
murders—the word daily cannot
convey this—the broken branch
on 16th Street two Novembers ago
is the link to the moment of one
of the two deaths

11
your honor
my thesis will be based
upon Myung Mi Kim's DURA
and Duras' Two by Duras
The Atlantic Man
The Slut of the Normandy Coast
a new world

12
how to refer to these two (Two)
will be the initial pivot
and probably final pivot
feeble insomnia
brick of the school

13
the elementary school
in e elementary evening

14
something like candy cities
—"*Waipo* stands for maternal grandma. *Wai* means "outside,"
"stranger." *Po,* "old woman."   (Wang Ping,"Female Marriage")

I want my Maypo.
outside means no snow
outside means stolen drawing from snow's friend
outside means Jean Valentine's "ghost guide"

15
I had this feeling
                    Sheldon was up
to something, Jane too—

maybe not Jane, maybe not Jean
—sometimes, from Jean's incredible
poem Ironwood

sometimes I thought I was
"the other Michael"—
                    I asked her
last November, finally,
after wanting to ask for

a long time, and she sort
of said she could not recall
who that was—were we walking
along arm in arm

after she gives this wonderful
reading of poems from this
book she is now thinking (May)

of calling HER LOST BOOK.
I don't believe her, about "the other
Michael," but it becomes vague now

like a snowy fact, like some of
the most interesting facts in poems
do—mask facts

literal light:

16
LAMB
   | cuban
   | panther
JASPER JOHNS—ANXIETY—A MAN WHO WANTED ME BUT I WAS
     WRONG
Street of pain
Someone is actually going to pay me to hang out in churches
"I don't want an adversarial relationship c̄ my writing, you have"
Don't sleep with your head in the sun here
"I COME FROM SECRETS" John Frazier
have told our dog a dog we had another dog we had a story we should not
LATIN "His friends did not see him for months."
too much house too much wind in the sense of wind against trees and house
The liability of the inside
Kim's "Large pond gives way"
Kim's Collect the years' duration
"AND YEARS AGO, TOO"   Melissa Hotchkiss   Could *not* see the ball
     coming
said his brother, and the rain helped the silent father understand his silence
again: the songs
little did you know i almost threw myself under the train tonight
little did you know
people claim people like objects
today the story of my friend the sea. Tomorrow, utter sexuality of the sea
YOU PROBABLY WON'T STEAL FROM YOUR MOTHER IN LAW

AGAIN FOR AWHILE

i was intimidated by weldon kees

painted digression 8500 ghosts today painted senators with money bags for
      faces

painted representatives with blades for ears painted soldiers with assholes

for brains painted murderers with US painted all over their hearing

painted punishments for another woman   painted brutality for another
      child

evening coast loan sudden reverse far scamper duck globe refrain to per
      drop

see my difficult gone he talked part door she broughtnightly crows

this bird was a sign or not unhate the hand the pelvis   hello blue moon

from *American Poetry Review*

Heartland

◇　◇　◇

And she saying, I cannot quite
hear what she says, but he, standing
in clothes washed too often still
to be warm, looks out at the land.

And she saying, I cannot hear
what follows his name, and he, "What's
it all meant, Lizzie? We've made
a living and no one doubts our name."

And he remembering the years
before the green combines and long,
open barns for machinery
and their hands on each other young.

And she saying, I cannot tell
whether or not it's comforting,
until he turns to a door that
is not a new house and goes in.

And she saying, I can hear now,
"If the words are old, let them be.
It's hard enough with a dream;
here, what can you see of a plan?"

And he nodding, I can no longer
hear what she says, the house shadowed

by combines and long open barns,
the fields planted and bare for rain.

from *The Nation*

Blouse of Felt

◇   ◇   ◇

Assembly tree and bowl of thorns
       You see these hanging vases we have flogged
Hooded bell saved, illustrations in
black on green, the Admirable clutched at his lapel
as I touched him
    thistle and all—organized by
a monk in spike breeches
of assurance these four-pointed stars aren't upset
        or a tad fish with savior heart—
          nettles imprinted

Pinwheel caught in the stillness of cremation
Spikes wedded, bathed umbrella

My collar holds a ball, mitts bulb-ended

     Capital of magnified balsam, the
plot opening season-burst
Someone has burned these poles!
Carted away my polestars!

Christmas is a Japanese hour   these barlamps
       of clay arranged
such that   to decipher their lay one must
be embalmed in a necklace of paperwhites

             Shoot moon-bleached, crush scattered
near garden's plump seizure

All the spiked blades of a flung disc   *and*
whirling at the center is a pom-pom
that spills its shadow   into this evening

for the Admirable assures me
armed with unfolding cabbages,
lilac javelin, and glockenbud

they can view us from the square portals atop
the nut-shaped hill itself balanced upon a stalk
Poppy vent, or the signs of a
mineral fall pulling sleep first

Three looking away, one begging to be penetrated
or the corolla of an albino dune-flower

What is that . . .?
—a perpetrator I found on my widower's mat

A white fever of tiger, cut by   Omen's shards,

tunnel babble, and weathered
the advancement of quickened speech—
floral listening

In one frame his hand reaches to pluck a raisin's past
In the next our cheeks are at the bottom
of a glaze toward his wall of tan and russet
In the last a ferret has gone limp on his lip

*A leaf then grew to house
the faint creature—oranges
secretly ripened as he nursed its
Prussian health*

From *Faucheuse*

Longing, a documentary

◇　◇　◇

Shot List

1. Night.
   River.

   subtitle:　　*It was for such a night she had waited.*

2. Trunk of her car is open and lit by a funnel of light from the porch.

3. She loads the trunk: 4x6 trays, photographic papers, strobe light.
   Strobe doesn't fit, she angles it into the backseat.

4. She is driving, concentrating, empty highway.

   subtitle:　　*She was not a person who aimed at eventual*
   reconciliation with the views of common sense.

5. She is at the river in deep reeds, watching.

6. She wades along the edge of the river, watching.

7. Night plucks her, she stumbles, stops.

8. She is bending beside the car, unpacking trays.

9. She drags the trays through deep reeds toward the river.
   Moon unclouds itself and plunges by.

subtitle: *Night is not a fact.*

10. She walks into the river.

subtitle: *Facts lack something, she thought.*

11. She positions the big trays on the riverbottom near the bank, just under the water, spreads photographic papers in them, adjusts it, moves back. Watches.

12. She stands by the strobe in deep reeds.

13. Flash of strobe surprises the riverbank.

14. She sits awhile in the reeds, arms on knees.

subtitle: *"Overtakelessness" (what facts lack).*

15. Moonlight sways down through black water onto the photographic papers.

16. She is driving, windows blowing, empty highway.

subtitle: *As usual she enjoyed the sense of work, of having worked. Other fears would soon return.*

from *The Threepenny Review*

Ceriserie

◊　◊　◊

Music: Sexual misery is wearing you out.

Music: Known as the Philosopher's Stair for the world-weariness which climbing it inspires. One gets nowhere with it.

Paris: St-Sulpice in shrouds.

Paris: You're falling into disrepair, Eiffel Tower this means you! Swathed in gold paint, Enguerrand Quarton whispering come with me under the shadow of this gold leaf.

Music: The unless of a certain series.

Mathematics: Everyone rolling dice and flinging Fibonacci, going to the opera, counting everything.

Fire: The number between four and five.

Gold leaf: Wedding dress of the verb *to have,* it reminds you of of.

Music: As the sleep of the just. We pass into it and out again without seeming to move. The false motion of the wave, "frei aber einsam."

Steve Evans: I saw your skull! It was between your thought and your face.

Melisse: How I saw her naked in Brooklyn but was not in Brooklyn at the time.

Art: That's the problem with art.

Paris: I was in Paris at the time! St-Sulpice in shrouds "like Katharine Hepburn."

Katharine Hepburn: Oh America! But then, writing from Paris in the thirties, it was to you Benjamin compared Adorno's wife. Ghost citizens of the century, sexual misery is wearing you out.

Misreading: You are entering the City of Praise, population two million three-hundred thousand . . .

Hausmann's Paris: The daughter of Midas in the moment just after. The first silence of the century then the king weeping.

Music: As something to be inside of, as inside thinking one feels thought of, fly in the ointment of the mind!

Sign at Jardin des Plantes: GAMES ARE FORBIDDEN IN THE LABYRINTH.

Paris: Museum city, gold lettering the windows of the wedding-dress shops
in the Jewish Quarter. "Nothing has been changed," sez Michael, "except
for the removal of twenty-seven thousand Jews."

Paris 1968: The anti-museum museum.

The Institute for Temporary Design: Scaffolding, traffic jam, barricade,
police car on fire, flies in the ointment of the city.

Gilles Ivain: In your tiny room behind the clock, your bent sleep, your
Mythomania.

Gilles Ivain: Our hero, our Anti-Hausmann.

To say about Flemish painting: "Money-colored light."

Music: "Boys On The Radio."

Boys of the Marais: In your leather pants and sexual pose, arcaded shadows of
the Place des Vosges.

Mathematics: And all that motion you supposed was drift, courtyard with the
grotesque head of Apollinaire, Norma on the bridge, proved nothing but
a triangle fixed by the museum and the opera and St-Sulpice in shrouds.

The Louvre: A couple necking in an alcove, in their brief bodies entwined near
the Super-Radiance Hall visible as speech.

Speech: The bird that bursts from the mouth shall not return.

Pop song: We got your pretty girls they're talking on mobile phones la la la.

Enguerrand Quarton: In your dream gold leaf was the sun, salve on the
kingdom of the the visible.

Gold leaf: The mind makes itself a Midas, it cannot hold and not have.

Thus: I came to the city of possession.

Sleeping: Behind the clock, in the diagon, in your endless summer night, in
the city remarking itself like a wave in which people live or are said to
live, it comes down to the same thing, an exaggerated sense of things
getting done.

Paris: The train station's a museum, opera in the place of the prison.

Later: The music lacquered with listen.

from *American Poetry Review*

Snow Day

◇   ◇   ◇

Today we woke up to a revolution of snow,
its white flag waving over everything,
the landscape vanished,
not a single mouse to punctuate the blankness,
and beyond these windows

the government buildings smothered,
schools and libraries buried, the post office lost
under the noiseless drift,
the paths of trains softly blocked,
the world fallen under this falling.

In a while, I will put on some boots
and step out like someone walking in water,
and the dog will porpoise through the drifts,
and I will shake a laden branch
sending a cold shower down on us both.

But for now I am a willing prisoner in this house,
a sympathizer with the anarchic cause of snow.
I will make a pot of tea
and listen to the plastic radio on the counter,
as glad as anyone to hear the news

that the Kiddie Corner School is closed,
the Ding-Dong School, closed,
the All Aboard Children's School, closed,
the Hi-Ho Nursery School, closed,
along with—some will be delighted to hear—

the Toadstool School, the Little School,
Little Sparrows Nursery School,
Little Stars Pre-School, Peas-and-Carrots Day School
the Tom Thumb Child Center, all closed,
and—clap your hands—the Peanuts Play School.

So this is where the children hide all day,
these are the nests where they letter and draw,
where they put on their bright miniature jackets,
all darting and climbing and sliding,
all but the few girls whispering by the fence.

And now I am listening hard
in the grandiose silence of the snow,
trying to hear what those three girls are plotting,
what riot is afoot,
which small queen is about to be brought down.

from *The Atlantic Monthly*

En Famille

◇   ◇   ◇

I wandered lonely as a cloud . . .
I'd seemingly lost the crowd
I'd come with, family—father, mother, sister and brothers—
fact of a common blood.

Now there was no one,
just my face in the mirror, coat on a single hook,
a bed I could make getting out of.
Where had they gone?

•

What was that vague determination
cut off the nurturing relation
with all the density, this given company—
what made one feel such desperation

to get away, get far from home, be gone from those
would know us even if they only saw our noses or our toes,
accept with joy our helpless mess,
taking for granted it was part of us?

•

My friends, hands on each other's shoulders,
holding on, keeping the pledge
to be for one, for all, a securing center,
no matter up or down, or right or left—

to keep the faith, keep happy, keep together,
keep at it, so keep on
despite the fact of necessary drift.
Home might be still the happiest place on earth?

•

You won't get far by yourself.
It's dark out there.
There's a long way to go.
The dog knows.

It's him loves us most,
or seems to, in dark nights of the soul.
Keep a tight hold.
Steady, we're not lost.

•

Despite the sad vagaries,
anchored in love, placed in the circle,
young and old, a round—
love's fact of this bond.

One day one will look back
and think of them—
where they were, now gone—
remember it all.

•

Turning inside as if in dream,
the twisting face I want to be my own,
the people loved and with me still,
I see their painful faith.

Grow, dears, then fly away!
But when the dark comes, then come home.
Light's in the window, heart stays true.
Call—and I'll come to you.

•

The wind blows through the shifting trees
outside the window, over the fields below.
Emblems of growth, of older, younger,
of towering size or all the vulnerable hope

as echoes in the images of these three
look out with such reflective pleasure,
so various and close. They stand there,
waiting to hear a music they will know.

•

I like the way you both look out at me.
Somehow it's sometimes hard to be a human.
Arms and legs get often in the way,
making oneself a bulky, awkward burden.

Tell me your happiness is simply true.
Tell me I can still learn to be like you.
Tell me the truth is what we do.
Tell me that care for one another is the clue.

•

We're here because there's nowhere else to go,
we've come in faith we learned as with all else.
Someone once told us and so it is we know.
No one is left outside such simple place.

No one's too late, no one can be too soon.
We comfort one another, making room.
We dream of heaven as a climbing stair.
We look at stars and wonder why and where.

•

Have we told you all you'd thought to know?
Is it really so quickly now the time to go?

Has anything happened you will not forget?
Is where you are enough for all to share?

Is wisdom just an empty word?
Is age a time one might finally well have missed?
Must humanness be its own reward?
Is happiness this?

from *Boston Book Review*

A Mown Lawn

◇   ◇   ◇

She hated a *mown lawn*. Maybe that was because *mow* was the reverse of *wom*, the beginning of the name of what she was—a *woman*. A *mown lawn* had a sad sound to it, like a *long moan*. From her, a *mown lawn* made a *long moan*. *Lawn* had some of the letters of *man*, though the reverse of *man* would be *Nam*, a bad war. A *raw war*. *Lawn* also contained the letters of *law*. In fact, *lawn* was a contraction of *lawman*. Certainly a *lawman* could and did *mow a lawn*. *Law and order* could be seen as starting from *lawn order*, valued by so many Americans. *More lawn* could be made using a *lawn mower*. A *lawn mower* did make *more lawn*. *More lawn* was a contraction of *more lawmen*. Did *more lawn* in America make *more lawmen* in America? Did *more lawn* make *more Nam*? *More mown lawn* made *more long moan*, from her. Or a *lawn mourn*. So often, she said, Americans wanted *more mown lawn*. All of America might be one *long mown lawn*. A *lawn* not *mown* grows *long*, she said: better a *long lawn*. Better a *long lawn* and a *mole*. Let the *lawman* have the *mown lawn*, she said. Or the *moron*, the *lawn moron*.

from *McSweeney's Quarterly*

Ma Ramon

◇　◇　◇

Ma Ramon would fall upon the floor
feigning death at her children's no's
when they were too grown to force the bending

M' pa palé anglé, she'd say, *no eenglees*
to tax collectors and those too dark to fall
within her notice. She a grand lady
of Abercrombie Street now the capital
was under the Queen and not the rusted
Republique. She did not
believe in London, the pappy show
that was the civil service, good jobs
for brown faces behind a desk.

She believed in land. Her own mystical origins
lay *en la France,* in red-haired green-eyed
aristocrats escaping *guillotines* and *egalité*
for seven mountains they would call their own
and though she had to marry black for money
she never forgot she was person of *qualité.*

She kept her parchment mother in lace and linen
photographed herself with all her siblings
maintained a piano in the parlor
for butter-skinned suitors with Creole tongues
to swirl the Castilian with dervish daughters
petticoats twining with worsted knickers.

Eh ben, Lucretia, *Allé* Ena, *Oú ça* John
Vini Vivi, *Dansé, dansé, li beau, nuh?*
Mes belles enfants, my beautiful cream children.

from *Callaloo*

The Cloud of Unknowing

◇   ◇   ◇

Is not a cloud at all
But a wall colored so efficiently
It seems to be an alley of trees
Some believe this cul de sac
Can be approached from every angle
While others consider it merely a frontage road
To remnants of summer, a disused
Anchorage inside the spiral jetty. But we
Have seen this cloud, you and I have,
Just before we set out to martinize the infidel
It was there, somewhere in the Sahara,
Hovering above an Italian restaurant
Perched on the edge of a depression. White-tunicked
Waiters with jet-black hair served us cannelloni
And Chianti yet at the same time did not
Serve us cannelloni and Chianti—but then
We were at sea as we always were in those days
On a ferry yes the Dover ferry
Everyone was heaving
Patches of sawdust everywhere on deck
Always followed by the cloud
The sun came out but it was still raining
North of Leningrad the tramline ends
We trudge through acres of mud between
Grim apartment blocks in a colorless landscape
Day for night whistling in the sleet
The mud becomes woods, beyond the woods
We finally reach the little wooden village on the far side of a hill—
Bent-bark roofs as in the poem—

With a little Orthodox church, a bit like St-Cloud
From a distance this is Old Russia I think
We meet the priest whom I like
Immediately we parted as old friends—
Never saw him again. Funny, like the
Facial expressions of the father-and-son
Pickpocket team in the Mexico City subway
June rush hour you all of a sudden turn to
Shake their hands "*¡Que pasa?!*" They looked
As if they had seen a ghost
Probably like my own face when I lost my passport
In a dream. I was in Heathrow and hung my coat
On the convenient too convenient rack outside the duty-free shops
The Pakistani woman at the gate was very helpful
But could not help me. For some reason
I was interested only in which languages she spoke
The truth was all I wanted was for her
To say Urdu, which she did.

from *Boston Review*

T.A.P.O.A.F.O.M.

(The Awesome Power of a Fully-Operational Memory)

◇   ◇   ◇

for Sharan Strange

1 ALIENATION

The cassette tape
you sent had a sloppy,
secret second coming on it,
not to mention

the magic-markered mugs
of afronauts
with new spaceships
not manufactured

up south
in any of those privately-owned,
aspirin-white ghettos
ringworming the ozone.

Thanks! You've been here.
You know what
artist colonization is like:
lunchmeataphobia

and black radioinactive levels
of love amnesia
dense as the cosmos.
A brotherloadless UFO.

Only me and Michael S. Harper.
Barely a sister either,
except Afro-Sappho:
Sapphire.

          All of one
day-one month
in the supergroovalistic guerrilla
Nipple Room
and nothing computes.

No wonder they call it Yaddo.
After Faber and Faber
it's the whitest, most minus-da-groove
diaperspace I go:

icka tit,
icka clit,
icka prick,
lickety-split.

Deeper still, I didn't come here to thighlight
empty memory's bangalang mutiny
to zeep then zapp
glitter's non-linear re-entry.

2 ANNIVERSARY

July 5, 1996. Central Park,
New York City. Both mobs up-in-here,
all of their survivors
and damn-near

half ours: you, me, Vera, Major
and Gelonia as well as
a few extended inkslingers.
I ran into Darius James

(who introduced me
to Pedro Bell) and Tracie Morris,
summer-swimming the crowd.
Pump up and down.

Ah underground angel!
Ah gaps and gadgets!
A limousine arrived from Mars.
Baldass Kabbabie babbled.

Remember? It was November 22, 1986.
I was writing a paper
on Jean Vigo,
and you, Sharan, you were looking

for one of Chris Marker's
films, on video.
Ten years is not a long time
for poetry, but it is for us.

Next we were all living together in Cambridge.
After that, freeing and reading black books.
Then, precious lord, James Baldwin died
and we became a church.

Ah! Those Dark Room Sundays
and their infinite, unrehearsed, double-mouthed
            marches toward the rear.
Some readings you really could hear
a rat piss on cotton

and on off weekends
workshops equally dark and feeling.

Your eloquent *Ash* was promoted there,
          in the funkcronomix,
between memory and experience.

Memory, Walcott says, moves backwards.
If this is true, your memory is a mothership
          minus the disco-sadistic silver
all stars need to shine. Tell the world.
A positive nuisance. Da bomb.

                    from *AGNI*

The Art of the Snake Story

◇   ◇   ◇

I.   In Greece in 1939, these kids had this little snake trapped in a
corner, kicking it and laughing. I charged in, all the hero, "Leave the
snake alone," and (I was very high at the time) picked it up and took it
outside. Suddenly I was in horrible pain. I looked down, and the snake
had its teeth in the web of skin between my thumb and first finger,
right here. I let go, and the snake just hung from my hand like some
weird tumor, giving off that glandular, musky smell of ingratitude. The
worst thing was, all the abominable children could see me from the
door. So I had to wait until I was out of sight before thrashing my arm
and screaming.

II.   He had almost made his cautious way across the waterfall. He
was shaking part of a fallen tree to test if it was a solid hand rail or not.
A medium-sized rattlesnake was sunning itself on a high branch, got
shaken off. In the air next to his head I saw it, the flabby gun-metal
body with its frightening marks making an S it was moving through, as
if the ink were sliding out of the letter. The snake landed audibly. Dead
leaf scramble, quite suddenly he was back on this side of the waterfall.
We had the following conversation. "What was it?" "A rattler." "Was it a
rattler?" "It was a rattler." "It was only a foot away from you. Are you all
right?" "It ran off." "Do you want to walk some more?" "No, I don't."

III.   It's coiled on a rock on the bank, it rears up and hisses at us. I
say leave it be, but Stu says no, someone else might pass by too close
and not see it. So he stands up in the boat with his oar and tries to
smash it. It's in the water and then in the boat, it must be six feet long,
and it is *mad*. But at last it's good and dead, so we take the beer out of
the cooler and coil it up in there and close the lid.

We're floating along, fishing and talking, we drift right up along-

side these three old geezers fishing off a dock, and they say, you catching anything? Stu, recognizing a priceless opportunity, says, yeah,
wanna see? and opens up the cooler. That cottonmouth comes shoot-
ing out of there like one of those joke snakes out of a can of nuts.
Nobody gets hurt except the snake, which we have to kill all over again.
Those old guys though, they don't stay and help. They pick up their
lawn chairs and leave, looking unhappy with the whole world.

I suggest throwing the snake overboard this time. Stu says he has
to keep it to show to his wife or she'll never believe us. So now we flop
and twist it into the cooler again, and buzz back to the house. His wife
says, as we come up carrying our burden, what did you catch for us,
and he says, lookie here. Well, you can guess what happens next. This
time, he gets bit on the ankle.

IV.   No, Felix died. I was out of town when it happened. In fact,
Greg decided he would save him until he could take him to the lab and
get him stripped down for the skeleton. But he didn't bother to tell me
that. The day after I came back, I went through the packages in the
freezer and had the shock of my life.

> Snake eternity. Because
> Of the way biting its tail made a circle.
> We're in Hall C,
> An illustration, c, of
> How no snake really did this.
> Never rolled downhill
> As a wheel, never bit off
> Its own ending.
> Or: you have heard
> Of the Gnostic snake? Wisdom-Jesus as a
> Serpent convinced
> The two to know.
> There's also the quaint idea
> Snakes are the spirits of dead
> Heros (this concerns us—we
> Are a museum.) Here is
> An artist's rendering of the dead hero's
> Spirit as it
> Might have landed
> On Matthew's head.

What are the elements of
  A successful snake story?
    A: **The snake must
      Seem animate.** The speaker
        Need not describe,
          Because the listener cannot help but see,
            That oblique, that
              Movement of head sideways to
                Go forward. You understand how
                  This violates the rules for
                    Artful language; the speaker
                    Cannot overestimate
                      Associations an audience brings to
                      This occasion.
                    If the snake is not alive,
                    The teller must
                  Have thought it was. A stuffed or
                Frozen snake need not detract
              From the story. And notice
            How the word gun-
          Metal is used
        Twice—surely significant.

V.   This last time I talked to Alice—Alice had been really depressed
lately, what with trying to finish her thesis and all, but this last time I
called she had just bought this snake and was all excited. It got kind of
boring to listen to, actually—my snake this, my snake that. Well. She
called me today in tears: the snake crawled into her computer. She can't
turn it on now, for fear of, you know, electrocuting him? She knows
he's in there because she blew some cigarette smoke into the opening,
and he stuck his nose out for a second. He hasn't eaten for a long time,
and she can't write her thesis without her computer, and what is she
going to *do?* I mean, this is getting too weird. I mean this snake thing.
Why didn't she get a hamster or something.

VI.   According to the Bangkok guidebook, they milked the cobras
at the cobra farm every day at two. But when I got there, the time had
been changed to twelve, and I had missed the whole thing.

VII.   I was working in the garden, and I almost tripped over a rat-tlesnake. I called pest control, and they were pretty condescending. They said it was probably a hog snake and that hog snakes were *good*. An hour later I called back and said that I had the hog snake trapped in a garbage can, where it was making distinctive rattling noises. They came out and killed it for me, and they were much more polite.

They said to cut the head off, throw the body away, and bury the head carefully so that it wouldn't be dug up again. It sounds like voodoo, but I guess the poison doesn't decay, and water can reconstitute it, and you can walk on it and absorb it right through your skin.

VIII.   This was back in Bombay when I was, oh, a very young boy. I was strictly forbidden to go into the attic, so of course when I found the door unlocked one day, I started up at once.

My friend, it was very dark. There was no electricity in the attic. But there was just enough daylight to make out an enormous cobra right in front of me, ready to strike. I froze. The cobra did not move. The cobra and I remained this way for about half an hour—the stuffed cobra, as it turned out.

IX.   This was when we, my family, lived in Michigan. We had a lot of barn cats, and it used to be my job to go out and fill a bucket with water for them. I had to refill it every day in the winter, because it would freeze over. So I went out to the barn and grabbed the bucket. I'd only taken a few steps when I knew that the weight was off some-how. I looked down, and there was a bronze snake coiled around the outside of the bucket. Evidently it had chosen this spot when it was warmer, and it was now frozen in place. To tell the truth, I never found out if it was alive or not. I screamed, threw the bucket down, and ran into the house. My mother came out with a hoe and chopped it into twenty pieces—strange. Why can't you just chop the thing in half and stop? It doesn't ever seem like a snake is dead enough, does it.

B: **The snake must
Startle.** These are
With one exception stories
    About not expecting snakes.
        Alice, for example, did
            Not really think

79

The snake would be
In the computer; she only looked because
She had been unsuccessful
Looking elsewhere.
For a brief moment when she
Saw the snake's nose, she even
Thought, "Snake!" before
Remembering it was a snake she wished to find.
C: **There must have actually been a snake.**
Grossest exaggeration,
While permissible, is not
Necessary.
Enough, if it
Is true, to say,
"I saw." No lie
Is more hideous than the
Invented snake encounter.
This belongs to (line up along the right, please)
An oral tradition. This word, said with a
Specific register of urgency is
Last bastion of
Word equals thing. You can see a squiggled line
In the raconteur's pupil.
More than that, the snake teller, perpetrating
Horrors, *becomes* a snake, like
Christabel's hiss—
Becomes, and you
Become him, or her, frozen.
These are not in fact stories,
But frames for the one instant,
When a blowing vine, dead stick
Vertiginously metamorphoses, oh,
Sickening, into something living. D: **The
Story reminds
You that anything at any time may be-
Come snake.** We petrify to
Make up for it.

X. They have these little brown snakes there, no longer than that. They like to coil up inside of flowers. You go to smell this pretty flower and you die. Also these giant spiders, this gun-metal blue-black color, like to build their webs across the trail. They kill you too. I tell you, I was a hell of a lot more scared of the wildlife then I ever was of the enemy.

This last was overheard by
            A herpetologist on
                        A train. She managed to photograph it: Here
                        Is the perpetrator. You can just tell what
                                    His friends call him, him with his
                                    Tale in his mouth.

from *Quarter After Eight*

Contemporary American Poetry

◇   ◇   ◇

Maybe when her eye first gave her trouble, but when I did not yet know
This was a growth that would spread through her brain, Mother sent me
Donald Hall's "Kicking the Leaves," which she'd torn from the *Times,*

One of the clippings that piled up around her feet while she read
To scout out the news for half-a-dozen people,
But particularly for her children, particularly for me.

Hall—so uncool—in a poem so humble and conventional,
Where the leaves are dying leaves, not pie plates,
And stand for what we always know they stand for.

In a way, this poem was my mother's leave-taking,
What she would have said to me if she wrote poems.
My darling, she tried to say, through Hall's poem,

I will soon be leaving you. When you hear about my death
You will be staring at a blood red leaf against a raw blue
October sky through a film of tears, and you will be

An orphan. The price you will have to pay
For having been loved—essentially without qualification—
By me. I am leaving you now with this clipping,

This poem about leaves from the editorial page of the Times,
Which I read daily, always with thoughts of you.
How I resented this poem, which moved me terribly,

Though it was completely without jokes or irony,
Unadorned and sad as a New England graveyard,
The anthem of our family, not designed for tragedy,

Other than the loss of each other, my mother signaling to me
Through the voice of her bearded Protestant avatar.
I diminish, not them, as I go first into the leaves

Taking the step they will follow, Octobers and years from now.
Mother, you'd be eighty-four, though younger than some of my students.
Like them, you'd listen skeptically to my praise for my contemporaries

Like Louise Glück. *Her mother, Bea, went to high school with me*
In the Twenties. She's added the umlaut. Remember
Her paintings at the library when she just got out of the hospital?

See, dear, you were never troubled or gloomy enough to be a poet,
Though, like Donald Hall, you have and will have losses.
Remember his poem about the leaves? I sent you a clipping once,

Though I know you always threw out my clippings.
Still, I sent them, messages for you piling up around my feet
Each night as I sat and read the Times *and thought of you.*

Now the poem's in our *Contemporary American Poetry* anthology,
One that puts old enemies, like O'Hara and Lowell, together
In an academy of poetry of the world to come.

And Hall, who looks healthy now, also had cancer,
And nearly died, but here he's still in his mid-forties,
Happy his long drought is over and he's writing again.

He's kicking the leaves, leaping and exultant, recovering from death,
And I am re-reading his poem, thinking of myself at thirty,
Scornful and envious, moved and suspicious, reading in his poem,

One of the few my mother ever cared to send me,
About what he calls *the pleasure, the only long pleasure*
Of taking a place in the story of leaves, which is one hundred percent grief.

The pleasure, if there is one, is knowing we have the dead inside us,
Where they have to make peace with us, and never leave us.
My mother, in class today, though dead way back,

Will go home to hang her coat in the closet of heaven and say:
What a wonderful class! I don't like much in contemporary American poetry,
Except for "Kicking the Leaves" by Donald Hall. But the teacher—

He's like that Louis Rukeyser on "Wall $treet Week"
I watch faithfully, though I leave the investing to Barney.
A man like that—anything he says is worth listening to.

from *Poetry*

Little Dantesque

◇ ◇ ◇

It turns out
The dogs were in control all along.

Hard by the hinges of hell—
A faculty party.

Everyone drifts
In their disastrous bodies.

Sudden furniture,
A hint of eucalyptus.

Someone plugs in the flowers.

1.
I've been a has-been.
Now I'm a was. I was
Promoted.

2.
The dogs were in control all along.
They saw everything.

3.
I had a happy medium—
Had her reading out of my palm.
The circus folded up and left—

A riot of life forms
And annoying colors whisked
Like bright scarves up a sleeve.

4.
The dogs want out.
How like them.

from *Fence*

Time

◊   ◊   ◊

There was too much, always, then too little.
Childhood: sickness.
By the side of the bed I had a little bell—
at the other end of the bell, my mother.

Sickness, gray rain. The dogs slept through it. They slept on the bed,
at the end of it, and it seemed to me they understood
about childhood: best to remain unconscious.

The rain made gray slats on the windows.
I sat with my book, the little bell beside me.
Without hearing a voice, I apprenticed myself to a voice.
Without seeing any sign of the spirit, I determined
to live in the spirit.

The rain faded in and out.
Month after month, in the space of a day.
Things became dreams; dreams became things.

Then I was well; the bell went back to the cupboard.
The rain ended. The dogs stood at the door,
panting to go outside.

I was well, then I was an adult.
And time went on—it was like the rain,
so much, so much, as though it was a weight that couldn't be moved.

I was a child, half sleeping.
I was sick; I was protected.

And I lived in the world of the spirit,
the world of the gray rain,
the lost, the remembered.

Then suddenly the sun was shining.
And time went on, even when there was almost none left.
And the perceived became the remembered,
the remembered, the perceived.

from *The New Yorker*

My Chakabuku Mama

a comic tale

◇   ◇   ◇

My first big love was cosmically correct:
vegetarian chili, herbal tea, feng shui.

I pretended to comprehend numerology,
graphology, phrenology and the phases of the moon.

We meditated on celestial seasonings about who
should do the laundry in an equal relationship.

I slept with my head facing north abiding a vicious draught.
My shoes sat outside the door crying to be let in.

We searched together for the higher ground
through macrobiotic bushes and abstinence.

I peered into her thick transcendental glasses.
She faced the way of the Wicca.

We chanted to find our center
beneath an azure blue candle from Key food.

We never separated without talking it all out
or allowed bad vibes to invade our space.

She made breakfast on alternate Sundays
and I gave up drinking gin.

We went on camping trips every Spring.
I read dense poets and kept copious journals.

I sprinkled a pinch of salt in the four corners of each room,
and loaned all of my favorite clothes to mere acquaintances.

I never eavesdropped when she talked on the phone.
I ate fresh fruit and only argued with Con Edison.

I cut my finger nails. We played kalimba duets.
I threw out my Salems. She threw out the roach spray.

We shuddered in unison at the mention
of french fries or Table Talk pies.

I never watched TV
or listened to James Brown.

I gave up aspirin and wore 100% cotton,
had my tarot read, meditated on a tatami bed.

I learned to love brown rice and Japanese slippers,
eat raw fish and burn patchouli.

She could squeeze the names of three
Egyptian goddesses into any general conversation.

Malice and jealousy beat a hasty retreat. Our life moved forth
on a path of righteous awareness and sisterhood.

Then she left me flat. Exiting serenely
on a cloud of universal love.

from *Callaloo*

Gulls

◊ ◊ ◊

Those neck-pointing out full bodylength and calling
outwards over the breaking waves.
Those standing in waves and letting them come and
                              go over them.
Those gathering head-down and over some one
                              thing.
Those still out there where motion is
primarily a pulsing from underneath
and the forward-motion so slight they lay
their stillness on its swelling and falling
and let themselves swell, fall . . .
Sometimes the whole flock rising and running just
as the last film of darkness rises
leaving behind, also rising and falling in
                              tiny upliftings,
almost a mile of white underfeathers, up-turned, white spines
                              gliding over the wet
sand, in gusts, being blown down towards
              the unified inrolling awayness
              of white. All things turning white through
breaking. The long red pointing of lowering sun
going down on (but also streaking in towards) whoever
might be standing at the point-of-view place
from which this watching. This watching being risen
from: as glance: along the red
blurring and swaying water-path:
to the singular redness: the glance a
being-everywhere-risen-from: everywhere
cawing, mewing, cries where a

single bird lifts heavily
just at shoreline, rip where
its wing-tips (both) lap
backwash, feet still in
the wave-drag of it, to coast
on top of its own shadow and then down to not
landing.

★

Also just under the wave a thickening where
sun breaks into two red circles upon the
                       carried frothing—
white and roiling, yes, yet unbreakably red—red pushed (slicked) under
                each wave (tucked) and, although breaking, always
                one—(as if from the back-end-of-distance red)—
and that *one* flowing to here to
slap the red it carries in glisten-sheets
up onto shore and (also as if *onto*)
my feet.

★

[Or onto my feet, then into my eyes] where red turns into "sun" again.
So then it's sun in surf-breaking water: incircling, smearing: mind not
knowing if it's still "wave," breaking on
itself, small glider, or if it's "amidst" (red turning feathery)
or rather "over" (the laciness of foambreak) or just *what*—(among
the line of also smearingly reddening terns floating out now
on the feathery backedge of foambroken
looking)—*it is.*

★

The wind swallows my words one
                    by
one. The words leaping too, over their own
                         staying.
Oceanward too, as if being taken
                 away

into splash—my clutch of
                    words
swaying and stemming from my
                    saying, no
echo. No stopping on the temporarily exposed and drying rock
                                        out there
to rub or rest where nothing else
                    grows.
And truly swift over the sands.
As if most afraid of being re-
                    peated.
Preferring to be dissolved to
                    designation,
backglancing stirrings,
wedged-in between unsaying and
                    forgetting—
what an enterprise—spoken out by
                    me as if
to *still* some last place, place becoming even as I speak
                                        unspeakable—
and so punctually—not even burnt
by their crossing through the one great
                    inwardness of
mind, not by the straining to be held (grasped) by my
                                    meanings:
"We shall have early fruit
this year" one of the shades along the way
                    calls out,
and "from the beginning" (yet further on). Words: always face-down:
listening falling upon them (as if from
                    above):
listening greedy, able to put them to death,
flinging itself upon them: them open and attached
                    so hard to
                    what they carry:
the only evidence in them of having
                    been.
And yet how they want to see behind themselves,
                    as if there is something
back there, always, behind these rows I

gnaw the open with,
feeling them rush a bit and crane to see beneath themselves,
and always with such pain, just after emerging,
twisting on their stems to see behind, as if there were a
                                        sun
back there they need, as if it's a betrayal,
this single forward-facing: reference: dream of: ad-
                            mission: re
semblance: turning away from the page as if turning to a tryst:
the gazing-straight up at the reader there filled with ultimate
                                        fatigue:
devoted servants: road signs: footprints: you are not alone:
slowly in the listener the prisoners emerge:
slowly in you reader they stand like madmen facing into the wind:
nowhere is there any trace of blood
spilled in the service of kings, or love, or for the sake of honor,
or for some other reason.

from *Conjunctions*

Waterborne

◇   ◇   ◇

1.

The river is largely implicit here, but part
                of what
        becomes it runs from east to west beside

our acre of buckthorn and elm.
                (And part
        of that, which rather weighs on Steven's mind,

appears to have found its way to the basement. Water
                will outwit
        a wall.) It spawns real toads, our little

creek, and widens to a wetland just
                across
        the road, where shelter the newborn

fawns in May. So west among the trafficked fields,
                then south, then
        east, to join the ample Huron on its

curve beneath a one-lane bridge. This bridge
                lacks every
        grace but one, and that a sort of throwback

space for courteous digression:
                your turn,
        mine, no matter how late we are, even

the county engineers were forced to take their road
                        off plumb. It's heartening
            to think a river makes some difference.

                              2.

Apart from all the difference in the world,
                        that is.
            We found my uncle Gordon on the marsh

one day, surveying his new ditch and raining
                        innovative
            curses on the DNR. That's Damn Near

Russia, since you ask. Apparently
                        my uncle
            and the state had had a mild dispute, his

drainage scheme offending some considered
                        larger
            view. His view was that the state could come

and plant the corn itself if it so loved
                        spring mud. The river
            takes its own back, we can barely

reckon fast and slow. When Gordon was a boy
                        they used to load
            the frozen river on a sledge here and

in August eat the heavenly reward—sweet
                        cream—
            of winter's work. A piece of moonlight saved

against the day, he thought. And this is where
                        the Muir boy
            drowned. And this is where I didn't.

3.

Turning of the season, and the counter-
        turn
        from ever-longer darkness into light,

and look: the river lifts to its lover the sun
        in eddying
        layers of mist as though

we hadn't irreparably fouled the planet
        after all.
        My neighbor's favorite spot for bass is just

below the sign that makes his fishing
        rod illegal,
        you might almost say the sign is half

the point. The vapors draft their languorous ex-
        curses on
        a liquid page. Better than the moment is

the one it has in mind.

from *The Atlantic Monthly*

The Singers Change, The Music Goes On

◇ ◇ ◇

No one really dies in the myths.
No world is lost in the stories.
Everything is lost in the retelling,
in being wondered at. We grow up
and grow old in our land of grass
and blood moons, birth and goneness.
A place of absolutes. Of returning.
We live our myth in the recurrence,
pretending we will return another day.
Like the morning coming every morning.
The truth is we come back as a choir.
Otherwise Eurydice would be forever
in the dark. Our singing brings her
back. Our dying keeps her alive.

from *AGNI*

Enough rain for Agnes Walquist

(five little fits of tears)

◇　◇　◇

We are all given something precious that we lose irrevocably.
—CAPRONI

1.

It happened at midnight.
—What I possessed and lost
or what I never possessed
and have nonetheless lost,
or what in any case I
was not born possessing
but received from another's mouth:
—a smooth stone
passed in a kiss from the mouth
of a Fate into my open mouth
amidst odors of metal
and slamming doors
at the dark end of a railway car
as the train was leaning
on a curve and slowing
to stop—is lost. Lost
in that dark!—*Dilectissima,*
the Fate showed me two ways,
male and female. Also a third:
Gessert's midnight path
to the wild *iris,*
an escaped garden among

thickets of poison oak
where rolls the stony Oregon
and hears no sound
except stone on stone.

2.

What, then, shall I give YOU?
My kiss-stone is lost.
But look! The vast world,
energetic and empty,
glows in the dark.
On the strip between the road
—gravel or macadam,
or an earthen path
(but in this case gravel)
and the settlement
or the side-hill field or forest
or other tangled right of way
for jews, gypsies, ghosts
(outcasts in any case)
there among weeds
springs up Gessert's
wild *iris tenax,* violet or pale yellow,
the bloom 3" to 5" across.
Gessert asks, "How in the world
did they come here?"
Then he says, "If you must
take these *iris,*
use a shovel. Root them
in your garden
and let them go to seed.
Gather the seed
in Fall
—October or November.
Drive out into the countryside.
Plant the seeds
on any half-sunny,
slightly eroded, roadside bank.

3.

Sow Gessert's *iris, dilectissima,*
Violet or ghostly yellow,
in the wild, universal garden
named "Shadowy Agnes Walquist,"
her midnight body
from which wild *iris*
and lilies grow.
To whom better entrust
pure loss?
To what breasts other
than the breasts
of Agnes Walquist!
—"Agnes! (Can you hear?)
when a man dies,
or a woman dies,
the whole world of which
he is the only subject
dies without residue
(or the whole world of which
she is the only subject
dies without residue).
'DID I EVER LIVE?'
'NEVER, NEVER.'
The world of each person,
man or woman,
is a dependency of the world
of another one.
When a man dies or a woman
the reason for confidence
with respect to any world
is diminished. (Weep! Weep!)
When the last person but one
dies, the last person,
though he continue to live,
ceases to exist!"
Agnes Walquist sighs.
Then she says,
YES!

4.

In my sleep I say, "Agnes! I will
give you rain
from my mystery store
of rain. The dead have buried
the dead and are forever
burying the dead.
But the dead do not remember
as the living do not know
the heart." I wake
in the hour before dawn
to the huge hammer of the rain
(hammer of sex
as the poet makes it)
which thunders enough, enough, enough."
Earth shudders and springs.
The East grows bright.
And Agnes Walquist whispers,
"Thank you."

5.

Sweet youth, sweet youth
(*dilectissima mea*)
go!
Punish thy pillow.
Your kiss-stone is among the stones
the stony Oregon rolls
and hears no sound
but stone on stone.
Blond Fate, the honey-blond,
no longer knows which one
is the stone of witness.
What follows is the wearing
out to dust.
The water mill deep down
in ocean grinds out salt
(truth, troth, death).

But sweeter than the body
of a man or a woman
(sweetness of that sweetness,
song of all those songs)
is the midnight garden
of Agnes Walquist.
Her breasts are sweet.
The huge hammer is an ancient memory
of water falling into water.
There is lightning all night
on distant mountains,
strike after strike
(violet, blue, red, ghostly yellow,
indigo).
And along the mountain paths,
asleep or dead,
are sprawled
nocturnal mountaineers.

from *The Southern Review*

DONALD HALL

Her Garden

◊　◊　◊

I let her garden go.
let it go, let it go
How can I watch the hummingbird
Hover to sip
With its beak's tip
The purple bee balm—whirring as we heard
It years ago?

The weeds rise rank and thick
let it go, let it go
Where annuals grew and burdock grows,
Where standing she
At once could see
The peony, the lily, and the rose
Rise over brick

She'd laid in patterns. Moss
let it go, let it go
Turns the bricks green, softening them
By the gray rocks
Where hollyhocks
That lofted while she lived, stem by tall stem,
Dwindle in loss.

from the *Times Literary Supplement* and *Tin House*

Sarabande on Attaining the Age of Seventy-Seven

◇   ◇   ◇

The harbingers are come. See, see their mark;
White is their colour, and behold my head.

Long gone the smoke-and-pepper childhood smell
Of the smoldering immolation of the year,
Leaf-strewn in scattered grandeur where it fell,
Golden and poxed with frost, tarnished and sere.

And I myself have whitened in the weathers
Of heaped-up Januaries as they bequeath
The annual rings and wrongs that wring my withers,
Sober my thoughts, and undermine my teeth.

The dramatis personae of our lives
Dwindle and wizen; familiar boyhood shames,
The tribulations one somehow survives,
Rise smokily from propitiatory flames

Of our forgetfulness until we find
It becomes strangely easy to forgive
Even ourselves with this clouding of the mind,
This cinerous blur and smudge in which we live.

A turn, a glide, a quarter turn and bow,
The stately dance advances; these are airs

Bone-deep and numbing as I should know by now,
Diminishing the cast, like musical chairs.

from *The New Yorker*

Nights

◇　◇　◇

Ooooh, oooooh, ooooh, says the voice of a girl:

I've been attacked by owls,
by owls with towels,
I've been attacked
by snakes with rakes.

It is just this kind of ridiculous language, banal but lacking even banality's
pretense at relevance and sense, that I hear in my sleep; I wake, feeling irritable and
depressed.

★

The sadness! the injustice!
It's true I want to know, I want to look
But what is it?

★

The fingers leave their owls in a calm
Sleep figures the features

Sleep speaks for the bird, the animal
For the round and the residual

Sleep soaks from experience
But why and what?

★

Suddenly I remember having rescued a spider from the bathtub in the morning. I imagined that I had established rapport with my environment. I observed the spider eerily. I was in harmony with life and my times. Not only will things go on but this going on will repeat.

After all, I can vow kindness in relation to something I cannot know.

The spider, when it appears within "a range of alternatives," will be rescued—dished out of the nicked and polished porcelain tub and knocked onto the shrubbery just outside the open window.

Of course, it will not be the same spider each time but a sequence of spiders.

★

The 23rd night was very dark.
It was cold.
My eyes were drawn to the window.

I thought I saw a turtledove nesting on a waffle
Then I saw it was a rat doing something awful
But anarchy doesn't bother me now any more than it used to

I thought I saw a woman writing verses on a bottle
Then I saw it was a foot stepping on the throttle
But naturally freedom can be understood in many different ways

I thought I saw a fireman hosing down some straw
Then I saw it was a horse grazing in a draw
But it's always the case that in their struggle to survive, animate objects must
    be aided

I thought I saw a rhubarb pie sitting on the stove
Then I saw it was the tide receding from a cove
But although I have strong emotions when I watch a movie, jealousy is never
    one of them.

I thought I saw a bicyclist racing down the road
Then I saw it was a note, a message still in code
But sense is always either being raised to or lowered from the sky

★

A voice says, The ambered bed flag fills.
A voice says, This is voltage island.
A voice says, The wall past which girls wander flicks is built of baffled face bricks.

★

I saw a juxtaposition
It happened to be between an acrobat and a sense of obligation
Pure poetry
Of course there is a great difference between withering and a napping man
And flailing in relation to fossils in a stone is different from a set of dominoes
Still I don't worry less about the same old worries

★

I'm of a mule age, I dare like a log.
I live where I live, and I'll bulk graciously

    —to zero.

★

But the worst of speaking in the dark is that the sounds we emit are strange and hollow.

★

The moon was solemnly full.
Jim Trotmeyer assertively declared, Emotions can't be governed by rules.
Millie Corcoran politely requested, Don't overwhelm me.
To this Jim Trotmeyer delightfully responded, But the azures of spring truly rush.
Millie Corcoran remarked astutely, Azures rush, yes, but composedly.
Jim Trotmeyer mused pensively, The clouds do indeed puzzle.
Millie Corcoran said sociably, They appear above the crowd.
Oswald Proskaniewicz interrupted furiously, You, Jim Trotmeyer, are not the radical you say you are.

★

109

As for me, I want to be Banambitan
and leave kind ships vitalities by art.
I am untouchable.

from *Conjunctions*

The Formation of Soils

◇　◇　◇

For forty million years   a warm, warm rain—

then the sea got up to try to relax.

Vulnerable volcanoes had just melted away.

He worked below, translating the author's imps and downs,
    his ups and demons—;
pines grew skyward though the pines were not.

Thus began long episodes of quiet,

nickel laterites not ready
for the slots.

It took periods of soft showers attacking the dream
under the silt-covered sun,

Osiris washing his fragments,
Leda swimming with her vagabonds.

Everyone is made essentially the same way.

Through notebooks of tight red dirt
Franciscans walked upside down under us:

aluminum oxides,   incidents of magma,

and I had to go down in the earth for something—

Iron sediments spread over the foothills where Caliban
had his flat;

I was wearing the brown sweater when we spoke,
my heart and the one below translating his heart out.

But by that time, what.

Experience had been sent up, at an angle.

from *The Journal*

In Praise of Coldness

◇ ◇ ◇

"If you wish to move your reader,"
Chekhov wrote, "you must write more coldly."

Herakleitos recommended, "A dry soul is best."

And so at the center of many great works
is found a preserving dispassion,
like the vanishing point of quattrocento perspective,
or the tiny packets of desiccant enclosed
in a box of new shoes or seeds.

But still the vanishing point
is not the painting,
the silica is not the blossoming plant.

Chekhov, dying, read the timetables of trains.
To what more earthly thing could he have been faithful?—
Scent of rocking distances,
smoke of blue trees out the window,
hampers of bread, pickled cabbage, boiled meat.

Scent of the knowable journey.

Neither a person entirely broken
nor one entirely whole can speak.

In sorrow, pretend to be fearless. In happiness, tremble.

from *Tin House*

JOHN HOLLANDER

What the Lovers
in the Old Songs Thought

◊　◊　◊

Thinking "In the beginning was the—(*What??*)"
Faust tried, for openers, *Wort . . . Sinn . . . Kraft . . . Tat*
("Word"? Meaning? Power?—all these reeked of creed:
He finally settled simply on "the Deed".)
But none of these would do for true Beginning:
Our ghosts were there before all those, and not
Playing love's game in which there is no winning,
But doing love's work, continuous creation
Of all the celebrated lovers' tales,
Of all the letters, all the conversation,
All the strange fictions that plain fact entails
And all the silences that bridge the void
Of words exhausted. Let us take possession
Of Origin, then like some crafty Freud
Saying "In the beginning was Repression"
Or like some cabbalist "First was the Name."
What could we literary lovers claim?

In the beginning was unlikeness? (*Good!*)
In the beginning was the opened door
Through which crept in the soul of all our sins?
In the beginning there was need for more?
In the beginning there was likelihood?—
The oldest gospel of our lives begins
"In the beginning there was metaphor."

from *The New Republic*

114

After 65

◊   ◊   ◊

The tragedy, Colette said, is that one
does *not* age. Everyone else does, of course
(as Marcel was so shocked to discover),
and upon one's mask odd disfigurements
are imposed; but that garrulous presence
we sometimes call the self, sometimes deny

it exists at all despite its carping
monologue, is the same as when we stole
the pears, spied on mother in the bath, ran
away from home. What has altered is what
Kant called Categories: the shape of *time*
changes altogether! Days, weeks, months,

and especially years are reassigned.
Famous for her timing, a Broadway wit
told me her "method": asked to do something,
anything, she would acquiesce *next year*—
"I'll commit suicide, provided it's
next year." But after sixty-five, next year

is now. Hours? there are none, only a few
reckless postponements before *it is time* . . .
When was it you "last" saw Jimmy—last spring?
last winter? That scribbled arbiter
your calendar reveals—betrays—the date:
over a year ago. Come again? No

time like the present, endlessly deferred.
Which makes a difference: once upon a time
there was only time (. . . *as the day is long*)
between the wanting self and what it wants.
Wanting still, you have no dimension where
fulfillment or frustration can occur.

Of course you have, but you must cease waiting
upon it: simply turn around and look
back. Like Orpheus, like Mrs. Lot, you
will be petrified—astonished—to learn
memory is endless, life very long,
and you—you are immortal after all.

from *Antioch Review*

Doubt

◊   ◊   ◊

Virginia Woolf committed suicide in 1941 when the German bombing campaign against England was at its peak and when she was reading Freud whom she had staved off until then.

Edith Stein, recently and controversially beatified by the Pope, who had successfully worked to transform an existential vocabulary into a theological one, was taken to Auschwitz in August, 1942.

One year later Simone Weil died in a hospital in England—of illness and depression—determined to know what it is to know.
She, as much as Woolf and Stein, sought salvation in a choice of words.

But multitudes succumb to the sorrow induced by an inexact vocabulary.

While a whole change in discourse is a sign of conversion, the alteration of a single word only signals a kind of doubt about the value of the surrounding words.
Poets tend to hover over words in this troubled state of mind.
What holds them poised in this position is the occasional eruption of happiness.

While we would all like to know if the individual person is a phenomenon either culturally or spiritually conceived and why everyone doesn't kill everyone else, including themselves, since they can—poets act out the problem with their words.

Why not say "heart-sick" instead of "despairing"?
Why not say "despairing" instead of "depressed"?

Is there, perhaps, a quality in each person—hidden like a laugh inside a sob—that loves even more than it loves to live?
If there is, can it be expressed in the form of the lyric line?

Dostoevsky defended his later religious belief, saying of his work "Even in Europe there have never been atheistic expressions of such power. My hosannah has gone through a great furnace of doubt."

According to certain friends, Simone Weil would have given every-thing she wrote to be a poet. It was an ideal but she was wary of charm and the inauthentic. She saw herself as stuck in fact with a rational prose line for her surgery on modern thought. She might be the arche-typal doubter but the language of the lyric was perhaps too uncertain.

As far as we know she wrote a play and some poems and one little prose poem called *Prelude*.

Yet Weil could be called a poet, if Wittgenstein could, despite her own estimation of her writing, because of the longing for a conversion through writing her ideas down. In *Prelude* the narrator is an uprooted seeker who still hopes that a transformation will come to her from the outside. The desired teacher arrives bearing the best of everything, including delicious wine and bread, affection, tolerance, solidarity (people come and go) and authority. This is a man who even has faith and loves truth.

She is happy. Then suddenly, without any cause, he tells her it's over. She is out on the streets without direction, without memory. Indeed she is unable to remember even what he told her without his presence there to repeat it, this amnesia being the ultimate dereliction.

If memory fails, then the mind is air in a skull.
This loss of memory forces her to abandon hope for either rescue or certainty.

And now is the moment where doubt—as an active function—emerges and magnifies the world. It eliminates memory. And it turns eyesight so far outwards, the vision expands. A person feels as if she is the figure inside a mirror, looking outwards for her moves. She is a forgery.

When all the structures granted by common agreement fall away and that "reliable chain of cause and effect" that Hannah Arendt talks about—breaks—then a person's inner logic also collapses.

Yet strangely it is in this moment that doubt shows itself to be the physical double to belief; it is the quality that nourishes willpower, and the one that is the invisible engine behind every step taken.
Doubt is what allows a single gesture to have a heart.

In this prose poem Weil's narrator recovers her balance after a series of reactive revulsions to the surrounding culture by confessing to the most palpable human wish: that whoever he was, he loved her.

Hope seems to resist extermination as much as a roach does.

Hannah Arendt talks about the "abyss of nothingness that opens up before any deed that cannot be accounted for." Consciousness of this abyss is the source of belief for most converts. Weil's conviction that evil proves the existence of God is cut out of this consciousness.

Her Terrible Prayer—that she be reduced to a paralyzed nobody—desires an obedience to that moment where coming and going intersect before annihilation.

And her desire: "To be only an intermediary between the blank page and the poem" is a desire for a whole-heartedness that eliminates personality.

Virginia Woolf, a maestro of lyric resistance, was frightened by Freud's claustrophobic determinism since she had no ground of defense against it. The hideous vocabulary of mental science crushed her dazzling star-thoughts into powder and brought her latent despair into the open air.
Born into a family devoted to skepticism and experiment, she had made a superhuman effort at creating a prose-world where doubt was a mesmerizing and glorious force.

Anyone who tries, as she did, out of a systematic training in secularism, to forge a rhetoric of belief is fighting against the odds. Disappointments are everywhere waiting to catch you, and an ironic realism is always convincing.

Simone Weil's family was skeptical too, and secular while attentive to the development of the mind. Her older brother fed her early sense of inferiority with intellectual put-downs. Later, her notebooks chart a superhuman effort at conversion to a belief in affliction as a sign of God's presence.

Her prose itself is tense from sustained and solitary concentration. After all, to convert by choice (that is, without a blast of revelation or a personal disaster) requires that you shift the names for things, and force a new language out of your mind onto the page.

You have to *make* yourself believe. Is this possible? Can you turn "void" into "God" by switching the words over and over again?
Any act of self-salvation is a problem because of death which always has the last laugh, and if there has been a dramatic and continual despair hanging over childhood, then it may even be impossible.

After all, can you call "doubt" "bewilderment" and suddenly be relieved?

Not if your mind has been fatally poisoned. . . .
But even then, it seems, the dream of having *no doubt* continues, finding its way into love and work. After all choices matter exactly as much as they don't matter—especially when history is on your side.

from *Seneca Review*

Sweet Reader,
Flanneled and Tulled

◊   ◊   ◊

Reader unmov'd and Reader unshaken, Reader unsedc'd
and unterrified, through the long-loud and the sweet-still
I creep toward you. Toward you, I thistle and I climb.

I crawl, Reader, servile and cervine, through this blank
season, counting—I sleep and I sleep. I sleep,
Reader, toward you, loud as a cloud and deaf, Reader, deaf

as a leaf. Reader: *Why don't you turn*
pale? and, *Why don't you tremble?* Jaded, staid
Reader, You—who can read this and not even

flinch. Bare-faced, flint-hearted, recoilless
Reader, dare you—Rare Reader, listen
and be convinced: Soon, Reader,

soon you will leave me, for an italian mistress:
for her dark hair, and her moon-lit
teeth. For her leopardi and her cavalcanti,

for her lips and clavicles; for what you want
to eat, eat, eat. Art-lover, rector, docent!
Do I smile? I, too, once had a brash artless

feeder: his eye set firm on my slackening
sky. He was true! He was thief! In the celestial sense
he provided some, some, some

(much-needed) relief. Reader much-slept with, and Reader I will die
without touching, You, Reader, You: mr. small-
weed, mr. broad-cloth, mr. long-dark-day. And the italian mis-

fortune you will heave me for, for
her dark hair and her moonlit-teeth. You will love her well into three-or-four cities, and then, you will slowly

sink. Reader, I will never forgive you, but not, poor
cock-sure Reader, not, for what you think. O, Reader
Sweet! and Reader Strange! Reader Deaf and Reader

Dear, I understand youyourself may be hard-
pressed to bear this small and un-necessary burden
having only just recently gotten over the clean clean heart-

break of spring. And I, Reader, I am but the daughter
of a tinker. I am not above the use of bucktail spinners,
white grubs, minnow tails. Reader, worms

and sinkers. Thisandthese curtail me
to be brief: Reader, our sex gone
to wildweather. YesReaderYes—that feels much-much

better. (And my new Reader will come to me empty-
handed, with a countenance that roses, lavenders, and cakes.
And my new Reader will be only mildly disappointed.

My new Reader can wait, can wait, can wait.) Light-
minded, snow-blind, nervous, Reader, Reader, troubled, Reader,
what'd ye lack? Importunate, unfortunate, Reader:

You are cold. You are sick. You are silly.
Forgive me, kind Reader, forgive me, I had not intended to step this
    quickly this far
back. Reader, we had a quiet wedding: he&I, theparson

&theclerk. Would I could, stead-fast, gracilefacile Reader! Last,
good Reader, tarry with me, jessa-mine Reader. Dar-
(jee)ling, bide! Bide, Reader, tired, and stay, stay, stray Reader,

true. *R.: I had been secretly hoping this would turn into a love poem.* Disconsolate. Illiterate. Reader,
I have cleared this space for you, for you, for you.

From *The Paris Review*

The Emperor of China

◊ ◊ ◊

I didn't know I was going to sleep until I woke up. . . .
—PAUL BOWLES

1

Remember the boy who played with a rope
in Kieslowski's film? He wrapped it around his hand
in the back of the taxi before he strangled the driver. Because.
Filmed through a filter, gray-green pallor of streets in a city,
moldy faces. Unnatural light the color of evil. It follows us now
when the sky is so steadily even in winter blue. Follows us
climbing the sanctified hill in Ein Kerem, the two mothers touching
each other's bellies, the unborn skimming across the valley
in their bees' wings, and a choir of children in the courtyard
of the Church of the Visitation singing Mozart.

2

Thin little squares of metal sewn in the hems of drapes
to make them hang straight. They are weighing me down.
Like the pigment and gravel in a Kiefer painting crushed
by the weight of its own excess. I don't want romance
in dung heaps, or Nuremberg with a blow-torch and traces
of blood. I don't want silence under the master's arches.
I want them to hear what I say. Disorder, chaos, the fibrillation
of my heart. I don't want us to fight the old wars.

3

"I was the eldest son of the Emperor of China. Our father
put me in a basket, summoned his mandarins in their funny caps
to rock me to sleep and fill me with nightmares about the war,
so when he died and I would be Emperor I'd be so scared
of war I'd never start one." When Uri was nine or ten in the camps
and his younger brother was frightened, he would tell him
the story again and again, how it all was a dream while he slept
in a basket and how nothing they went through was real.

4

"Enjoy your life," said our friend on her eightieth birthday,
"whether you like it or not." On the road to the *Peace*
and Other Dreams Writers' Conference in Beersheva,
a blue glass *hamsa* dangles from the rear view mirror
against the evil eye. There are fields of sunflowers
on both sides of the road. Their quivering faces follow us
down the highway, rimmed with light. They will be harvested
for oil and seeds the birds haven't stolen. I'm glad for the yellow,
that it's not at the center, that it sways and shines all the way
to the edge as long as the eye remembers.

5

The shape of a sound, your voice and the vowels as I saw them
in the first years, lips slightly open over mine and your warm
tongue bringing me here. The place of beginnings. We never
thought about the End. Where we are is only where we have been.
Diamond edge of the mind, our selves coming out of the rock
like spiked thistles. Something older than bodies that live
for a moment under the blankets, their moist skin touching.
Diamond and coal the same pure element of carbon. How you
talked about Lawrence when we first met. I want you to feel my
heart at the back of your throat. We can't go on with the quarrels
near the rubble of the next war. If we could only remember

how we started, perhaps the words would remember us
the way we found the road home in a blackout.

6

Oh love, for the young wolf caught in a foot trap in Sinai
who pulled the trap out of the ground and dragged herself
with the trap attached over our border, now healed and set free
in the desert; for the red heifers they'll never breed pure enough;
for the tiny knuckles of freesia and hyacinth breaking out of
the cold earth before it is spring; for us in our cheerfulness
and fury, for days when we're still who we were from the beginning,
unrecognized; for the Emperor of China, for dreaming and waking
though we're all dying, whether you like it or not, enjoy.

7

We're bent in the garden planting spring bulbs, pulling up
weeds, and I'm wondering how much longer we'll crouch here
on our knees in the damp soil sorting things out. Guardians
of shrubs and flowers, the first wild cyclamen sipping the sun.
We watch over each other as we watch over our garden,
woolly branches of cacti, fiery pokers of aloes in winter.
Especially during a long drought, after a snowfall, or following
the arcs of missiles on our screen. Flurries of extra caring.
Some mornings we hang on to each other as if we're afraid to let go.

8

What lasts is what we are up against. We are dividing
the city after the walls came down. Raising new barriers.
I explain why I did what I did you explain why you said
what you said and that makes it worse it gets obsessive
like our neighbor across the street who sweeps the stone path
to his front door every day and now that it's snowing
sweeps it every few hours. He's out there still in the numbing cold
wearing shorts black socks and sandals, making neat little mounds

of dirty snow. First he sweeps every pine needle out to the curb
and cleans up the sidewalk. Then he turns on the hose
and washes it down. We watch from our windows
as the soft flakes fall and he wipes them off with a rag,
wrings out the rag and wipes them again.

from *American Poetry Review*

The Quick
and the Dead

◊ ◊ ◊

At the hayfield's edge, a few stalks
of grass are twitching; I bend close
and find the plump body of the vole.
He's dead, I lobbed him here myself,
after snapping him in a mousetrap to halt
his forays through the flower beds. Yet now
he lives: he jerks, he heaves, he shudders,
as if the process of decomposition
had quickened in him and turned violent,
or he were struggling with something
blocking an attempt at resurrection—
or could it be that something
unimaginable happens, something
worse than death, after death.

I prog him, tilt him, peer under him
and see: he's being buried, by beetles—
bright-yellow or red chevrons
laid across their black wings—
carrion beetles, sexton beetles,
corpse-eating buriers who delve
and undergrub him, howking out
the trench his sausagey form settles into.

Now a beetle moils across him,
spewing at both ends, drooking him

in chemical juices. The reek of him
is heavy, swampy, surely savory,
luring from afar not only beetles
but those freeloaders of the afterlife
the midden flies, who arrive
and drop their eggs in, too,
before the covering of the grave.

Scummaging down into an ever
more formfitting last resting place,
the vole by now has dwelt almost
a full day in death, and yet somehow he's
still looking good. His gape drawn back,
he bares his teeth: uppers
stubby and old-folks yellow, lowers
an inch long, curled inward, like uppers
of beavers if forced to subsist on soft food.
At the last day, when souls go back
to their graves and resume the form
and flesh once theirs, this one
could jump and jig, as if simply
risen from a good night's dead sloom.

The flies' eggs hatch, the larvae squirm
in and out of the eyeholes; in and out
of the ears; in and out of the snout,
which slorped too often the airy auras
of our garden flowers; in and out of the mouth,
which, even cluttered with bent choppers,
snipped flowers and dragged the blossoms
stem first through gaps in the stone wall—
all but the peony blossom, which stuck
and stoppered the hole for a week
like a great gorgeous cork; and in and out
of the anus, like revenant turds,
that go in to practice going out.

The last half of the vole's tail
still sticks out, as if it might be left

that way, like a stalk of grass, to make
the site look natural. At the grave's edge
a cricket stands in glittering black,
ogling it all. Shocking to find
this hearth critter here, like a Yankee
town father spectating at a cross burning.

A larger beetle, the pronotum behind
her head brilliant red, noggles
into view; pushing the grass down
on either side she plouters
without pause past the tobacco-ish
teeth and down into the underroom
of the self-digesting birth banquet,
to deposit her eggs, to wait, and then
to peel tidbits from the carcass and feed
her hatchlings mouth to mouth, like a bird.

Soon this small plot will be unfindable:
every blade of grass will look
like a vole's tail, every smither
of ungrassed earth like burial ground,
day won't feel exactly like day, nor night
like night, and in the true night,
when we have our other, more lunatic day,
I may hear in the dunch of blood
a distant, comforting, steady shovelling,
but I will know—when a human body
is drained of its broths and filled
again with formaldehyde and salts,
or unguents and aromatic oils, and pranked
up in its holiday best and laid out
in a satin-lined airtight stainless-steel
coffin and stowed in a leakproof concrete vault—
I will know that if no fellow-creatures
can pry their way in to do the underdigging
and jiggling and earthing over and mating
and egg laying and birthing forth,
then the most that can come to pass

will be a centuries-long withering
down to a gowpen of dead dust, and not ever
the crawling of new life out of the old,
which is what we have for eternity on earth.

from *The New Yorker*

Dear Derrida

◇　◇　◇

My new grad-school roommates and I are attending
　　　　our first real lecture, which has gone okay,
we guess, since none of us understands it,
　　　　　　　when one of our professors rises,
a somewhat prissy fellow
　　　　with a mild speech impediment,
and says he takes issue with the speaker's tone,
　　　　　　　which he characterizes as one of "sar, sar,"
and here he raises his voice a little,
　　　　"sar, sar, sar," and wipes his mouth

with a handkerchief, "sar," and turns red
　　　　　　　and screams, "sar, sar, sar—DAMN EET!—sarcasm!"
The four of us look at each other
　　　　as if to say, Hmmmm, nothing like this
at the cow colleges we went to!
　　　　　　　After that, whenever we'd spill our coffee
or get a sock stuck in the vacuum cleaner,
　　　　we'd look at the mess ruefully
and say, "da, da, da—SARCASM!—damn eet!"

　　　　　　　Our lives were pretty tightly sealed,
　　　　and if we weren't in class or the library,
either we spent our time in wordplay
　　　　　　　or cooking: what with girlfriends
and passersby, we always had a pot
　　　　of water boiling on the back of the stove
(it's like you're ready to deliver babies,
　　　　　　　somebody said once), either for spaghetti

or sausages, though one evening Chris,
        the English student from England, came by

for a sausage supper, and after he left,
            we ran up on the roof to pelt him
with water balloons, though when we did,
        he fell down as though he'd been shot,
and one of us said, Jeez, what's wrong
            with Chris, and somebody else said,
You know, Chris eats nothing *but* sausage,
            and a third party said, Hmmmm,
        maybe we ought to vary our diet a little.

        And that was our life: school, the boiled messes
    we made on that stove, and hanging around
that crummy apartment talking about,
            I don't know, Dr. Mueller's arm,
I guess, which hung uselessly
        by his side for reasons no one
fathomed—polio, maybe, or some
            other childhood disease—though Paul
said he thought it was made of wood.
        Can't be made of wood, said Michael,

you can see his hand at the end
            of it, to which Paul replied,
Yeah, but you can have a wooden arm
        and a real hand, can't you?
And that was what our life was like,
            because mainly we just sat around
and speculated like crazy while
        the snow piled up outside,
    so much so that by the time spring came,

        I'd had it, so I moved out of there and in with Grant
        and Brian and Poor Tom, who were philosophy
students but also genuine bad asses,
        believe it or not, because at that time
you more or less had to be an existentialist,
        i. e., tough, and not a deconstructionist,

which was a few years down the road yet
            and which would have left everyone
paralyzed, since all texts
            eventually cancel themselves out.

Of the new roomies, I hit it off best
            with Grant, who became one of the big-brother
types I seemed to be looking for at that period in my life,
            and in fact he rescued me
on more than one occasion, such as the time I was talking
            to a local girl outside a bar
called Jazz City and her three brothers
            decided to "teach me a lesson" and would have
            if Grant hadn't punched one of them

                across the hood of a parked car, or the night
            he and I were in this other place where
a biker gang called Quantrill's Raiders
                hung out and into which wandered
a well-dressed couple so unaware
            of their surroundings that they asked the bartender
to please make them some hot toddies,
            which set everybody to laughing,
only the Quantrills decided we were laughing at them
            and jumped up to "teach us a lesson"

and would have, too, if Grant had not thrown
            a table at them and dragged me
out of there to dive behind some garbage cans
            and choke on our own laughter
while the drunk, fucked-up bikers howled
            and swore and punched each other since they
couldn't punch us. All this was therapy,
            I figured, since grad school was stressful enough
            to send three people I knew to the clinic

                with barbiturate overdoses (two made it,
            one didn't), and I'm not even listing here
all the divorces I know of that were directly
            attributable to that constant pressure

to be the best, be publishable, hireable,
            lovable, that came from professors and sweethearts
and parents but mainly from ourselves,
                        as though each of us were two people,
a good and capable slave, on the one hand,
            and, on the other, a psychotic master

who either locked us up with our pots
            of boiling water or sent us out to dance
with the devil in the streets of Baltimore.
            That year magi appeared from the east:
Jacques Lacan, Tzvetan Todorov,
            Roland Barthes, and Jacques Derrida
brought their Saussurean strategies
            to the Hopkins conference on "The Language
of Criticism and the Sciences of Man,"

            where they told us that all language
is code and thus separate from reality,
and therefore everything
            is a text as long as there is nothing
more than this half-conscious
            linguistic interplay between perceiver
and perceived, which is another way
            of saying that language is the only reality
or at least the only one that counts.
            As different as these thinkers are,

each was telling us that there is no us:
            that cultural structures
or the media or Western thought
            or the unconscious mind
or economic systems make us
            what we are or what we seem to be, since,
in fact, we are not, which isn't such bad news,
            if you think about it, because it means
we don't have to take ourselves so seriously.

            Derrida and company make it impossible
for anyone today to read a book

as they had before, but we didn't know that then.
     Grant didn't, that's for sure;
four years later, he put a gun in his mouth
   and blew the back of his skull off,
and sometimes it makes me sad
     when I think of how long it takes
for new ideas to catch on, because,
   yeah, deconstruction might have saved us.

from *The Kenyon Review*

The Ashes

◇　◇　◇

For William Gass

This elderly poet, unpublished for five decades,
Said that one day in her village a young girl
Came screaming down the road,
"The Red Guards are coming! The Red Guards . . .
Are Coming!" At once the poet
Ran into her house and stuffed the manuscript
Of her poems into the stove. The only copy.
When the guards arrived they took her into the yard
For interrogation. As they spoke
The poet's mother tried to hang herself in the kitchen.
That's all I know about the Red Guard.
It is enough.

The elderly poet is bitter—and why not?
She earned her Ph.D. at an Ivy League school
And returned to China in 1948. Bad timing.
She is bitter with me
Because I've chosen to translate a younger poet,
Young enough to be her child or mine.
The truth is, her poems are forced,
But not flowering. The good work died in the stove.
She knows this. She wants me to recompose them
From the ashes. She wants the noose
Around her mother's neck untied by me.
She wants—oh she wants!—to have her whole life over:

Not to leave America in 1948;
To know me when we are both young promising poets.
Her rusty English now is flawless,
My Mandarin, so long unused, is fluent.
No dictionaries needed. A perfect confidence
Flowing between us. And the Red Guard,
Except as the red sword-lilies
That invigilate the garden,
Unimagined by us both:
I, who believe the Reds are agrarian reformers,
She, who believes she will be an honored poet,
Her name known to everyone, safe in her fame.

from *The Texas Review*

To World War Two

◇ ◇ ◇

Early on you introduced me to young women
   in bars
You were large, and with a large hand
You presented them in different cities,
Made me in San Luis Obispo, drunk
On French seventy-fives, in Los Angeles, on
   pousse-cafés.
It was a time of general confusion
Of being a body hurled at a wall.
I didn't do much fighting. I sat, rather I stood,
   in a foxhole.
I stood while the typhoon splashed us into
   morning.
It felt unusual
Even if for a good cause
To be part of a destructive force
With my rifle in my hands
And in my head
My serial number
The entire object of my existence
To eliminate Japanese soldiers
By killing them
With a rifle or with a grenade
And then, many years after that,
I could write poetry
Fall in love
And have a daughter
And think
About these things

From a great distance
If I survived
I was "paying my debt
To society" a paid
Killer. It wasn't
Like anything I'd done
Before, on the paved
Streets of Cincinnati
Or on the ballroom floor
At Mr. Vathé's dancing class
What would Anne Marie Goldsmith
Have thought of me
If instead of asking her to dance
I had put my BAR to my shoulder
And shot her in the face
I thought about her in my foxhole—
One, in a foxhole near me, has his throat cut
    during the night
We take more precautions but it is night and it
    is you.
The typhoon continues and so do you.
"I can't be killed—because of my poetry. I have
    to live on in order to write it."
I thought—even crazier thought, or just as
    crazy—
"If I'm killed while thinking of lines, it will be
    too corny
When it's reported" (I imagined it would be
    reported!)
So I kept thinking of lines of poetry. One that
    came to me on the beach in Leyte
Was "The surf comes in like masochistic lions."
I loved this terrible line. It was keeping me
    alive. My Uncle Leo wrote to me,
"You won't believe this, but someday you may
    wish
You were footloose and twenty on Leyte
    again." I have never wanted
To be on Leyte again,
With you, whispering into my ear,

"Go on and win me! Tomorrow you may not
    be alive,
So do it today!" How could anyone ever win
    you?
How many persons would I have had to kill
Even to begin to be a part of winning you?
You were too much for me, though I
Was older than you were and in camouflage.
    But for you
Who threw everything together, and had all
    the systems
Working for you all the time, this was trivial. If
    you could use me
You'd use me, and then forget. How else
Did I think you'd behave?
I'm glad you ended. I'm glad I didn't die. Or
    lose my mind.
As machines make ice
We made dead enemy soldiers, in
Dark jungle alleys, with weapons in our hands
That produced fire and kept going straight
    through
I was carrying one,
I who had gone about for years as a child
Praying God don't let there ever be another war
Or if there is, don't let me be in it. Well, I was
    in you.
All you cared about was existing and being won.
You died of a bomb blast in Nagasaki, and
    there were parades.

from *Harper's Magazine*

NOELLE KOCOT

Consolations Before an Affair, Upper West Side

◇   ◇   ◇

The ticking minutes shed their sound.
Our ill-matched grammar claps like thunder
Over plates of noctilucent steam.
Strange, you were rich in a poor country
And now you are its mirror.
My catechism was the digital whim of this city.
I feasted on a diet of its most numinous scraps.
It seems neither one of us has obeyed
The edicts of arranged existence.
Earlier tonight I walked here with you,
Unperplexed on the perimeter of what is,
As the nimble sentences springing from your face
Revived my collection of darknesses
Strung around me like a smashed necklace of shells.
Always, this part of the city
Fills with the scent of old ghosts,
And now the tumult of new ones.
For you the undulant tomorrows seem image-laden, plaintive,
And I want to say please, be careful, but I have no right
As your hair is already stricken a little with gray.
I want to find a way to burn it into you from across the table,
Across these fine dressings of civility,
That what I have at any given moment
Is a limbo cloaking my heavy shoulders
Like a balm that soothes the phoenix.

from *Another Chicago Magazine*

Songs of the Valley

◇ ◇ ◇

There are two choirs, one poised in space,
Compelled by summer and the noise of cars
Obscured behind the green abundance of the leaves.
The other one is abstract, kept alive by words
Deflected from their courses, gathered
And assembled in the anonymity of someone's room.
Their crescendos mount like mountains of desire,
Like bodies floating through a spectral haze
Of unimagined sounds, until the masks drop,
And the face of winter gazes on the August day
That spans the gap between the unseen and the seen.
The academies of delight seem colder now,
The chancellors of a single thought
Distracted by inchoate swarms of feelings
Streaming like collegians through the hollow colonnades.
Fish swim in the rivers. Olives ripen on the trees.
And the wind comes pouring through the valley
Like the flowing monologue of the mirror,
Celebrating the rocks and hills beyond the window.
The clouds are stones set in the inner sky
Where the nights and days distill their contradictions,
The piano is the minor of a dream, and distant
Fires transmit their codes from ridge to ridge.
It is a pageant of the wistful and the real, sound
And sense, archaic figures and the eyes that see them
In absentia. Morning is a different dream,
Waking to the embarrassment of a face,
To a paradox created in the semblance of a person
Who remains a pessimist of the imagination,

Caught up in the coarse mesh of thought
Through which life flows, and is celebrated.

from *Southwest Review*

Seven Deadly Sins

◇   ◇   ◇

SLOTH

If you're one of seven
Downfalls, up in your kingdom
Of mulberry leaves, there are men
Betting you aren't worth a bullet,

That your skin won't tan into a good
Wallet. As if drugged in the womb
& limboed in a honeyed languor,
By the time you open your eyes

A thousand species have lived
& died. Born on a Sunday
Morning, with old-world algae
In your long hair, a goodness

Disguised your two-toed claws
Bright as flensing knives. In this
Upside-down haven, you're reincarnated
As a fallen angel trying to go home.

ENVY

Icarus imitated the golden plover,
Drawn toward a blue folly
Above, looping through echoes
Of a boy's prankish laughter,

Through an airy labyrinth
Of conjecture. A lifetime
Ahead of Daedalus, with noon sun
In his eyes, he outflew the bird's

Equilibrium, wondering how this
Small creature of doubt braved
The briny trade winds. Surely,
In a fanfare of uneclipsed wings

Driven by dash & breathless style,
He could outdo the plover's soars
& dares. But he couldn't stop
Counting feathers against salty sky.

PRIDE

Crowned with a feathered helmet,
Not for disguise or courtship
Dance, he looks like something
Birthed by swallowing its tail,

Woven from a selfish design
& guesswork. As if masked
With a see-through caul
From breast to hipbone,

His cold breath silvers
Panes of his hilltop house
Into a double reflection.
Silhouetted almost into a woman,

He can beg forgiveness now
As he leans against a window
Overlooking Narcissus's pond
Choked with a memory of lilies.

LUST

If only he could touch her,
Her name like an old wish
In the stopped weather of salt
On a snail. He longs to be

Words, juicy as passionfruit
On her tongue. He'd do anything,
Would dance three days & nights
To make the most terrible gods

Rise out of ashes of the yew,
To step from the naked
Fray, to be as tender
As meat imagined off

The bluegill's pearlish
Bones. He longs to be
An orange, to feel fingernails
Run a seam through him.

GLUTTONY

In a country of splendor & high
Ritual, in a fat land of zeros,
Sits a man with string & bone
For stylus, hunched over his easel,

Captured by perfection.
But also afflictions live behind
Electric fences, among hedges
& a whirlwind of roses, down

To where he sits beside a gully
Pooling desires. He squints
Till the mechanical horizon is one
Shadowplay against bruised sky,

Till the smoky perfume limps
Into undergrowth. He balls up
Another sheet in unblessed fingers, always
Ready to draw the thing that is all mouth.

Avarice

At six, she chewed off
The seven porcelain buttons
From her sister's christening gown
& hid them in a Prince Albert can

On a sill crisscrossing the house
In the spidery crawlspace.
She'd weigh a peach in her hands
Till it rotted. At sixteen,

She gazed at her little brother's
Junebugs pinned to a sheet of cork,
Assaying their glimmer, till she
Buried them beneath a fig tree's wide,

Green skirt. Now, twenty-six,
Locked in the beauty of her bones,
She counts eight engagement rings
At least twelve times each day.

Anger

We can cut out Nemesis's tongue
By omission or simple analysis.
Doesn't this sin have to marry
Another, like a wishbone

Worked into meat, to grow
Deadly? Snared within
The blood's quick night,
Our old gods made of sex

& wit, of nitrate & titanium,
Hurl midnight thunderbolts
& lightning. Are we here
Because they must question

Every death in an alley,
Every meltdown? We know
We wouldn't be much, if thorns
Didn't drive light into wet blooms.

from *Poetry*

Wedding Day

◇　◇　◇

1.

I have an appointment with elsewhere
I told the crater
which was filling with water and fragrant debris.
But that's just me.

All the impatient green bottles were pairing off,
a few stuffed with dainty Spanish galleons.
I doused my rag in silvery butane.
I had a picnic to attack: lamb chops; childhood.

Mine was a wedding of pipeline and pomp.
My bride pranced barefoot in the rime-dusted marsh.
She who sold me her eventual surrender
before losing herself in the blades.

She was a pristine evasive gesture.
She was a prissy evasive jester.
Troubled by a prolonged fondling
at the construction bin she called home.

2.

A confidential grimace in the ditch.
A brass band with its mouthpieces removed.

She in dejection
swung in one hand her broken heels
at the stone altar and in the other
tugged her ringlets.

The turbulent breeze had found me
and asked me to slumber in its physicist's truck.
I liked trucks. And this one's treads
had been scooped of sand with a sparkling trowel.

3.

One of the emotions not included
showed up on my fruit plate
like a seed but more like a listening
device. You've swallowed all

the mints, whispered my mate to me.
The mint with the imprint of a slave ship
and its masts and its slaves floundering at sea,
oh never to be reproduced.

Home: the chaff of stereotypical daylight,
potatoes in the closet, the waxy floor;
and squatting in shadows beneath the fuse box,
distracted by trumpets, my only lonely bride.

4.

It was solstice inside the atom
and I took a stroll
to the sandy atoll
where I hired a girl for a whirl.

There was room for me inside her and her family.
She was swollen with particles of Emerson.
She had a packet of locomotive stamps
that she longed to sell me in the future.

This is the future I said and she with longing replied:
You sir have bought yourself a shiny train.

from *Northwest Review*

SARAH MANGUSO

The Rider

◇　◇　◇

Some believe the end will come in the form of a mathematical equation.
Others believe it will descend as a shining horse.
I calculate the probabilities to be even at fifty percent:
Either a thing will happen or it won't.
I open a window,
I unmake the bed,
Somehow, I am moving closer to the equation or to the horse with everything I do.
Death comes in the form of a horse covered in shining equations.
There will be no further clues, I see.
I begin to read my horse.
The equations are drawn in the shapes of horses:
Horses covered in equations.
I am tempted to hook an ankle around the world as I ride away.
For I am about to ride far beyond the low prairie of beginnings and endings.

from *American Letters & Commentary*

J. D. MCCLATCHY

Tattoos

◇　◇　◇

1.

Chicago, 1969

Three boots from Great Lakes stumble arm-in-arm
　　　　Past the hookers
　　　　And winos on South State
To a tat shack. Pissed on mai tais, what harm
　　　　Could come from the bright slate
Of flashes on the scratcher's corridor
Wall, or the swagger of esprit de corps?

Tom, the freckled Hoosier farmboy, speaks up
　　　　And shyly points
　　　　To a four-inch eagle
High over the Stars and Stripes at sunup.
　　　　A stormy upheaval
Inside—a seething felt first in the groin—
Then shoves its stubby subconscious gunpoint

Into the back of his mind. The eagle's beak
　　　　Grips a banner
　　　　Waiting for someone's name.
Tom mumbles that he'd like the space to read
　　　　FELIX, for his small-framed
Latino bunkmate with the quick temper.
Felix hears his name and starts to stammer—

He's standing there beside Tom—then all three
        Nervously laugh
      Outloud, and the stencil
Is taped to Tom's chest. The needle's low-key
       Buzzing fusses until,
Oozing rills of blood like a polygraph's
Lines, there's a scene that for years won't come off.

Across the room, facedown on his own cot,
        Stripped to the waist,
      Felix wants Jesus Christ
Crucified on his shoulder-blade, but not
       The heart-broken, thorn-spliced
Redeemer of punk East Harlem jailbait.
He wants light streaming from the wounds, a face

Staring right back at those who've betrayed him,
        Confident, strong,
      With a dark blue crewcut.
Twelve shading needles work around the rim
       Of a halo, bloodshot
But lustrous, whose pain is meant to prolong
His sudden resolve to fix what's been wrong.

(Six months later, a swab in Viet Nam,
        He won't have time
      To notice what's been inked
At night onto the sky's open hand—palms
       Crawling with Cong. He blinks.
Bullets slam into him. He tries to climb
A wooden cross that roses now entwine.)

And last, the bookish, acned college grad
        From Tucson, Steve,
      Who's downed an extra pint
Of cut-price rye and, misquoting Conrad
       On the fate of the mind,
Asks loudly for the whole nine yards, a "sleeve,"
An arm's-length pattern of motives that weave

And eddy around shoals of muscle or bone.
                    Back home he'd signed
          On for a Navy hitch
Because he'd never seen what he's since grown
          To need, an *ocean* which. . . .
But by now he's passed out, and left its design
To the old man, whose eyes narrow, then shine.

By dawn, he's done. By dawn, the others too
                    Have paid and gone.
          Propped on a table-top,
Steve's grappling with a hangover's thumbscrew.
          The bandages feel hot.
The old man's asleep in a chair. Steve yawns
And makes his way back, shielded by clip-ons.

In a week he'll unwrap himself. His wrist,
                    A scalloped reef,
          Could flick an undertow
Up through the tangled swash of glaucous cyst
          And tendon kelp below
A vaccination scallop's anchored seaweed,
The swelling billow his bicep could heave

For twin dolphins to ride toward his shoulder's
                    Coppery cliffs
          Until the waves, all flecked
With a glistening spume, climb the collar-
          Bone and break on his neck.
When he raises his arm, the tide's adrift
With his dreams, all his watery what-ifs,

And ebbs back down under the sheet, the past,
                    The uniform.
          His skin now seems colder.
The surface of the world, he thinks, is glass,
          And the body's older,
Beckoning life shines up at us transformed
At times, moonlit, colorfast, waterborne.

2.

Figuring out the body starts with the skin,
   Its boundary, its edgy go-between,
The scarred, outspoken witness at its trials,
   The monitor of its memories,
Pleasure's flushed archivist and death's pale herald.
   But skin is general-issue, a blank
Identity card until it's been filled in
   Or covered up, in some way disguised
To set us apart from the beasts, whose aspects
   Are given, not chosen, and the gods
Whose repertoire of change—from shower of gold
   To carpenter's son—is limited.
We need above all to distinguish ourselves
   From one another, and ornament
Is particularity, elevating
   By the latest bit of finery,
Pain, wardrobe, extravagance, or privation
   Each above the common human herd.
The panniered skirt, dicky, ruff, and powdered wig,
   Beauty mole, Mohawk, or nipple ring,
The pencilled eyebrow above Fortuny pleats,
   The homeless addict's stolen parka,
Face lift, mukluk, ponytail, fez, dirndl, ascot,
   The starlet's lucite stiletto heels,
The billboard model with his briefs at half-mast,
   The geisha's obi, the gigolo's
Espadrilles, the war widow's décolletage . . .
   Any arrangement elaborates
A desire to mask that part of the world
   One's body is. Nostalgia no more
Than anarchy laces up the second-hand
   Myths we dress our well-fingered goods in.
Better still perhaps to change the body's shape
   With rings to elongate the neck, shoes
To bind the feet, lead plates wrapped to budding breasts,
   The Sadhu's penis-weights and plasters,
The oiled, pumped-up torsos at Muscle Beach,

Or corsets cinched so tightly the ribs
Protrude like a smug, rutting pouter pigeon's.
They serve to remind us we are not
Our own bodies but anagrams of their flesh,
And pain not a feeling but a thought.

But best of all, so say fellow travellers
In the fetish clan, is the tattoo,
Because not merely molded or worn awhile
But exuded from the body's sense
Of itself, the story of its conjuring
A means defiantly to round on
Death's insufferably endless emptiness.
If cave men smeared their bones with ochre,
The color of blood and first symbol of life,
Then peoples ever since—Egyptian
Priestesses, Mayan chieftains, woady Druids,
Sythian nomads and Hebrew slaves,
Praetorian guards and kabuki actors,
Hell's Angels, pilgrims, monks, and convicts—
Have marked themselves or been forcibly branded
To signify that they are members
Of a group apart, usually above
But often below the rest of us.
The instruments come effortlessly to hand:
Fish bone, razor blade, bamboo sliver,
Thorn, glass, shell shard, nail, or electric needle.
The canvas is pierced, the lines are drawn,
The colors suffuse a pattern of desire.
The Eskimos pull a charcoaled string
Beneath the skin, and seadogs used to cover
The art with gunpowder and set fire
To it. The explosion drove the colors in.
Teddy boys might use matchtip sulfur
Or caked shoe polish mashed with spit. In Thailand
The indigo was once a gecko.
In mall parlors here, India ink and tabs
Of pigment cut with grain alcohol
Patch together tribal grids, vows, fantasies,

Frescos, planetary signs, pinups,
Rock idols, bar codes, all the insignia
    Of the brave face and the lonely heart.

The reasons are both remote and parallel.
    The primitive impulse was to join,
The modern to detach oneself from, the world.
    The hunter's shadowy camouflage,
The pubescent girl's fertility token,
    The warrior's lurid coat of mail,
The believer's entrée to the afterlife—
    The spiritual practicality
Of our ancestors remains a source of pride.
    Yielding to sentimentality,
Later initiates seek to dramatize
    Their jingoism, their Juliets
Or Romeos. They want to fix a moment,
    Some port of call, a hot one-night-stand,
A rush of mother-love or Satan worship.
    Superstition prompts the open eye
On the sailor's lid, the fish on his ankle.
    The biker makes a leather jacket
Of his soft beerbelly and nailbitten hands.
    The callgirl's strategic butterfly
Or calla lily attracts and focuses
    Her client's interest and credit card.
But whether encoded or flaunted, there's death
    At the bottom of every tattoo.
The mark of Cain, the stigma to protect him
    From the enemy he'd created,
Must have been a skull. Once incorporated,
    Its spell is broken, its mortal grip
Loosened or laughed at or fearlessly faced down.
    A Donald Duck with drooping forelock
And swastikas for eyes, the sci-fi dragon,
    The amazon's griffon, the mazy
Yin-yang dragnets, the spiders on barbed-wire webs,
    The talismanic fangs and jesters,
Ankhs and salamanders, scorpions and dice

All are meant to soothe the savage breast
Or back beneath whose dyed flesh there beats something
   That will stop. Better never to be
Naked again than not disguise what time will
   Press like a flower in its notebook,
Will score and splotch, rot, erode, and finish off.
   Ugly heads are raised against our end.
If others are unnerved, why not death itself?
   If unique, then why not immortal?
Protected by totem animals that perch
   Or coil in strategic locations—
A lizard just behind the ear, a tiger's
   Fangs seeming to rip open the chest,
An eagle spreading its wings across the back—
   The body at once both draws death down
And threatens its dominion. The pain endured
   To thwart the greater pain is nothing
Next to the notion of nothingness.
   Is that what I see in the mirror?
The vacancy of everything behind me,
   The eye that now takes so little in,
The unmarked skin, the soul without privileges . . .
   Everything's exposed to no purpose.
The tears leave no trace of their grief on my face.
   My gifts are never packaged, never
Teasingly postponed by the need to undo
   The puzzled perfections of surface.
All over I am open to whatever
   You may make of me, and death soon will,
Its unmarked grave the shape of things to come,
   The page there was no time to write on.

3.

New Zealand, 1890

Because he was the chieftain's eldest son
      And so himself
      Destined one day to rule,

The great meeting-house was garishly strung
          With smoked heads and armfuls
Of flax, the kiwi cloak, the lithograph
Of Queen Victoria, seated and stiff,

Oil lamps, the greenstone clubs and treasure box
          Carved with demons
          In polished attitudes
That held the tribal feathers and ear drops.
          Kettles of fern root, stewed
Dog, mulberry, crayfish and yam were hung
To wait over the fire's spluttering tongues.

The boy was led in. It was the last day
          Of his ordeal.
          The tenderest sections—
Under his eyes, inside his ears—remained
          To be cut, the maze run
To its dizzying ends, a waterwheel
Lapping his flesh the better to reveal

Its false-face of unchanging hostility.
          A feeding tube
          Was put between his lips.
His arms and legs were held down forcibly.
          Resin and lichen, mixed
With pigeon fat and burnt to soot, was scooped
Into mussel shells. The women withdrew.

By then the boy had slowly turned his head,
          Whether to watch
          Them leave or keep his eye
On the stooped, grayhaired cutter who was led
          In amidst the men's cries
Of ceremonial anger at each
Of the night's cloudless hours on its path

Through the boy's life. The cutter knelt beside
          The boy and stroked
          The new scars, the smooth skin.

From his set of whalebone chisels he tied
    The shortest one with thin
Leather thongs to a wooden handle soaked
In rancid oil. Only his trembling throat

Betrayed the boy. The cutter smiled and took
        A small mallet,
        Laid the chisel along
The cheekbone, and tapped so a sharpness struck
    The skin like a bygone
Memory of other pain, other threats.
Someone dabbed at the blood. Someone else led

A growling chant about their ancestors.
            Beside the eye's
        Spongy marshland a frond
Sprouted, a jagged gash to which occurs
        A symmetrical form,
While another chisel pecks in the dye,
A blue the deep furrow intensifies.

The boy's eyes are fluttering now, rolling
            Back in his head.
        The cutter stops only
To loop the blade into a spiralling,
        Puckered, thick filigree
Whose swollen tracery, it seems, has led
The boy beyond the living and the dead.

He can feel the nine Nothings drift past him
        In the dark: Night,
    The Great Night, the Choking
Night, the All-Brightening Night and the Dim,
        The Long Night, the Floating
Night, the Empty Night, and with the first light
A surging called the War Canoe of Night—

Which carries Sky Father and Earth Mother,
        Their six sons borne
    Inside the airless black

The two make, clasped only to each other.
Turning onto his back,
The eldest son struggles with all his force,
Shoulder to sky, straining until it's torn

Violently away from the bleeding earth.
He sets four beams,
Named for the winds, to keep
His parents apart. They're weeping, the curve
Of loneliness complete
Between them now. The old father's tears gleam
Like stars, then fall as aimlessly as dreams

To earth, which waits for them all to return.
Here is the care
Of the dead, and his tears
Seep into her folds like a dye that burns.
One last huge drop appears
Hanging over the boy's head. Wincing, scared,
He's put his hand up into the cold air.

from *The Paris Review*

Mae West Chats It Up with Bessie Smith

◇   ◇   ◇

You hadn't oughta kiss a girl if you're carrying a gun.
—RAYMOND CHANDLER

once I found a cowboy   who thought he could
ride me into the New   West and God
put rollers on the bed   to make his journey smoother
last time I saw him   he looked the worse for wear
hair all but gone   gut eating his belt
he was a sight   all laid out in a new suit
(same one I bought him)

honey he had a corvette   and the morals
of a chinchilla   but just enough
gangster to satisfy my   Kansas City longings
oh he was handsome   as you know the devil was
in his eyes and his clothes   slick as sharkskin
some kinda silk worn close   and groin sweet
like morning rain   inside a buttercup

cept he dropped his pants and showed me
something for the cat to play with

thought he'd stopped me on the road
he did but when I said come up and see me
I was already heading in another direction

then there was that business   with some woman
he wouldn't name   now would naming matter sugah
you gotta know who you're aiming for   just aim
for the light   of one cigarette to the next
always someone there with a match   and an itch
to scratch   what hurts long as your voice holds

from *Crab Orchard Review*

My One

◇　◇　◇

and only: money

minus one. No noun
like a pronoun!—best of all

the jealous kind. Come, come,
company doll, cide with a coin,

one moan, one
more, honey

bunch.

from *Jubilat*

HARRYETTE MULLEN

Music for Homemade Instruments

◊ ◊ ◊

improvising with Douglas Ewart

I dug you artless, I dug you out. Did you re-do? You dug me less, art. You dug, let's do art. You dug me, less art. Did you re-do? If I left art out, you dug. My artless dug-out. You dug, let art out. Did you re-do, dug-out canoe? Easy as a porkpie piper-led cinch. Easy as a baby bounce. Hop on pot, tin pan man. Original abstract, did you re-do it? Betting on shy cargo, strutting dimpled low-cal strumpets employ a hipster to blow up the native formica. Then divide efficiency on hairnets, flukes, faux saxons. You dug me out, didn't you? Did you re-do? Ever curtained to experiment with strumpet strutting. Now curtains to milk laboratory. Desecrated flukes & panics displayed by mute politicians all over this whirly-gig. Hey, you dug! Art lasts. Did you re-do? Well-known mocker of lurching unused brains, tribal & lustrous diddlysquats, Latin dimension crepe paper & muscular stacks. Curtains for perky strumpets strutting with mites in the twilight of their origami funkier purses. Artless, you dug. Did you re-do? For patting wood at flatland, thanks. For bamboozle flukes at Bama, my seedy medication. Thanks for my name in the yoohoo. Continental camp-out, percolating throughout the whirly-gig on faux saxon flukes. You dug art, didn't you? Did you re-do?

from *Facture*

Our Kitty

◇   ◇   ◇

She is swinging in a contraption above the heads
of the audience,
>> Reflected in the glass lamps on the tables.

She sits in one of those fin-de-siècle gilded sleighs
hung from the ceiling
>> by braids of sparkling hemp.

Here come all the poet-accountants pushing in
to talk about cate-
>> gories of experience. Wine, sex.

The ceiling is hammered tin, alight and jumping
with her shadow
>> cast upward by the table lamps.

As she swings, she rubs herself, adjusts herself
in the seat, so she
>> can be seen through the see-through bottom.

Pink cheeks has Kitty. A pop-open camisole. Mother
is striking her
>> name from the family bible. But

she has to eat, does Kitty. She is so petite and incautious
that all the poet-
>> accountants are taking copious notes.

They can use her: she may be the littlest
Whore of the imagination.
                    She might even be how they imagine

The twentieth century's end: just like the end
of the last century,
                    the dream of body parts floating

Above cigar smoke. In other words, *more war.*
Kitty inspires all
                    of them to think about triage.

The end of the twentieth century. Artist or banker—
who should be saved?
                    The artist in his same old tourniquet? The banker

With a dented skull? Try to guess. The poet-
accountants have
                    already guessed. They know the price of

this ending. They've seen the banker and his surgeons,
the poet bleeding
                    all over the sterile gauze. Who wants to be

John Keats? Well, the poems, yes—but not the death.
Now they hear Kitty
                    coughing. I'm Keats, she gasps.

I'm John Fucking Keats returned in Kitty's body.
Forlorn she cries *Forlorn*
                    but they refuse to listen to her

As she swings, pale and beautiful, glittering above them
holding out her
                    living hand, warm, capable—as ever, untaken.

from *The Evansville Review*

ALICE NOTLEY

Where Leftover Misery Goes

◇　◇　◇

if its a spiritual offense does it as wrongdoing take place more in more in the second
leftover

or spiritual world and is the significance of the double now that i might be might the one who offends in other circumstan or that it takes two to make an offense but how was i used and why were the others not usable was it because they were always too selfinvolved to be exploited. oh keep this mostly masked as always these events are of the sort are replayed over and over in the second world perhaps in the overlap the border was it a spiritual offense and did it take place more in the second world than in the first it surely does now. it only takes place in my and keep this masked keep it low shes awaiting attention acceptance as exceptional her face corroding i have to avoid her like poison but i have to keep remembering shes poison there is a machine that allows memory to be memories to taken into the futur i have to remember shes pois and that isnt a known a universally accepted fact that shes poison to me wants to poison me and make me hers of her emotional her emotional camp make me live of the camp of she thinks but she is poison shes acting like she isnt and i can barely remember the last time i was poisoned and now in the now in the second world there is no linear time no many years past and i dont know when they last said in the first world accept her poison bu because its only you dont bother us on the cold wintry avenue in your coat lined with papers another wild looking night darker than the last one which was purple this ones deep navy with slivver moon behind a raggy cloud in this wind the buildings are dangerously high and here and there a gold lights tossed i didnt see the two strangers my former fr is that possible strangers until i suddenly did staring at me but the real point is that i'm not them nor her i'm not the double and i want to be hard about this i am only the double as i must straddle two worlds but i am th not the double who did wrong to me i am not thee there is no key for the brilliant red lake in the top of the rectangle map of me which seems to be a sort of early area is desperation a pleasure i'm so thirsty and i'm suppose in joy but do i believe remem desperation joy or guilt approach me from a side street trying to make me talk to them i'm singing a song and the he double says not enough facts in that song though theres a lot of poetry one word has become coeur of me what word it must be poet coeur de coeur no longer no longer a word we have driven up high to this mountain town where the gypsies live but must leave live but must leave he asks me to talk to him but i wont now an she all fuzzed up in the head wants to give me an entire shelf of old books as a bribe to poison knowledge of her mind but i'm resolutely in black fur burning into a snowbank a dream a tall snowbank that is taller than i am and its hard to walk hard to walk here in the death you are helping i am being assimilated and wear a long dress and shawl watch me make love as a prostitute so i can be your friend because youve only ever wanted to see my body what you think of me the villagers want to circumcize me sunday so i can be everyones theyre gypsies in the mountains on luna something street i used to live there but i have since cut up the sidewalk and carry it with me carry luna something street with me wherever i go and lay it down so i can walk towards or away what away from what i must walk away from them again board the ship my other sister life will go to the camp where the actress a second a

second

demonic womans face must be kept out of the movie you cant know about her you cant know in the first world and in the second thus there are these dreams which play out shadows on the street useless kindness curiously useless until the play the playing out is over in the head of what you did used me to stay you and so i'm a gypsy again wait for the camp to break up in the mountains encased in crystal you used me but said you were use in the first world on the street on the street of poison words b was it only words no there was the deathhole that was burned into the snow it was supposedly another who died not die because i was never the one was i never the focus was other so how could you ever affect me when you were trying to ki fight another and only poison me lightly who died not die but there was the deathhole burned into the snow here in the second world as i play it out play it out in the crystal a lighter story now where i never die have only died to that world. no one believes in poison thats why we cant breathe. someone has left me a book highlighted in black always do that leave a book and the letters hop and try to transform but tha they cant nor can the shelf of old book of esoterica change the nature of poison which goes towards because only because only thinks of self thinks story so the poison flows outwards in the bad air in winter tinged with yellow and corroded face bookstore bookstore ever if the double lives in a book. others support her because i have never needed story and the letters hop and try to transform they are snow the letters try again i dont know how to tell you this letters i dont care about your transitional stages i dont care why you used pois i dont care whose real name or person i dont have to be tain tained certain of the action of self without salt keep doing this keep doing this so old. because it happened once in the first world and in the second doesnt quite go away the actions in the first and the real story as dream as dream in the seconds milder haunt where who died not i but died to the first and died to that camp and died to that bookstore and died to that oh keep this mostly masked dont feel a thing or be pois get poisoned theyre still all waiting for that i dreamed i lived them they wore black robes and lived in a cluster of wooden houses in a clearing but there may have been woods and i was being assimilated i wore a long black dress and shawl the narrator cut in to say that i was prostitute and my boyfriend john watched me make love with the village men there seem to be many and tenderfaced what does prostitution symbolize half of the villagers are leaving and then i will be circumcized because he dies or somethi take part in the rite of becoming a woman can withstand of pain of that she tries to poison again wants me to be on a side and not in i wake up for a few minutes fall back asleep many years ago they are gypsies this movie will star us and the stars are familiar in the part where i'm taken away on a ship with other prisoners but am no one just movie stars just parts and theres no point in falling in love with the commandant hes just a star and i'll die anyway theres no point in and when she says love theres no love. this is a spell to get out of here how long will it take the border is endless. wants me to be on another side she wants t wants me to be on her side of the border and i stay on the side of the second world always but am still in the border the border where the nightmare sucks me into its feeling want to say her keep saying

saying

about her because no has believed it and so say it and say and so remain in the border

will the circumcized women feel after death will the real w will the real e include
sensation that cant be manipulated by ones feel fellowcreatures on the street denying
me to the point of point because i think they like and if you maintain sides you are
always near the border and never in the snows come again and the purple sinister sky
so i can die and read the books they leave me always alive the letters and the letters letters
hop about and try to change but never do because no one wants them to change.

from *Chain*

His Costume

◇　◇　◇

Somehow I never stopped to notice
that my father liked to dress as a woman.
He had his sign language about women
talking too much, and being stupid,
but whenever there was a costume party
he would dress like us, the tennis balls
for breasts—balls for breasts—the long
blond wig, the lipstick, he would sway
his body with moves of gracefulness
as if one being could be the whole
universe, its ends curving back to come
up from behind it. Six feet, and maybe
one-eighty, one-ninety, he had the shapely
legs of a male Grable—in a short
skirt, he leaned against a bookcase pillar
nursing his fifth drink, gazing
around from inside his mascara purdah
with those salty eyes. The woman from next door
had a tail and ears, she was covered in Reynolds Wrap,
she was Kitty Foyle, and my mother was in
a tiny tuxedo, but he always won
the prize. Those nights, he had a look of daring,
a look of triumph, of having stolen
back. And as far as I knew, he never threw
up, as a woman, or passed out, or made
those signals of scorn with his hands, just leaned,
voluptuous, at ease, deeply
present, as if sensing his full potential, crossing

over into himself, and back,
over, and back.

from *The New Yorker*

KATHLEEN OSSIP

The Nature of Things

◇ ◇ ◇

(after paintings by Robert Lostutter)

For ages and ages, they couldn't have seemed less simpatico—street songs turned Brahms' insane cadenza turned sharpening crack.

Which reminded you of all the novels you might have inhabited, of your daddy the routeman, of Easter's spice-flavored jelly eggs, of the rowdy oleander, of the women at the xerox place, so petty. How privately (you simmered) Time can walk, or fall.

Heart. Couldn't. Break. That was the problem here. A lonely boy. You were, just.

There must be no self-pity, your pal said then. *And that means NO self-pity. Can we not do this anymore, please?* Emanation of a wood fire, blue of blue, singleton, scamp: We live not only in a world of thoughts, but also in a world of things.

He did you a favor, your pal, when he told you this secret: *First become ordinary, if you ever wish to become anything else.* By Tuesday, you were so splendid the bees rose.

from *Barrow Street*

Here

◊   ◊   ◊

Here I am in the garden laughing
an old woman with heavy breasts
and a nicely mapped face

how did this happen
well that's who I wanted to be

at last   a woman
in the old style   sitting
stout thighs apart under
a big skirt   grandchild sliding
on   off my lap   a pleasant
summer perspiration

that's my old man across the yard
he's talking to the meter reader
he's telling him the world's sad story
how electricity is oil or uranium
and so forth   I tell my grandson
run over to your grandpa   ask him
to sit beside me for a minute   I
am suddenly exhausted by my desire
to kiss his sweet explaining lips

from *The Massachusetts Review* and *Poetry Daily*

MICHAEL PALMER

Untitled (February 2000)

◇   ◇   ◇

The naked woman at the window
her back to you, bowing the violin

behind the lace curtain
directly above the street

is not a fiction
as the partita is not a fiction

its theme and variations
ornaments and fills

not a fiction
as the one-way street still

wet from all this
rain is no fiction

and nakedness not a fiction.
It reads us like a book

as we listen to its music
through milky eyes wide shut.

And what does this fiction think of us?
The rain, the notes, both softly fall.

Slight errors of intonation do not matter
in the faded green

notebooks where we record these
things, and conceal other things.

What's the name of that tree, anyway,
with yellow flowers, small silver leaves,

planted in the concrete—
I used to know.

As for today, Leap Year Day,
the window was empty.

from *Conjunctions*

A Metal Denser Than,
and Liquid

◇　◇　◇

What sets the worst architect apart from the best bee is this:
the architect builds his structure in imagination before he
erects it in reality.

—MARX, *CAPITAL*

Had he sat there, a witness?
at Posen, the speech in which Himmler
spoke the abomination,
a darkness within darkness.

He tried to believe he had not.
There was enough in him
that he had to go on living.
And so he would not remember.

There had been talk, briefly,
of his being made successor.
Before the complexities.
He didn't talk about that.

Then there was the hospital,
when he had nearly died
from the task and the unspoken.
No one did that task better.

Doing it better became
his way of foxing the wolves

who pranced around him. But
how much had he taken on

else, and where had it led him?
He worked from that bed till he broke.
Then lift-off, out of his body:
light, rich appointments, warm colors,

the doctors did a ballet,
and at last, there at last
he felt for his wife how much,
he smiled the withheld, he fully

was who he knew he was
and knew he could go. But was sent back.

His prison chaplain, although
supposing the story might be
fantasy, knew it came with
the urgent stink of Lazarus.

Ach it was all in his mind
laughed Frau Speer. If only
she too could have seen it:
he'd nearly found the exit

from his squeeze, he'd skirted
the suck of the great change.

And one of my own tribe: when
transferred for interrogation
to Versailles, what saved him
was an English parachute major
taking him for a drive
to Paris.
                    We went through
St. Germain and Bougival
where in years past I dined
with Vlaminck, Alfred Cortot—
then we walked along the quais

and looked at the stalls. I was
horribly sad, but I bought
a print like any tourist
and—so silly—it made
me feel human.

    And if I briefly abhor
this fantast while pitying him
the hole in his feeling, with
art as surrogate—if
his uncontrollable falseness
even to himself, the untracked
changeability,
alarms and disgusts me?
                        Then
somewhere near right here
I have lost the treasure
of shaming accuracy
about myself.
                  His decades
of fox-introspection
kindle several days
of fascination and
gnawing discomfort and
discernment in my corner,

while a voice both sharp and soothing
intervenes: *discernment*
is not judgment!
                May it
be so. But this rankling rawness?

Cicero did not warn us:
Aesop makes tricky reading.

Art is not surrogate,
but the gate. The gate stands
to be passed through. The passage
is to truth truly lived

whatever the means, however
mean, for what is great
and shines quiveringly is
self-presence from the soul.

Where the treasure lies
there lie the means also.
The metallurgist's kit
went with the gold galleons
to the bottom. Divers brush
scum from lakes of it there,
push at it, play with it,
quivering mercury—

a comeliness past that
of gold, because it lives,
a mirror to the will
to undergo all change.

Unloved, the master in him
went seeking a mad attachment.

Suddenly undersea,
the day, the room, strangely
rich in appointments, when evil
seems to shake far beyond me.

Mirror, mirror, on the floor,
which beast in me shall I adore

judiciously?
            May his rootless soul
have felt, somewhere, compassion.
Let compassion rise
and quiver in me. And let me
turn again to the sun.

from *AGNI*

LUCIA PERILLO

The Ghost Shirt

◊   ◊   ◊

*—Museum of Natural History, NYC, 5/1/92,
the first day of the riots*

The blue whale swam through blue air in the basement
while upstairs the elephants twined together tusk by tusk,
and the enormous canoe was being rowed by the Tlingit

as they have rowed without moving for years through the dusk
in the Hall of the Americas. Empty space
was brocaded by schoolkids' shrieks

as teachers pantomimed in front of each glass case,
and I turned a corner and came up smack against the ghost shirt,
worn by a mannequin with no legs and no face—

                                        at first
it almost didn't register;
it was not what books had led me to expect: no beads
no ornament no chamois leather

or those shiny cornets made from rolled up snuff-tin lids.
Instead it was just a cotton shift
negotiating grimly between blue and green and red,

with some glyphs scrawled amateurishly across the breast
in ordinary pen: a thunderbird and some lightning,
a buffalo and its hoofprint,

one tree, one little man puffing
on a flume-sized pipe. Pentagram stars formed a cloud
atopside a smaller species of stippling

that I had to stare at a long time before I understood
meant bullets. Then I found myself checking for broken threads
to see if any of the holes were rimmed in blood—

but no: time or moths or bullets, it was anybody's guess.
A quote on the wall from the Paiute messiah
said *Indians who don't believe in the ghost dance*

will grow little, just about a foot high,
and stay that way. Then some of those
will be turned into wood and burned in fire—

and I left the museum wondering about which was worse:
to display a man's blood here
so every kid can practice crumpling as if falling off a horse

(& the kid knows exactly how to clutch the new air
entering his heart). Or to clean the shirt
as if the ghost blood had never been there.

★★★

This is the kind of story you could carry around
like a beaded key chain from a tourist trap:
how the ghost dance became a thunderstorm
that even summoning Buffalo Bill out
to the Standing Rock agency could not slake—
until the schoolhouses were empty
and the trading stores were empty
and the winter wheat went bony in the field
and the War Department had no idea what it meant
but that the Sioux had gone mad with their dancing
and that Yellow Bird wore a peculiar shirt when he chanted
Your bullets will not go toward us right before they did.

★★★

From the museum, I take the subway downtown
and change trains where the tunnels all converge
below Times Square, in one dank cavern underground

whose darkness seems so large it does not have edges.
Even at midafternoon, the shade there seethes
with people marching in a lockstep through that passage;

sometimes, when directed back over a shoulder, a mouth
on someone's profiled face will drop
and I'll see the tongue dart nervously along the teeth . . .

then the march becomes a gallop
when the walls begin to pound with an arriving train,
its riders rushing toward us in a yellowness crushed up

against the glass. And we board like cattle, one person
driving an elbow into another's gut
as we jam in (and we jam in . . .)

and coming up at Grand Central, I find it likewise knotted
with people ranged in single files,
shuffling toward the ticket counters in fits and stops

that give them time to paw the vast floor with their heels.
But what strikes me most is how loudly the silence
murmurs off the marble tiles

as if we were all underwater, hearing backward our own breath.
Then I remember that I bought a return on my way in
and hurry back down two flights of steps

to the lower level, where the train for Croton
sits almost full, though not scheduled to leave for half an hour
yet. Soon all the seats are gone

but the train keeps filling, arms and legs the mortar
in a wall of breasts and double-breasts. I avoid the gaze
and glare of those who hang on straps over

my head, and it isn't until the train begins to wheeze
from its hydraulics and slowly labors
past the gate that everyone around me will unfreeze

enough to speak: about a city bus and its passengers
rocked onto its flank and set aflame, a hundred black
and Spanish kids aswarm with Molotovs and crowbars . . .

which is the story we sow along the darkness, until the track
rises into daylight above Ninety-seventh Street,
where the broken windows have been boarded back

with plywood, each painted with its own domestic scene
—curtains gathered primly or potted geraniums on the sills—
though otherwise, everything looks to me as it has always been,

with the same nimbuses of spray paint on the trestles,
the alphabet stuffed like heavy furniture
reciting its addition on the same brick walls

. . . until we cross the East River
where everybody lets their breath go with relief,
the wheels droning their steady whuckerwhuckerwhucker

as the train settles into its top speed
and we skitter along the Hudson, where nothing is except
water on one side, on the other side a ravine

overstudded with junk: a Cadillac sunk axle-
deep a shopping cart the front wheels of a stroller
menacingly airborne like the forelegs of *Tyrannosaurus rex*—

and it's here the train zippers
to an abrupt stop (though we haven't come to any station),
steeping us anxiously awhile in quiet, until the whispers

blossom like umbrellas opening before the rain:
first *they're blocking the engine* then *they're lying down*
on the tracks, rumors that ripple through the train

like a wave sweeping upstream, then back down,
by which time the muttering has escalated to a shout
that goes *Keep going!* and *We've got to run those fuckers down!*

★★★

Between the train and whoever lies down in its path,
you could say there's a ghost shirt,
whatever it is that makes the locomotive stop
if the engineer can see far enough ahead.
I think it is a dotted line
looping the outskirts of our being human—
ghostly because of the ease with which
its perforations can be ripped. Also
because the sole proof of its presence
lies in the number of days we go unhurt,
a staggering number, especially when you consider
how much bigger the world is than a train.
And how something even as small as a bullet
can pick out of elsewhere's 359 degrees
one shape, and suddenly everything is changed,
though the calx of what didn't happen
remains in curiously enduring traces
like the stone casts that larval caddis flies
leave behind them in the stream
(& *larvae:* from the latin word for ghost).
What you have is always less
a history of a people, any people,
than a history of its rocks: first a heap
then a cathedral and soon a heap again,
while the names get amortized like money.
Like Damian Williams, the one they called Football,
who held his bloody cinderblock aloft
and danced as if he were stomping out a hundred

baby flames: Rodney King, Reginald Denny,
William Cody, Stacey Koon. And Black Coyote,
who refused to give up his Winchester
after Yellow Bird danced the first few steps
before Colonel Forsythe's pony soldiers
broke all hell loose. And Black Coyote,
whom Turning Hawk said was crazy,
"a young man of bad influence and in fact a nobody."

★★★

I want to say that we weren't all white on that train,
but mostly we were—
and when without explanation the engine started up again,

those who weren't fell away to the edge of the herd
and got off where the conductor squawked out *Spuyten Duyvil,
Marblehead* and *Yonkers* . . .

and as we rolled I strained to imagine the sound a wheel
would make as it milled through someone's ribs,
listening for them bedded down in every mile

until I got off way out in the suburbs.
From the station I called my father to come pick me up
and waited for him half-hidden in some shrubs

so that when he arrived I could make my usual leap
into his Mercedes so no one sees me getting in.
I remember what it was like in that town, growing up

so out of it I didn't even see the affluence back then—
and how we kids rolled our eyes whenever our parents
started in on the WPA and the Great Depression

and being glad for a day's honest work even if that meant
no more than laying a stone and piling another on top
—part of a war we waged in serial installments,

mostly over what we put on our backs, or feet, or not:
the tattered clothes we wore to ape a poverty
about which our folks claimed we did not know shit

(though like every kid in that town I toted around my copy
of a gospel that one week was *Soul on Ice*
and the next week *Bury My Heart at Wounded Knee*)

—which maybe explains why it still makes me nervous,
though twenty years have passed: to be riding around in a car
that cost more than, elsewhere, someone's house,

while I'm trying to explain to my old father
what it meant to me to see the ghost shirt
just before Wall Street shut down and every broker

fled. And not just fled, but reverted,
as if what made us human had been only a temporary crust
on our skins, as if there were no way to stop the backward

march into the swamp. Pretty soon we'd all be just
like rats but bigger, and combat ready . . .
but here again my father claimed I didn't know whereof

I spoke: all day the television had showed the city
eerily at peace. And the only fires were the tiny flames
of people holding candles, outside the public library.

from *Pequod*

The Clearing

◇   ◇   ◇

Had the light
changed, possibly—or,

differently, was that how I'd
seen it

    always, and not
looking? Was I meant for

a vessel? Did I only
believe so and,

so, for a time, was it true but

only in that space which belief makes
for its own wanting?

*What am I going to
do with you*
        —Who just

said that?

Whose the body—where—that voice
belongs to?

      Might I turn,
toward it, whinny

into it?

My life
a water,

or a cure for
that which no water
can cure?

His chest
a forest, or a lush
failure—

Even now, shall I choose? Do I
get to?

Dearest-once-to-me

Dearest-still-to-me

Have I chosen
already,

        or is choice a thing
hovering yet, an

intention therefore, from
which, though
late, could I hurry back?

What am I going to do with you—   or

how?
Whom for?

        If stay my hand—where

rest it?

from *Callaloo*

193

Jersey Rain

◇　◇　◇

Now near the end of the middle stretch of road
What have I learned? Some earthly wiles. An art.
That often I cannot tell good fortune from bad,
That once had seemed so easy to tell apart.

The source of art and woe aslant in wind
Dissolves or nourishes everything it touches.
What roadbank gullies and ruts it doesn't mend
It carves the deeper, boiling tawny in ditches.

It spends itself regardless into the ocean.
It stains and scours and makes things dark or bright:
Sweat of the moon, a shroud of benediction,
The chilly liquefaction of day to night,

The Jersey rain, my rain, soaks all as one:
It smites Metuchen, Rahway, Saddle River,
Fair Haven, Newark, Little Silver, Bayonne.
I feel it churning even in fair weather

To craze distinction, dry the same as wet.
In ripples of heat the August drought still feeds
Vapors in the sky that swell to drench my state—
The Jersey rain, my rain, in streams and beads

Of indissoluble grudge and aspiration:
Original milk, replenisher of grief,
Descending destroyer, arrowed source of passion,
Silver and black, executioner, font of life.

from *The Atlantic Monthly*

CLAUDIA RANKINE

A short narrative of breasts and wombs in service of Plot entitled

◊   ◊   ◊

Liv lying on the floor looking at

The Dirty Thought

[The womb similar to fruit that goes uneaten will grow gray fur, the breasts a dying rose, darkening nipples, prickling sickness as it moves toward mold, a spongy moss as metaphor for illness.]

Liv, answer me this: Is the female anatomically in need of a child as a life preserver, a hand, a hand up? And now, and now do you want harder the family you fear in fear of all those answers?

Could you put fear there as having to do with the price of milk, as having to do with prudence? To your health. Cheers. Or against the aging body unused, which way does punishment go?

"Let us not negotiate out of fear . . ." butbutbut . . . Then the wind touched the opened subject until Liv finding herself in light winds, squalls, was without a place to put her ladder.

From the treetop something fell, a bundle, a newspaper, a bug, a bag, still nobody's baby. The sound was desperation dropped down, a falling into place, and not way away—

Statistics show: One in what? One in every what? A child in every pot will help the body grow? No matter, all the minutes will still slip into the first then the ashes will shiver.

Liv, is the graffitied mind sprained? Who sprayed an answer there? Which cancer? What dirtied up intention? No matter. Anyway, which way does your ladder go?

Toward? Or away in keeping with that ant crawling on your ankle? Oh mindless hand, rub hard. Not quite in pain because pain is shorthand for what? One in every what? Cradle all.

Or kiss it up without facing yourself. Knowing the issue, Liv slouches, her chin resting on her folded hands. She thinks: blunt impact, injury. She tosses a but against the wall,

she tosses: boom. boom.

from *Verse*

Architect

◊   ◊   ◊

Nothing he had done before
      or would try for later
            will explain or atone
this facile suggestion of cross-beams
languid elevations traced on water
his stake in white colonnades cramping his talent
                  showing up in
facsimile mansions overbearing the neighborhood
his leaving the steel rods out of the plinths
      (bronze raptors gazing from the boxwood)
You could say he spread himself too thin   a plasterer's term
            you could say he was then
skating thin ice   his stake in white colonnades against the thinness of

ice itself   a slickened ground
            Could say he did not then love
his art enough to love anything more
Could say he wanted the commission so
badly betrayed those who hired him   an artist
            who in dreams followed
                  the crowds who followed him

Imagine commandeering those oversize those prized
      hardwood columns to be hoisted and hung
by hands expert and steady on powerful machines

            his knowledge using theirs as the one kind does the other
                        (as it did in Egypt)

—while devising the little fountain to run all night
   outside the master bedroom

from *The Paris Review*

Vectors: Forty-five Aphorisms and Ten-second Essays

◇   ◇   ◇

1.

It's so much easier to get further from home than nearer that all men become travelers.

2.

Of all the ways to avoid living perfect discipline is the most admired.

3.

Idolaters of the great need to believe that what they love cannot fail them, adorers of camp, kitsch, trash that they cannot fail what they love.

4.

Say nothing as if it were news.

5.

Who breaks the thread, the one who pulls, the one who holds on?

6.

Despair says *I cannot lift that weight.* Happiness says, *I do not have to.*

7.

What you give to a thief is stolen.

8.

Impatience is not wanting to understand that you don't understand.

9.

Greater than the temptations of beauty are those of method.

10.

Harder to laugh at the comedy if it's about you, harder to cry at the tragedy if it isn't.

11.

Patience is not very different from courage. It just takes longer.

12.

Even at the movies, we laugh together, we weep alone.

13.

I could explain, but then you would understand my explanation, not what I said.

14.

If the saints are perfect and unwavering we are excused from trying to imitate them. Also if they are not.

15.

Easy to criticize yourself, harder to agree with the criticism.

16.

Tragic hero, madman, addict, fatal lover. We exalt those who cannot escape their dreams because we cannot stay inside our own.

17.

Every life is allocated one hundred seconds of true genius. They might be enough, if we could just be sure which ones they were.

18.

Absence makes the heart grow fonder: then it is only distance that separates us.

19.

How much less difficult life is when you do not want anything from people. And yet you owe it to them to want something.

20.

Where I touch you lightly enough, there I am also touched.

21.

If we were really sure we were one of a kind, there would be no envy. My envy demeans both of us—no wonder it is the hardest sin to confess. It says I am not who I think I am unless I have what you have. It says that you are what you have, and I could have it.

22.

Laziness is the sin most willingly confessed to, since it implies talents greater than have yet appeared.

23.

If you reason far enough you will come to unreasonable conclusions.

24.

The one who hates you perfectly loves you.

25.

What you fear to believe, your children will believe.

26.

Of our first few years we remember nothing: experience only slowly gives us the power to be formed by experience. If this were not true, our characters would be completely determined by our infant hours of darkness, pain and helplessness, and we would all be the same. For her first six months my daughter cried continuously, who knows why. Yet she is as happy and trusting and kind as if all that had never happened. It never did.

27.

The road not taken is the part of you not taking the road.

28.

We invent a great Loss to convince ourselves we have a beginning. But loss is a current: the coolness of one side of a wet finger held up, the faint hiss in your ears at midnight, water sliding over the dam at the back of your mind, memory unremembering itself.

29.

If I didn't spend so much time writing, I'd know a lot more. But I wouldn't know anything.

30.

The wounds you do not want to heal are you.

31.

When my friend does something stupid, he is just my friend doing something stupid. When I do something stupid, I have deeply betrayed myself.

32.

If I didn't have so much work to keep me from it, how would I know what I wanted to do?

33.

My deepest regrets, if I am honest, are not things I wish were otherwise, but things I wish I wish were otherwise.

34.

I lie so I do not have to trust you to believe.

35.

Opacity gives way. Transparency is the mystery.

36.

To me, the great divide is between the talkative and the quiet. Do they just say everything that's on their minds, even *before* it's on their minds? Sometimes I think I could just turn up my head like a Walkman so what's going on there could be heard by others. But there would still be a difference. For inside the head they are talking to people like them, and I am talking to someone like me: he is quiet and doesn't much like being talked at; he can't conceal how easily he gets bored.

37.

Anger has been ready to be angry.

38.

It's easier to agree on the future than the past.

39.

Only half of writing is saying what you mean. The other half is preventing people from reading what they expected you to mean.

40.

They gave me most who took most gladly of my love.

41.

Back then I wanted to be right about my estimate of my abilities. Now I want to be wrong.

42.

Time heals. By taking even more.

43.

Self-love, strange name. Since it feels neither like loving someone, nor like being loved.

44.

What I hope for is more hope.

45.

To feel an end is to discover that there had been a beginning. A parenthesis closes that we hadn't realized was open).

from *Ploughshares*

What We Heard About the Japanese

◊ ◊ ◊

We heard they would jump from buildings
at the slightest provocation: a low mark

On an exam, a lovers' spat
or an excess of shame.

We heard they were incited by shame,
not guilt. That they

Loved all things American.
Mistrusted anything foreign.

We heard their men liked to buy
schoolgirls' underwear

And their women
did not experience menopause or other

Western hysterias. We heard
they still preferred to breastfeed,

Carry handkerchiefs, ride bicycles
and dress their young like Victorian

Pupils. We heard that theirs
was a feminine culture. We heard

That theirs was an example of extreme
patriarchy. That rape

Didn't exist on these islands. We heard
their marriages were arranged, that

They didn't believe in love. We heard
they were experts in this art above all others.

That frequent earthquakes inspired insecurity
and lack of faith. That they had no sense of irony.

We heard even faith was an American invention.
We heard they were just like us under the skin.

What the Japanese
Perhaps Heard

Perhaps they heard we don't understand them
very well. Perhaps this made them

Pleased. Perhaps they heard we shoot
Japanese students who ring the wrong

Bell at Hallowe'en. That we shoot
at the slightest provocation: a low mark

On an exam, a lovers' spat, an excess
of guilt. Perhaps they wondered

If it was guilt we felt at the sight of that student
bleeding out among our lawn flamingos,

Or something recognizable to them,
something like grief. Perhaps

They heard that our culture
has its roots in desperate immigration

And lone men. Perhaps they observed
our skill at raising serial killers,

That we value good teeth above
good minds and have no festivals

To remember the dead. Perhaps they heard
that our grey lakes are deep enough to swallow cities,

That our landscape is vast wheat and loneliness.
Perhaps they ask themselves if, when grief

Wraps its wet arms around Montana, we would not prefer
the community of archipelagos

Upon which persimmons are harvested
and black fingers of rock uncurl their digits

In the mist. Perhaps their abacus echoes
the shape that grief takes,

One island
bleeding into the next,

And for us grief is an endless cornfield,
silken and ripe with poison.

from *Verse*

Furtherness

◇　◇　◇

An oak coffin covered with vines
carried on moss in a farm cart

A dusty coffin in a yellow wagon
with bright red wheels going down
the painted road

A glass coffin stifled by roses

Raining, and in the film version
an unknown god stood at a distance
watching, got in his car and left

The little black urn before
a spray of orchids in the alcove

They laid a bunch of violets at her throat
closed the white coffin
carried it out the rear door
through buttercups down to the grave

The musicians are drunk and play
loudly, stumbling down the street

Six men with sore arms

The family in a rowboat:
the coffin inhabiting the mind

Or ashes streaming like a scarf from the convertible

Or, the chorus breaks out in excelsis

Or, the soloist sang like a dilated eye

Stunning din of a sob

Salt pork on a wound

Is it ordure to speak of the widow's grief?

Who drags herself back
through a field so thick with vetch
it gives a purple tint over two or three acres
You could run through them for hours
but one thing is certain from her face
she does not want you to

Furthermore, there are pies on the table waiting

from *American Letters & Commentary*

JAMES SCHUYLER

Along Overgrown Paths

◇ ◇ ◇

The road crowds houses almost into the lake.
On one side one day they may go plop
a short drop down a bluff a mere bank.
On the other side houses cling to it
(the road) for dear life, passing in cars
one might roll right in, well, at
the door. A first arrival by lunar eclipse:
it won't ever lose an aura of mystery
of a moon eroding and changing to the orange
of bloodroot sap. One of those roasting hot
Easters. Trilliums popped out of the ground
and unfurled at your feet before your eyes.
It was that hot. "I want," the man said,
"my stairs twice as wide as other stairs."
That was one day in 1823. They still are.
Not so high as some, wider than most,
beds can go up and down in ease and do.
Far better a hall than that extra room.
Far better a dining room than a nook.
Or a nook than a cranny or a cranny
than nothing, unless enclosed as in
this roadside hall, with wide stairs
to descend and walk out onto violets
blue, blue-violet, white, and brickish-pink
and the private houses could touch
if they'd a mind to put out their hands.

from *The New Yorker*

Night Picnic

◇   ◇   ◇

There was the sky, starless and vast—
Home of every one of our dark thoughts—
Its door open to more darkness.
And you, like a late door-to-door salesman,
With only your own beating heart
In the palm of your outstretched hand.

All things are imbued with God's being—
She said in hushed tones
As if his ghost might overhear us—
The dark woods around us,
Our faces which we cannot see,
Even this bread we are eating.

You were mulling over the particulars
Of your cosmic insignificance
Between slow sips of red wine.
In the ensuing quiet, you could hear
Her small, sharp teeth chewing the crust—
And then finally, she moistened her lips.

from *Boston Review*

Apple

◇   ◇   ◇

If I could come back from the dead, I would come back
for an apple, and just for the first bite, the first
break, and the cold sweet grain
against the roof of the mouth, as plain
and clear as water.

Some apple names are almost forgotten
and the apples themselves are gone. The smokehouse,
winesap and York imperial, the striped
summer rambo and the winter banana, the little
Rome with its squat rotunda and the pound apple

that pulled the boughs to the ground.
The sheep's nose with its three-pointed snout,
the blue Pearmain, speckled and sugared.
Grime's golden, cortland, and stamen.
If an apple's called "delicious," it's not.

Water has no substance
and soil has no shell,
sun is all process
and rain cannot rise.
The apple's core carries

a birth and a poison.
Stem and skin, and flesh,
and seed, the apple's name,
no matter, is work
and the work of death.

If you wait for the apple, you wait
for one ripe moment. And should
you sleep, or should you dream, or
should you stare too hard in the daylight
or come into the dark to see

what can't be seen, you will drop
from the edge, going over into
coarse, or rot, or damping off.
You will wake to yourself, regretful,
in a grove of papery leaves.

You need a hillside, a small and steady wind,
a killing frost, and, later, honey-bees.
You need a shovel, and shears, and a ladder

and the balance to come back down again.
You will have fears of codling moths
and railroad worms, and aphids.

Scale and maggots and beetles
will come to do their undoing.
Forests will trap the air

and valleys will bend to gales—
cedars will bring on rust, so keep them
far in the distance. Paradise,

of course, was easy, but you and I live
in this world, and "the fruit of the tree
in the midst of the garden"

says nothing specific about apples;
the "apples of gold" in Proverbs
are probably oranges instead.

And so are the fruits
Milanion threw down:
an apple does not glitter.

If you're interested in immortality
it's best to plant a tree, and even
then you can't be sure that form

will last under weather.
The tree can break apart in a storm
or be torqued into pieces over many

years from the weight of its ruddy labor.
The state won't let you burn the wood
in the open air; the smoke is too dense

for breathing. But apple-wood
makes a lovely fire, with excellent
heat and aroma.

Fire will take in whatever it can
and heat will draw back
into earth. "Here is the fruit,
your reward and penalty
at once," said the god

to the waiting figures.
Unbearable, the world
that broke into time.
Unbearable, the just-born
certainty of distance.

You can roast late apples
in the ashes. You can run
them in slices on a stick.
You can turn the stem to
find the letter of your love

or chase them down with
your chin in a tub.
If you count the seeds to tell
the future, your heart will
sense more than your

tongue can say. A body
has a season, though
it may not know it
and damage will bloom
in beauty's seed.

If I could come back from the dead, I would—
I'd come back for an apple,
and just for one bite, one break,
and the cold sweet grain on the tongue.
There is so little difference between

an apple and a kiss, between desire
and the taste of desire.
Anyone who tells you otherwise is a liar, as bad
as a snake in the quiet grass.

You can watch out for the snake and the lie.
But the grass, the green green wave
of it, there below the shadows of the black
and twisted boughs, will not be
what you thought it would be.

from *TriQuarterly*

Meteor

◇   ◇   ◇

I chose this. To be this
stone, grow nothing. I wanted this
absolute position in the heavens
more than anything, than you,
my two, too beautiful, my children.
A man I knew once
muttered in his terrors of the night,
no, no, no, instead of yelling.
It was this, this dismal low,
that made me leave him. I will leave them.
All the butterflies the lord above
can muster, all their roses.
I will leave whatever colors
struggle to be noticed. To leave,
to leave. That's the verb I am,
have always been, always will be,
heading, like a dewdrop, into steamy
confrontation, my train of neutral green
lasting half a second
before casting off its freight—his arms
outside the sheet, how warm they were,
like Rome the year it burned,
Nero at the window, loving no one,
fusion crust. I fly because
my space is crossed

with fear and hair and tail and hate,
the bowels of a lioness,
iron in her roar.

from *The Journal*

The Diagnosis

◊   ◊   ◊

Lincoln was sixty years old when the doctor told him he only had forty more years to live. He didn't tell his wife, with whom he confided everything, or any of his friends, because this new revelation made him feel all alone in a way he had never experienced before. He and Rachel had been inseparable for as long as he could remember and he thought that if she knew the prognosis she would begin to feel alone, too. But Rachel could see the change in him and within a couple of days she figured out what it meant. "You're dying," she said, "aren't you?" "Yes, I'm dying," Lincoln said, "I only have forty years." "I feel you drifting away from me already," she said. "It's the drifting that kills you," Lincoln whispered.

from *LIT*

I stopped writing poetry . . .

◊   ◊   ◊

Poetry gives no adequate return in money, is expensive to print by reason of the waste of space occasioned by its form, and nearly always promulgates illusory concepts of life.
—MYLES NA GCOPALEEN (FLANN O'BRIEN)

No one is more confident than a bad poet.
—MARTIAL

I stopped writing poetry
When I was just starting to get good at it. First
I got good at rhyme, so I cast it away.
Then I got good at line and stanza construction—
So good I hardly needed to *say* anything at all.
My meanings emerged
     in the spaces between.
So I got rid of that, too. Metaphor, metonymy,
Allusive echoes of my betters—well, frankly,
I was a whiz at that stuff pretty early on.
So I emptied out the file-drawers
Of rhetorical strategy, musical form,
Continuity or criticism of tradition,
And I just wrote. Finally I found
I was writing . . . *prose,* like everyone else.
But it was prose with a difference: prose with a rich,
Totally hidden other life lying behind it, unglimpsed
(I think) by the reader. Not like a prostitute
Who reforms and becomes a nun. I've seen
That movie. More like a nun who becomes a prostitute.

I stopped writing poetry
at 16 (seriously), then again at about 20
but only for six months, once again
at 27, then at 32, 35, 40, and 42.
I'll keep you posted.

i stopped writing poetry
when i realized that i understood romantic and symbolist
poetry sound sculpture objective verse conceptual art
pure language the confessional and elegiac modes and still
everything i wanted to do in poetry pretty much everything
i wanted anyone at all to do had been done already and much
better by don marquis in the archy and mehitabel poems

I stopped writing poetry
when everyone else did—in the early 90s, when television
became more interesting than culture.

I stopped writing poetry
when they came and deactivated my poetry button

I stopped writing poetry
when I got married—I mean settled down—
since the laws of the state of Maryland do not allow me
to marry the love of my life—though I'm not here
to whine about it—and maybe marriage would ruin me
as it seems to have ruined others—but one thing I know—
it is certainly nice to have someone to blame
for taking it easy and resisting inspiration when it inconveniently
insists on arising occasionally no matter what you do
(PS thanks for the dashes Emily Dickinson)

I stopped writing poetry
because the last thing I ever wanted
was to develop some obnoxious false
self masquerading as *voice* the way artists
as soon as their style becomes identifiable
are stuck in it and in what it will allow them
to think style isn't a correlative of personality
or a way to explore transcendent issues

that lie beyond mere worldly content style is
exhaustion ennui and fashion and death

I stopped writing poetry
when I received the praise of people I admired.
It's a terrible thing to receive exactly the attention you want
when you are unprepared to admit you might deserve it.
Of the many ways in which poets are always going on
about how poetry not only receives inspiration from love
but imitates it in form and feeling, this just may be the worst.

I stopped writing poetry because I saw what it was doing to people's prose style.
  Yikes.

I stopped writing poetry—
well, basically, because I'm white. I don't
like being white, it isn't a choice I'd make freely,
and to get argumentative I don't think it's entirely fair
that I have to be white right now when it's so 10 minutes ago
when if I'd been born fifteen years earlier most racists
would have considered me anything but, what with
the whole Jew-as-vermin thing, but OK, OK, I concede
the point, I'm culturally white, or whatever, *dammit,*
and in case you haven't noticed, this just isn't
white people's moment, poetry-wise. Don't even
get me *started* on the griot tradition and that stuff,
I mean, just look at rap—poetry that communicates
exquisitely within its chosen boundaries of class
and common interest, and hardly at all outside it,
except for those to whom it stands as aspiration to cool.
Just like Shakespeare and Donne. What have white people
contributed to culture recently? *Postmodernism?* Please.
My own revelation came when I realized
Little Red Corvette meant more to me than any poem
published since the early 1970s. On the not-very
mean streets where I learned versification, poetry
wasn't a mode of expression spontaneously developed
from living people's lived experience, it was a *regime.*
Well, that's over now. Get over it.

I stopped writing poetry
When I just ran out of steam.
It's really not a whole lot
More complicated than that.

I stopped writing poetry
When my friends started dying. Some of my friends
Wrote beautifully about the conditions of their illness,
And insightfully about mortality and their own impending
Death. Some wrote angrily about their invisibility
And created a literature of testimony in which we learn
What it was like to walk in the streets of American cities
As a ghost. Some wrote poems to memorialize their lovers,
Or to embarrass right-wing senators or arts funding agencies.
But I just counted 67 people I knew and was fond of
Who've died of "AIDS-related illness," and not once
Have I genuinely felt I could respond to their suffering or death
In poetry. Is it poetry? Is it me? The era? I am willing to believe
That if Milton and Shelley and Tennyson could do it,
It can still mean something. Why should I think their ages
Made death any more manageable a subject than mine?
But whenever I sat down to try, I stopped in despair.
Whatever the political advantages of slogans
Of the time, it wasn't the right words I looked for
But some way to make silence heard in lines
Of verse, and I never found it.
                                        Now even that
Sounds like a device to me, like special pleading.
Fuck it. Just fuck it. Let someone else do it.

I stopped writing poetry
but I still love the stanza. All that other cool stuff—
tropes, the caesura, enjambment—I can live without.
But the *stanza*—wow.

I stopped writing poetry
after I went to my first MLA conference,
where they were attacking a way of reading
and understanding literature they called
"mainstream" and "dominant" that I'd never even

encountered. It was like what they meant by "book"
was totally different from what I meant by "book"—
as different as "washing machine" and "golf ball."
I stopped writing poetry when it was eclipsed by criticism
for purely sociological and economic reasons.
I stopped writing poetry when people began writing
scholarly articles explaining how to read Frank O'Hara's
Lunch Poems and it never occurred to them to mention
that you should read them during lunch. I stopped
writing poetry when it became popular. I realize
Robert Frost read at Kennedy's inauguration but now
Ethan Hawke is telling *Vanity Fair* that he keeps
your book by his bed, and poetry as adjunct
to commercial culture and the veneration of celebrity
is so much more deliciously embarrassing for everyone
than even poetry in the service of the state.
I stopped writing poetry when taking it seriously
started seeming more likely to indicate
intellectual complacency than intellectual liveliness.
I stopped writing poetry when it got boring.

I stopped writing poetry
when the internet replaced the telephone
(since now that *everyone* has a phone,
and takes it *everywhere,* it's obvious
the telephone is *over*). Ted Berrigan I thought
destroyed the sonnet by inviting the beloved
to just pick up the phone and call him
sometime—thus no more need to plead
and seduce through verse—so the *channel*
changed: it works both ways. Now we are all
(gay str8 bi-curious) pleading and seducing
in lower case as only the freest verse used to
hitting reply b4 the intimacy of communication
has time even to register killing off poetry
by creating the first real audience for it in centuries

I stopped writing poetry
because I promised to. I read something
at the Ear Inn around 1984 in which I encouraged everyone

to give up writing—as I engaged to—and it went over
real big. Afterwards any time I ran into any of the
poetry crowd they'd always ask me if I was still
not writing. I understood it was a performance piece
and so did they but I kept getting this gnawing feeling
I was abandoning a principle by continuing to write.
It was entirely superstition, like actually feeling sick
when you call in sick, but I suppose I have been a victim
of the terrible conviction that you must mean what you say.

I stopped writing poetry
when I had dedicated poems to everyone I knew, at least everyone I wanted to
        impress.
I promise to start writing poetry again as soon as I meet some new people.
Interesting people, anyway.
Interesting people I can't just come out and *say* things to, anyway.

I stopped writing poetry
but as satisfying as it has been to turn my back on it
as on a distant homeland fallen under the spell of a fascist party
still a breeze reaches me from time to time fragrant of verse
and suddenly I am as nostalgic as an exiled Russian
grand duke waiting on tables in Paris in a screwball comedy
sometimes I wonder would it really be so terrible
if I wrote just one more line

from *Antioch Review*

DEAN YOUNG

Sources of the Delaware

◇ ◇ ◇

I love you he said but saying it took twenty years
so it was like listening to mountains grow.
I love you she says fifty times into a balloon
then releases the balloon into a room
whose volume she calculated to fit
the breath it would take to read
the complete works of Charlotte Brontë aloud.
Someone else pours green dust into the entryway
and puts rice paper on the floor. The door
is painted black. On the clothesline
shirt-tails snap above the berserk daffodils.
Hoagland says you've got to plunge the sword
into the charging bull. You've got
to sew yourself into a suit of light.
For the vacuum tube, it's easy,
just heat the metal to incandescence
and all that dark energy becomes a radiance.
A kind of hatching, syntactic and full of buzz.
No counter-indications, no laws forbidding
buying gin on Sundays. No if you're pregnant,
if you're operating heavy machinery because
who isn't towing the scuttled tonnage
of some self? Sometimes just rubbing
her feet is enough. Just putting out
a new cake of soap. Sure, the contents
are under pressure and everyone knows
that last step was never intended to bear
any weight but isn't that why we're standing there?
Ripples in her hair, I love you she hollers

over the propellers. Yellow scarf in mist.
When I planted all those daffodils,
I didn't know I was planting them
in my own chest. Play irretrievably
with the lid closed, Satie wrote on the score.
But Hoagland says he's sick of opening
the door each morning not on diamonds
but piles of coal, and he's sick of being
responsible for the eons of pressure needed
and the sea is sick of being responsible
for the rain, and the river is sick of the sea.
So the people who need the river
to float waste to New Jersey
throw in anti-depressants. So the river
is still sick but nervous now too,
its legs keep thrashing out involuntarily,
flooding going concerns, keeping the president
awake. So the people throw in beta-blockers
to make it sleep which it does, sort of,
dreaming it's a snake again but this time
with fifty heads belching ammonia
which is nothing like the dreams it once had
of children splashing in the blue of its eyes.
So the president gets on the airways
with positive vectors and vows
to give every child a computer
but all this time, behind the podium,
his penis is shouting, Put me in, Coach,
I can be the river! So I love you, say
the flashbulbs but then the captions
say something else. I love you, says
the hammer to the nail. I love Tamescha,
someone sprays across the For Sale sign.
So I tell Hoagland it's a fucked-up ruined
world in such palatial detail, he's stuck
for hours on the phone. Look at those crows,
they think they're in on the joke and
they don't love a thing. They think
they have to be that black to keep
all their radiance inside. I love you,

the man says as his mother dies
so now nothing ties him to the earth,
not fistfuls of dirt, not the silly songs
he remembers singing as a child.
I love you, I say meaning lend me twenty bucks.

from *Volt*

RACHEL ZUCKER

In Your Version of Heaven
I Am Younger

◇　◇　◇

In your version of heaven I am blond, thinner,
but not so witty. In the movie version of your version
of heaven you fight God to come back to me.
It is a box office hit because you are an unbelievable character.
Nothing is real except the well-timed traffic accident
which costs 226 thousand dollars.

In real life, I am on a small bridge over a small creek.
Then it isn't a bridge but a stadium. Then a low table.
A sense of knowing the future.
There is no clear location of fear.
I want you to say you will abandon your dissertation.
I want you to ask the man in the green scrubs if I was pregnant.

Put on the preservers! they announce. *They are under your seats!*
Time to tell your wife a few last things. People are puking
in the rows around us. The jackets sweaty and too big.
We are, in this version, an image of hope.
The broadcasters are just now sniffing us out.
I am pregnant but don't know it and can't know
that the fetus would have been, in any event, not viable.
No one survives. No one comes down with cancer.
The fade-out leaves a black screen over the sound of water.

The review says it is a *film noir.* The letter to the editor
says the reviewer should go back to college. The reviewer

is in graduate school writing a thesis about movies
that were never made. If they are made he will not get tenure.
If we die he has a small chance at success. A young woman
writes in: *it should, more properly, have been called an embryo.*

You say I have a dark vision. You buy me coffee and muffins
and cross the street safely. In this version you are there
when I come home. Night after night in bed
beside me. By day I watch the world your eyes watch:
the blondes, the redheads, the light blue baby jogger.
In this version the camera has a tiny light leak and the film,
after reediting, has no blond and no plane and no preservers.
No metaphysical struggle, no hero, no chance for financial success.

from *American Poetry Review*

CONTRIBUTORS'
NOTES AND
COMMENTS

NIN ANDREWS was born in Charlottesville, Virginia, in 1958. She has published three books of poetry: *The Book of Orgasms* (a new expanded version of which is just out from Cleveland State University), *Spontaneous Breasts* (Pearl Editions, 1998), which won the Pearl Chapbook Contest, and *Why They Grow Wings* (Silverfish Press, 2001), winner of the Gerald Cable Prize of 2000. She lives in Poland, Ohio.

Of "Notes for a Sermon on the Mount," she writes: "A couple of years ago I was at a Buddhist retreat where the teacher lectured on the sacredness of the body, which she said was the same as the holiness of Mother Earth. 'We need to start respecting every aspect of our physical selves,' she said. She led us on a guided meditation in which we were supposed to feel gratitude for our every body part and 'to imagine it as an aspect of God, herself.' The woman sitting next to me had a lot of trouble with the exercise. She told me afterwards that she got stuck on the genitals and never made it to any other part of her body. She kept thinking of pornographic magazines and feeling slimy. The more she tried to think nice thoughts, the more uncomfortable her thoughts became. 'I just can't imagine the pussy as a part of God,' she complained. When I giggled, she told me I should write a poem with the title 'How the Pussy Is Like a God.' I had no intention of doing so. Then one day, weeks later, I was seated at this coffee shop in Poland, Ohio, trying to write my Buddhist friends when someone turned the radio on. A zealous Christian preacher was broadcasting over the airwaves. The preacher kept bellyaching about God and our Satanic New Age. Even Christianity, he said, is becoming demonized by the worship of crystals and angels. 'Thou shalt put no other gods before thee,' he kept announcing in his heavy southern accent, and I decided I needed him in the poem. I made a few changes of course, beginning with 'Thou shalt put no other pussies before thee.' And 'Thou shalt not take the name of the pussy in vain.' This poem includes the notes from that summer afternoon."

RAE ARMANTROUT has published seven books of poetry, including *Made To Seem* (Sun & Moon, 1995), *writing the plot about sets* (Chax, 1998), *Necromance* (Sun & Moon, 1991), *Couverture* (Les Cahiers de Royaumont, 1991). Her prose memoir, *True,* was published by Atelos in 1998. A new collection of poetry, *The Pretext,* is forthcoming from Green Integer. Wesleyan University Press will publish her selected poems, *Veil,* in 2001. *A Wild Salience: The Writing of Rae Armantrout,* featuring essays by Robert Creeley, Hank Lazer, Bob Perelman, Charles Alexander, Ron Silliman, Brenda Hillman, Fanny Howe, and others has recently appeared from Burning Press. Armantrout has taught writing courses at UC San Diego since the early 80s. This year she is writer in residence at the California College of Arts and Crafts. She lives in San Diego.

Armantrout writes: " 'The Plan,' like many of my poems, is written in three quasi-independent sections. Each section is separate in that each has a different context, literally refers to a different situation. What interests me is the way such separate parts can interpenetrate (affect/inflect) one another. The first section is a take on the Garden of Eden story. The second might be located in a hotel where a pair of kinky lovers meet. I'm interested in seeing what sparks fly when such scenarios bump into each other."

JOHN ASHBERY was born in Rochester, New York, in 1927. *Some Trees,* his first book, was selected by W. H. Auden for the Yale Younger Poets Prize of 1956. Ashbery lived in Paris for ten years. During part of that time he was art critic for the *International Herald Tribune.* He won the Pulitzer Prize, the National Book Award, and the National Book Critics Circle award in poetry for *Self-Portrait in a Convex Mirror* (1975). He is the Charles P. Stevenson, Jr., Professor of Language and Literature at Bard College. *Other Traditions* (Harvard University Press, 2000) consists of the Norton lectures he gave at Harvard on such poets as John Clare, Thomas Lovell Beddoes, Raymond Roussel, David Schubert, and Laura Riding. *Your Name Here* (Farrar, Straus and Giroux, 2000) is his latest book of poems. In 2001 he was named state poet of New York. He divides his time between Hudson, New York, and New York City. He was guest editor of *The Best American Poetry 1988.*

ANGELA BALL was born in Athens, Ohio, in 1952. She cites her good luck in having, pro forma, to attend college right there, at Ohio University, where Victor Depta suggested to her that her tiny works were more ur-poems than ur-stories, and Stanley Plumly taught her the ineffables that make a poem. She later earned an M.F.A. from the University of Iowa and a Ph.D. from the University of Denver. She now teaches in the Center for Writers at the University of Southern Mississippi, where she is an editor for *Mississippi Review* (her World Poetry issue appeared in spring 2000). In spring 1999, she was poet in residence at the University of Richmond. She has received grants from the Mississippi Arts Commission and the National Endowment for the Arts. Her books include *Kneeling Between Parked Cars* (Owl Creek Press, 1990); *Possession* (Red Hen Press, 1995); *Quartet,* consisting of four long poems in the voices of Sylvia Beach, Nora Joyce, Nancy Cunard, and Jean Rhys (Carnegie Mellon University Press, 1995); and *The Museum of the Revolution,* a collage poem on Cuba (Carnegie Mellon University Press, 1999). "Jazz" is part of a recently completed manuscript, *Sleepy Girl.*

Ball writes: "I think I'd call 'Jazz' a mood poem. I find I'm interested more and more in a poetry of passing moods because I believe (with Wallace Stevens) that that's where we live. It's also a tribute to mixing: imitation, theft, borrowing—generally running away with the music. I love running away with a little Charles Mingus—his brilliant elegy for Lester Young, 'Goodbye Pork Pie Hat.' And a little of the Blues, part of my long-adopted Mississippi. Also, I've realized lately that the appearance of food in my life as compared to my work has been very disproportionate, and (between meals) I want to correct that."

MARY JO BANG was born in Waynesville, Missouri, in 1946, and grew up in St. Louis. She earned a B.A. and M.A. in sociology from Northwestern University; a B.A. in photography from Westminster University (London), and an M.F.A. in poetry from Columbia University. She has published three books of poems. *Apology for Want* (University Press of New England, 1997) was awarded the Bakeless Prize and the Great Lakes Colleges Association New Writers Award; *Louise in Love* (Grove, 2001) received an Alice Fay di Castagnola Award from the Poetry Society of America; and *The Downstream Extremity of the Isle of Swans* (University of Georgia Press, 2001) won the University of Georgia Press Contemporary Poetry Series Competition. She has been a poetry editor at *Boston Review* since 1995. In 1999–2000, she was a Hodder Fellow at Princeton University. She currently teaches at Washington University in St. Louis.

Of "Crossed-Over, Fiend-Snitched, X-ed Out," Bang writes: "Like many of my poems, this one is an amalgamation of a number of seemingly unrelated events—here, the televised aftermath of the fatal plane crash of John F. Kennedy Jr. and his wife, Carolyn Bessette Kennedy, and her sister, Lauren Bessette, which occurred in July 1999; a visit to the Freud Exhibit at the Jewish Museum in New York City; a listing in a catalogue of the Freud Museum which reads, '99C. (O) Napkin ring with the portrait of the newly married couple'; and a comment by the Chinese painter, He Gong, that the tail of a small plane seen through a window in his painting, *The Un-Biblio Story,* represents the beginning of the Twentieth Century (the first flight by the Wright Brothers was in 1903). Freud and the Kennedys and aviation coalesce as a way of talking about a century's ending which, in turn, becomes a way of talking about many different kinds of endings, public and private. About the way the fevered hopes of early life invariably give way to death, and death to eventual erasure. But tonally the poem chooses ironic detachment over lament. Freud would undoubtedly have much to say about such a choice."

CAL BEDIENT was born in Grand Coulee, Washington, in 1935. He did graduate work at Cornell University and the University of Washington and went on to become a professor of English at UCLA. He has published one book of poetry, *Candy Necklace* (Wesleyan, 1997), and four books of criticism: *Architects of the Self: George Eliot, D. H. Lawrence, and E. M. Forster* (University of California Press, 1972); *Eight Contemporary Poets* (Oxford University Press, 1974); *In the Heart's Last Kingdom: Robert Penn Warren's Major Poetry* (Harvard University Press, 1984); and *He Do the Police in Different Voices: The Waste Land and its Protagonist* (University of Chicago Press, 1986). *Eight Contemporary Poets* was nominated for a National Book Award. Bedient is an editor of the New California Poetry Series (University of California Press).

Bedient writes: "I thought I saw the phrase 'when the gods put on meter' while browsing in the Upanishads (S. Radhakrishnan's edition for Indus/HarperCollins), but haven't since been able to find it. Death lay like unbreathable smoke over the antique cabin camp in the Cascades that summer: Earl and Jeanne Smith, the owners, died as summer began, a short time apart, suddenly, senselessly. (A cancellation sign seemed to run through the camp itself, a rustic survival from the 1920s that the Smith family had built by hand from local cedar where two wild rivers meet.) The individual life is a sacrifice to what? What not on earth could merit the pains of a life, or, to turn it around, the tribute of formal beauty, formal behavior, exalted language? Is the universe as a great Fate beauty or horror?

"Looking back on the poem, I think it moves to get to the place in such questioning that Adorno thought the very essence of art, namely a prehistoric shudder. At least it doesn't want to rest short of that—that in which there is no rest."

ELIZABETH BISHOP (1911–79) was born in Worcester, Massachusetts, grew up in New England and Nova Scotia, and was educated at Vassar College. She lived for long periods in Key West, Florida, and in Brazil. She won the Pulitzer Prize for *A Cold Winter* (1955), the National Book Award for *Questions of Travel* (1965), and the National Book Critics Circle Award for *Geography III* (1976). *The Complete Poems, 1927–1979* was published by Farrar, Straus and Giroux in 1983. A year later the same publisher brought out her *Collected Prose*.

Like the majority of Bishop's poems, "Vague Poem" was published first in *The New Yorker*. It is among the fifty or sixty unfinished poems found in her papers at the Vassar College library, and it will appear in a volume of posthumous works that Farrar, Straus and Giroux will publish under the title *Edgar Allan Poem and the Jukebox*. As her friend Lloyd Schwartz has observed, in her lifetime Bishop published very few poems with an explicitly sexual content. Since her death, however, many of the poems that have surfaced, either completed or nearly completed, have been quite strikingly sexual.

ROBERT BLY was born in Minnesota in 1926. He has lived for various times in New York, in England, and in Scandinavia. In 1958 he launched *The Fifties*, which became *The Sixties* and *The Seventies*. He introduced the poets of his generation to many poets otherwise unknown such as Neruda, Vallejo, Tranströmer, Kabir, Machado, and Ponge. His recent books include *Morning Poems* (HarperCollins, 1977) and *Eating the Honey of Words: New and Selected Poems* (HarperCollins, 1999). Also in 1999 he published, in collaboration with Sunil Dutta, a volume of poems by the nineteenth-century Indian poet Ghalib under the title *The Lightning Should Have Fallen on Ghalib* (Ecco/HarperCollins). The poem included here is from his new book of poems, *The Night Abraham Called to the Stars*, which was published in May by HarperCollins. He was the guest editor of *The Best American Poetry 1999*.

Of "The French Generals," Bly writes: "After I looked at 'The French Generals' for a while, I decided the poem probably amounts to a meditation on the word 'many.' Napoleon, lying in his moist Elba bed, appears in it, just to throw you off. Those who follow every detail in a poem to its source are sure to be left behind in Elba. The mood of the poem is influenced by my admiration for the ghazals of Ghalib and Hafez in which there is no straight thread through the poem and each stanza can be read as a separate poem. Where the poem as a whole is going is a problem that the reader has to solve. I notice this poem has too many plural nouns in it, but perhaps one can forgive that because it's a poem about 'many.' I published an earlier version of the poem in the *TLS* under a different title. David Lehman has asked me to set down that version here as well. It seems that Jesus got into the title instead of Napoleon."

JESUS AT THE WELL

Whenever Jesus appears at the murky well,
I am waiting with my five hundred husbands.
It takes him all day to mention their names.

The growing soul longs for mastery, but
The small men inside pull it into misery.
It is the nature of shame to have many children.

We love our dark, greedy home. The serpent
Sends out his split tongue and waves it
In the air scented with many dark Napoleons.

The general goes to live in a small cottage
With damp sheets and useless French franc notes;
He keeps his old plans of attack under the mattress.

This world we love is the serpent's house.
We bring in newspapers to make his nest cozy.
It's the nature of wanting to have many wives.

So many rafters in lifejackets are pulled down
Till their toes touch the bottom of the Rogue River.
Wherever there is water there is someone drowning.

LEE ANN BROWN was born October 11, 1963, at Johnson Air Force Base, Saitama-ken, Japan. She was raised in Charlotte, North Carolina, and now resides in New York City. She is the author of *Polyverse* (Sun & Moon Press, 1999), which won the 1996 New American Poetry Series

Competition, and *The Sleep That Changed Everything,* forthcoming from Wesleyan University Press. She is the editor and publisher of Tender Buttons, a press that features experimental women's poetry. She received an M.F.A. in creative writing from Brown University in 1993 and has received fellowships from the New York Foundation for the Arts and the Fund for Poetry. She is currently an associate of Bard College's Institute for Writing and Thinking and an assistant professor of English at St. John's University.

Of "Sonnet Around Stephanie," Brown writes: "This poem was written upon hearing of the suicide of my girlhood friend, Stephanie Harrison, whom I had seen a few months before her death, in 1987. Elizabeth Robinson liked the poem and published a version of it in her Providence-based poetry newsletter, *Cold Water Business,* named for Lorine Niedecker's line. I pulled the poem out again in the past year as I was writing my second collection, which contains a number of elegies."

MICHAEL BURKARD was born in Rome, New York, in 1947. He currently teaches in the M.F.A. program at Syracuse University and in the summer program at the Fine Arts Work Center in Provincetown, where he also participated in MAKE: POEM, a showing of writer's drawings and paintings at the Schoolhouse Center for the Arts, and The C-Scape Mapping Project. He has taught in the past at Sarah Lawrence College and the University of Louisville, among other colleges, and has also worked as a psychiatric aide, an alcoholism and addictions counselor, and a proofreader for Bloomingdale's catalogues. He has been writing songs for many years. His books of poetry include *Unsleeping* (Sarabande Books, 2001), *Pennsylvania Collection Agency* (New Issues Press, 2001), *Entire Dilemma* (Sarabande Books, 1998), *My Secret Boat* (W. W. Norton, 1990), *Fictions from the Self* (W. W. Norton, 1988), *The Fires They Kept* (Metro Book Co., 1986), *Ruby for Grief* (University of Pittsburgh, 1981), *None, River* (Ironwood, 1979) and *In a White Light* (L'Epervier, 1977). He received two fellowships from the National Endowment for the Arts, two grants in poetry from the New York Foundation for the Arts, and, in 1988, a Whiting Writer's Award. Recent poems have appeared in *American Poetry Review, Fence, 3rd Bed,* and *Jubilat.* He is married to the artist Mary Alice Johnston.

Of "Notes About My Face," Burkard writes: "I wrote the poem in May of 1998; partly because of the fragments in the sequence I did not get much of a feel for what I had written for quite a while. I wrote into #7 and then returned to the poem the next day. A few of the fragments in #s 1–6 came from scattered notes. Except for this somewhat arbitrary reaching, I was improvising. The poem took more timing in #7—Jean Valentine had sent me a copy of a manuscript in progress and I had spent much very interested time with it. Her poems triggered a thought that I could turn to the reading event #7 talks to. And there had been a terrible brutal murder in New York City: the bodies of two young boys had just been discovered. I felt feeble beside this. I also wondered about some of the origins of my own wanting to write poetry, reasons for, perhaps suspect of . . . the pressures of school early on, later on . . . many different sources started crossing the poem perhaps as a way of using other art and poetry and poets as bridges, and some implicit admission that I am often much more comfortable and more truly my face with fragments from here and there without too much of a context. And wanting to state more of my political face? I looked at the notes a few times during the next year or so, and somewhere in 1999 the improvisation really began beckoning. I recopied it."

TRENT BUSCH was born in Brohard, West Virginia, in 1937. He has lived in Georgia for the past thirty years and owns a small place out in the country where he writes poetry and makes furniture. His poems have appeared in *Poetry, The Nation, Hudson Review, North American Review, Kenyon Review, Shenandoah, American Scholar,* and elsewhere. He is just now completing a book of poems entitled *Cuts from the Shop Floor.*

Of "Heartland," Busch writes: "If I could have heard half of what the woman says in this poem, I would be a little more qualified to speak about it. I have been involved in one way or another with farming all my life. One day being driven past a small house, long barns, and green tractors, I felt relieved they did not belong to me. I said so to my friend who was driving. Later, I wrote this poem about the couple we passed there."

AMINA CALIL was born in Stockton, California, in 1970. She lives in Oakland and Bangkok, and makes her living as a gardener and a midwife.

Of "Blouse of Felt," Calil writes, "After midnight, Schubert to play just a bit longer in the adjoining room his scofflaw narratives of children romping in metropolitan parks, I placed a massive picture book of plant forms on my lap, turned very slowly through its pages, and seemed to overhear 'Blouse of Felt' from the entities depicted there, and from those still active in my yard and body. The tones derive from psychic dilation. I am indebted to Flavor Flav for some of the cadences."

ANNE CARSON was born in Toronto, Canada, in 1950. She is a professor of classics at McGill University and has also taught recently at the University of Michigan and at Berkeley. Her books include *Glass, Irony and God* and *Men in the Off Hours* (Knopf, 2000). Her most recent book is *The Beauty of the Husband* (Knopf, 2001). She has received a Guggenheim Fellowship. Her work appears in *The Best of the Best American Poetry, 1988–1997*, edited by Harold Bloom. An article about Carson appeared in the *New York Times Magazine* in March 2000. "I'm conserving the past—it's what classicists are supposed to do," Carson told the reporter. "But there are ways to conserve it. One way is to say 'Nothing new is any good.' But you don't learn anything when you're still up on the window ledge, safe. The other way is to jump from what you know into empty space and see where you end up. I think you only learn things when you jump."

JOSHUA CLOVER was born in Berkeley, California, in 1962.

Of "Ceriserie," Clover writes: "While writing this poem I listened to 'Reasons To Be Beautiful' and 'Boys on the Radio' by Hole, 'The Everlasting' by Manic Street Preachers, 'Teardrop' by Massive Attack, 'Are You Still Mad?' and 'So Pure' by Alanis Morissette, 'Stolen Car' and 'Central Reservation (The Then Again Version)' by Beth Orton, and 'My Brother and Me' by Bruce Robison."

BILLY COLLINS was born in New York City in 1941. His books of poetry include *Picnic, Lightning* (University of Pittsburgh Press, 1998); *The Art of Drowning* (University of Pittsburgh Press, 1995), a finalist for the Lenore Marshall Poetry Prize; and *Questions About Angels* (William Morrow, 1991), which was selected by Edward Hirsch for the National Poetry Series and was reprinted by the University of Pittsburgh Press in 1999. This year Random House will publish his new and selected poems, *Sailing Alone Around the Room*. He has won the Bess Hokin Prize, the Frederick Bock Prize, the Oscar Blumenthal Prize, and the Levinson Prize—all awarded by *Poetry* magazine. A recipient of a Guggenheim Fellowship and a grant from the National Endowment for the Arts, he is a professor of English at Lehman College (City University of New York) and a visiting writer at Sarah Lawrence College. He lives in northern Westchester County. His poems have appeared in the 1992 and 1993 editions of *The Best American Poetry* and in each of the last four books in this series.

Of "Snow Day," Collins writes: "Long since recovered from the trance of writing this poem, I now have an outsider's view of it, which enables me to see all sorts of things that had little or nothing to do with its composition. For example, I see the poem as a series of steps that take us from a collective experience to a private one. The poem begins with the public event of snow (which Joyce would describe as 'general') and ends with three imagined girls whispering secrets. First, we are offered a kind of Marxist notion of snow as having the power to subvert civic life. Then we move to the domestic scene of speaker, tea, dog, radio. The poem gets strangely bogged down in the names of closed schools (all of which were lifted from the Yellow Pages), which leads us to a playground and finally into an intimate circle of conspiratorial little girls. In Chinese poetry this technique is called 'The Shepherd' because figuratively you begin with a widely dispersed flock and end in the enclosure of a sheepfold. If I step back further, I might say that a possible grandfather to this poem is Coleridge's 'Frost at Midnight' with its similar attention to winter and childhood. But if I took another step backwards, I might trip over a piece of furniture."

ROBERT CREELEY born in 1926, is a New Englander by birth and disposition although he has spent much of his life in other parts of the world, including Guatemala, British Columbia, France, and Spain. In the 1950s he taught at Black Mountain College and edited *The Black Mountain Review.* In 1966 he began teaching at the State University of New York in Buffalo. *For Love, Windows,* and *Selected Poems* are among his collections of poetry. He has also written a novel (*The Island*) and a collection of stories (*The Gold Diggers*).

Of "En Famille," Creeley writes: "This poem was written expressly for a collaboration with the photographer Elsa Dorfman. In fact, you can see what came of it at this site: http:// www.granarybooks.com/ books/dorfman/dorfman2.html.

It all began when Ellie gave me a great batch of her portraits—from which I first made a selection of ten for the so-called narrative of the poem, then an additional six for either end, making twelve—so twenty-two in all. I was up in Maine by myself, and I put the whole sequence on our big kitchen table, and then just sat and looked at them. Outside our place there's a big hayfield sloping down, with woods going off on all sides. I guess that's how Wordsworth got in there, with that opening line—and then, later, the wind. I would write two quatrains for each portrait, then move to the next—closing with old friend Bill Alfred's wise look (now gone, alas) and his dear friend Faye Dunaway. Perhaps because I was alone there, these dear people all became my company. They certainly made me recognize that I, like all, much needed it."

LYDIA DAVIS was born in Northampton, Massachusetts, in 1947. She is the author of *The Thirteenth Woman* (Living Hand Editions, 1976), *Sketches for a Life of Wassilly* (Station Hill Press, 1981), *Story and Other Stories* (The Figures, 1983), *Break It Down* (Farrar, Straus and Giroux, 1986), *The End of the Story* (Farrar, Straus and Giroux, 1995), and *Almost No Memory* (Farrar, Straus and Giroux, 1997). She has also translated numerous books from the French, including works by Maurice Blanchot, Michel Leiris, and Pierre-Jean Jouve. Her translation of Proust's *Swann's Way* will be published by Penguin UK in 2002. She lives in upstate New York.

Of "A Mown Lawn," Davis writes: "Towns lawns all mown, some poisoned, all free of weeds, all free of cover, some planned plantings, no loose small animals, no loose insects, some pets, some penned dogs, some tied and housed dogs, some pests, in effigy: effigy of raccoon, effigy of deer, effigy of Canada goose (no nibbling, no nuisance, no ruin of planned plantings), unmoving goose flock feed on poisoned mown lawn, red bows on necks come holiday."

R. ERICA DOYLE was born in Brooklyn, New York, in 1968 to Trinidadian parents. Her work has appeared in *Callaloo, Ms. Magazine, Black Issues Book Review, Blithe House Quarterly,* and *Sinister Wisdom,* and is forthcoming in the anthology *Other Countries: Voices Rising.* She received her M.F.A. in poetry from the New School in New York City. While living in Washington, DC, for twelve years, she taught creative writing and developed literacy curricula for young children at Children's Studio School; taught community writing workshops; and worked as a lesbian peer counselor, a paralegal, and a domestic violence activist. She has received grants and awards from the DC Commission on the Arts and Humanities and the Humanities Council of DC, and is a fellow of Cave Canem: A Retreat and Workshop for African. American Poets. She lives with her partner in Tel Aviv, Israel.

Of "Ma Ramon," Doyle writes: "My great-grandmother was a mean and manipulative person, and I wrote this poem as the antithesis and antidote to every 'grandmother' poem I'd ever read. She was the most singularly influential person in our family; her iron will, deviousness, tyranny, arrogance, and generosity are legendary, the ties she created still existent. Using the fragments of our family's oral history I pieced together a portrait of an ancestor who intrigued me as much for her political being as for her position in the histories as an emotional or nostalgic figure. Her machinations seemed to be as much a function of her will and personality as they were essential for her survival and, ultimately, success. She was a person who occupied multiple linguistic, geographic, legal, temporal, and cultural spaces and who operated, at least at the beginning of her life, from a position where her only privilege was the color of her fair skin. In the process of putting the pieces of her story together I saw a 'w/hole' that the great leveler of archetypal American popular culture was intent on erasing, given its inability to handle complexity and the tendency to romanticize a cruel past. She embodies the betweenness I carry within myself, a habitual and existential multiplicity."

CHRISTOPHER EDGAR was born in Pasadena, California, in 1961. His poems have appeared in *The Germ, Shiny, Lincoln Center Theater Review, The Portable Boog Reader,* and *The Best American Poetry 2000,* and he won the 2000 *Boston Review* poetry prize. An editor of *The Hat,* a literary magazine, Edgar is the translator of *Tolstoy as Teacher: Leo Tolstoy's Writings on Education* (Teachers & Writers Collaborative, 2000) and has coedited a number of books on teaching writing, including *Classics in the Classroom: Using Great Literature to Teach Writing* (Teachers & Writers Collaborative, 1999). He is publications director of Teachers & Writers Collaborative, a nonprofit arts organization in New York City, where he lives.

Of "The Cloud of Unknowing," Edgar writes: "I have always liked poems about travel, especially those of Valéry Larbaud, Blaise Cendrars, and Kenneth Koch. One day I was thinking about writing a poem about travel. I gazed dumbly at the bookshelf waiting for something to happen when *The Cloud of Unknowing* popped out from among the other spines. The central idea of this book, a treatise on knowledge by medieval English mystics, is (crudely) that in order to see one must first blur one's vision for a time. This seemed like something I could use, so I went with it, and wrote the rest of the poem without stopping. The events and places in the poem are mostly, but not all, from my own experience—a few are made up or lifted from others' accounts. The particular details weren't so important to me, though; I wanted to write a poem of many parts in one continuous zigzagging segue to approximate the experience of travel. Losing one's way, and having the freedom to do so, is a real pleasure, and when one feels relatively weightless—at sea in a port town or in a poem by Pierre Reverdy—a certain sense of recognition is sometimes heightened. Ending the poem in Heathrow seemed appropriate, since it's sort of a way station between Old and New Worlds, between our current, homogenized, post-International-style world and what came before."

THOMAS SAYERS ELLIS—or Sayers (after Gale) as he is known to family and friends—was born in Washington, DC, in 1963. Educated at Harvard University and Brown University, where he earned the M.F.A. in 1995, he is the author of *The Good Junk* (Take Three, Graywolf, 1996) and a chapbook, *The Genuine Negro Hero* (Kent State University Press, 2001). His poems have most recently appeared in *Giant Steps: The New Generation of American Writers; The New Young American Poets; American Poetry: The Next Generation,* and *The New American Poets: A Breadloaf Anthology.* A member of the core faculty of the Bennington Writing Seminars, he currently resides in Cleveland, Ohio, where he is an assistant professor of English at Case Western Reserve University.

Ellis writes: "I began 'T.A.P.O.A.F.O.M.' as a celebration and exploration of crossed and not yet crossed crossroads at Yaddo in the Nipple Room (West House), where Phillip Roth wrote *The Breast,* and I finished it in a park in Cleveland, Ohio, only days before Parliament-Funkadelic, a.k.a. P-Funk, was inducted into the Rock and Roll Hall of Fame. I wanted to write a poem for *That Fuss Was Us,* whose content and structure demonstrated the many nuances of difficulty I had witnessed navigating the languages and styles of form and formlessness, fake-ass freedom, between funky and unfunky worlds, and one that would juxtapose the twentieth anniversary of the landing of P-Funk's mothership with the tenth anniversary of The Dark Room Collective, which was officially founded the minute I met Sharán Strange. In the poem, I am working on my own brand of literary activism, which I call Genuine Negro Heroism. Genuine Negro Heroism (GNH) is the opposite of HNIC (Head Negro In Charge), and incorporates pee-pure modes of black freak, black folk, and black soul behavior such as signifying, shouting out, cursing, and playing the double-mouthed dozens like 'Yo momma ate-out Coretta Scott King, and got Ralph Abernathy on her chin.'

"I also intended for 'T.A.P.O.A.F.O.M.' to have three sections instead of two and to be the first poem with an afterparty. Regrettably, 'Afterparty' wouldn't surrender. Run and tell it like you run and tell everything else."

AMY ENGLAND was born in Alamorgordo, New Mexico, in 1962, and grew up in Illinois. She taught English as a second language in Tokyo and Chicago, and received a Ph.D. in creative writing from the University of Denver. Her first book of poems, *The Flute Ship Castricum,* was released by Tupelo Press in April of 2001. She edits Transparent Tiger Press, which publishes poetry chapbooks, and will be a visiting lecturer next year in Naropa University's writing and literature program.

England writes: "I've always been interested in the line that divides poetry from prose. 'The Art of the Snake Story' is the culminating piece in a manuscript *Victory and Her Opposites: a Guide,* which explores this division; the nominal subject is an archeological site in Greece. In doing research on this excavation and the history of the cult that was practiced there, I repeatedly came across images of snakes, which gave me the idea of combining a poem about the significance of those images with stories people had told me. I would like here to thank the sources of these stories: Eric Elshtain, Matthew Michael, Jim Bequette, Carol Loftin, Valerie Leppert, Barrett Shukla, and Carmen Curton."

ALAN FELDMAN was born in New York City in 1945. As an undergraduate at Columbia he edited *Columbia Review;* Columbia Review Press published his book of poems, *The Household* (1966). His second collection, *The Happy Genius* (SUN, 1978), won the annual Elliston Book Award for the best book of poems by an independent press in the United States. *The Personals,* a chapbook, came out in 1982, and *Anniversary,* self-published with color drawings by his wife, Nan Hass Feldman, in 1992. He is a professor of English at Framingham State College and also teaches writing at the Radcliffe Seminars, Harvard University. His most recent book, *State College 101: A Freshman Writing Class,* (www.xlibris.com), is about the "ignored middle"—working-class suburban kids who are first-generation college students—and the efforts of his colleague, professor Elaine Beilin, to educate them.

Feldman writes: "I wrote 'Contemporary American Poetry' immediately after delivering a visiting lecture on contemporary poetry at a Radcliffe Seminar. Some of the students were almost ninety, and they were finishing a two-year survey of great books. To prepare for me, they'd each brought a recent poem they liked. I kept thinking how perfectly my mother would have fit into such a group; like them she was well read, receptive, but (in a healthy way) somewhat skeptical, too. When she sent me Donald Hall's 'Kicking the Leaves' years ago, I didn't want to admire the poem. I felt my mother had gone over to the enemy. As a fan of New York poets Kenneth Koch and Frank O'Hara, I believed that poems could be more moving by being funny. Since then, whatever schism in American poetry this represented must have healed. When my poem appeared in *Poetry,* I received a gracious letter from Hall saying how much it pleased him. He reads it as being in-tune with his poem (different as the styles may be) and, I hope, as a tribute.

"My mother died in 1976, more than twenty years before I taught that poetry class. I don't claim to commune with spirits, but she can speak to me the way fictional characters do, dictating her own dialogue, which is what she began to do. Does she really believe that being 'troubled' is essential to the making of a poet, or is she just making excuses for me, thinking I should have devoted myself to poetry more single-mindedly? Though simpler than it was when she was alive, ours is still a loving but complicated relationship."

JAMES GALVIN was born in Chicago in May 1951. He teaches in the University of Iowa Writers' Workshop. He is the author of *The Meadow* and *Fencing the Sky* (both from Holt) and *Resurrection Update* (Copper Canyon Press). His earlier books include *God's Mistress* (Harper & Row) in 1984 and *Elements* (Copper Canyon Press) in 1988.

LOUISE GLÜCK was born in New York City in 1943. She is the author of ten books of poetry including, most recently, *The Seven Ages* (Ecco/HarperCollins, 2001). She received the National Book Critics Circle Award in poetry for *The Triumph of Achilles* (Ecco, 1985) and the Pulitzer Prize for *The Wild Iris* (Ecco, 1992). Her other poetry volumes include *Firstborn* (1968), *The House on Marshland* (1975), *The Garden* (1976), *Descending Figure* (1980), *Ararat* (1990), *Meadowlands* (1996), and *Vita Nova* (1999). A prose book, *Proofs and Theories: Essays on Poetry,* appeared in 1994. She has taught at Williams College since 1984. She received the Bollingen Prize in 2001. She was guest editor of *The Best American Poetry 1993.*

"My compositional process," Glück told Brian Phillips, who interviewed her in 1999, "almost always begins in a kind of despondency, or hopelessness, or desolation, usually born of a conviction that I will never write again. That I will at long intervals turn out little mechanical B+ poems, but that I'll never again feel that I am at the throat of the dog, that I'm at something essential. This pattern really hasn't varied, though my first book was more diligently written. But even then there were long hiatuses of silence and periods of despondency, life in the desert, that have come to seem to me the norm of my aesthetic life . . . which isn't to say those passages are not brutal. So that each of my books really begins with a prayer, you know: Appear to me again. Let me be suffused with the wish to, and ability to, make meaning out of language."

JEWELLE GOMEZ was born in Boston, Massachusetts, in 1948. A novelist, poet, and essayist, she makes her living as an administrator for arts and philanthropic organizations. She is the author of six books, including three collections of poetry. *The Gilda Stories* (Firebrand Books, 1991), a novel, was the winner of two Lambda Literary Awards, for fiction and science fiction. A recent collection of short stories, *Don't Explain* (Firebrand Books) appeared in 1999.

Gomez writes: "Whenever I read 'My Chakabuku Mama' it always gets uproarious laughter of recognition from people who identify with either the smugly self-righteous partner or with the puzzled, eager innocent who gets left behind. I love the response, but I always find the poem a bit sad because of the betrayal it represents. While it is a story told about a romance, to me it embodies many other types of exploitative relationships, especially between U.S. workers and corporate entities, or between lecturers and academic institutions, or between consumers and manufacturers. The personal is political, always."

JORIE GRAHAM was born in New York City in 1950. She grew up in Italy, studied in French schools, and attended the Sorbonne, New York University, Columbia University, and the University of Iowa. Her most recent collections of poetry are *The Dream of the Unified Field: Selected Poems 1974–1994* (Ecco, 1995), for which she received the Pulitzer Prize; *The Errancy* (Ecco/HarperCollins, 1998); and *Swarm* (Ecco/HarperCollins, 2000). A new collection, titled *Never,* is forthcoming in spring 2002. She is currently Boylston Professor at Harvard University. A MacArthur Fellow, she was the guest editor of *The Best American Poetry 1990.*

Of "Gulls," Graham writes: "The poem so evidently *is* what it *does,* it doesn't seem to require much explication. It attempts an acute act of description, tries to enact the emotional and spiritual states awakened thereby, and, finally, turns 'back' on those two 'first acts' in a final motion into meditation. It feels like an act of self-portraiture. It was, in its first draft, written *en plein air*—not unlike how painters, especially those of the Romantic period, happily place their easels and painting-boxes 'out' in 'nature.' It is, of course, in the trawling of such actions 'inside' (as well as 'indoors') that the problem of subjectivity—with which the poem, in its attempts at objectivity, is so strenuously involved—is brought into focus. It feels moving and urgent, as a process, to me. As I undertake it, sitting on the shore, peering intently, pen in hand, it feels like all the human history of inwardness is recapitulating itself in such attempted acts of representation. Then it just turns into a poem again and I really don't know much about it, except how vividly the wind came up as the sun went down."

LINDA GREGERSON was born in Elgin, Illinois, in 1950, and was educated at Oberlin College, the University of Iowa, and Stanford University. Her most recent book of poems, *The Woman Who Died in Her Sleep* (Houghton Mifflin, 1996), was a finalist for both the Poets' Prize and the Lenore Marshall Award. She is also the author of *Fire in the Conservatory* (Dragon Gate, 1982), *The Reformation of the Subject* (Cambridge University Press, 1995), and *Negative Capability: Contemporary American Poetry* (University of Michigan Press, 2001). Her third book of poems, *Waterborne,* will be published by Houghton Mifflin in 2002. Gregerson has received the Levinson Prize from *Poetry* magazine, the Consuelo Ford Award from the Poetry Society of America, the Isabel MacCaffrey Award from the Spenser Society of America, and a Guggenheim Fellowship. She teaches Renaissance literature and creative writing at the University of Michigan.

Of "Waterborne," Gregerson writes: "I am capable of shameful oblivion toward the world around me, especially the world of nature, but the dawn mists that gather on the surface of the Huron River in the spring and fall are the loveliest thing I see all day. Why those seasons in particular? Something to do with the temperature differentials between the water and the air? Thank heaven there are people who know more about these things than I do. And about bridge building (ours is quite decrepit; the school buses are no longer allowed to cross it) and the drainage of cornfields. I took a liberty in section two, omitting to mention that the river in question has temporarily metamorphosed into the Wisconsin River, some sixty miles north of Madison, where my uncle Gordon and my father and their siblings grew up. My neighbor tells me he'll take carp or walleye when he can't get bass, and he didn't take me for an agent of the DNR when I pulled over to ask."

LINDA GREGG was born in Suffern, New York, in 1942. Her fifth book of poems, *Things and Flesh,* was published by Graywolf Press in 1999. Her first two books, *Too Bright to See* and *Alma,* will be republished jointly in fall 2001. Also, this fall she is teaching at Princeton University. She currently lives in New York City.

Of "The Singers Change, The Music Goes On," Gregg writes: "This poem is trying to make a whole out of a contradiction. The permanence in myths, shards, temples and song, but also the permanence that was lived in the body and place. Love and revelations. Lasting, because of its heartbreaking momentariness."

ALLEN GROSSMAN was born in Minneapolis, Minnesota, in 1932. His most recent publications are *The Ether Dome* (1991), *The Philosopher's Window* (1995) and *How to Do Things with Tears* (2001), all available from New Directions. *The Long Schoolroom: Lessons in the Bitter Logic of the Poetic Principle* was published by the University of Michigan Press in 1997. He is the Mellon Professor in the Humanities at Johns Hopkins University.

Of "Enough rain for Agnes Walquist," Grossman writes: " 'Agnes' was the first name I ever knew. Her body was the first body I could name. I could think, 'Agnes is here' or I could think, 'Agnes is not here.' I have thought for most of a long life, 'Agnes is not here.' Agnes is, herself, the beginning and the end of my memory. I remember because she remembered. What she remembered I remember—as it happened, the sound of night rain.

"Some months ago I found a postal envelope among some other papers thrown away but not quite lost. It was addressed by my mother to Agnes Walquist. The envelope was empty. So I could make a poem for that envelope empty otherwise and send it off, the action of gratitude, making remembered in the world what she remembered. Remember what she remembered.

"All the names in this poem and in the book of which this poem is a part (*How to Do Things with Tears*) are like this."

DONALD HALL was born in New Haven, Connecticut, on September 20, 1928. He has earned his living as a freelance writer since 1975, the year he moved to a family farm in New Hampshire with his wife, the late poet Jane Kenyon. He had previously held a tenured professorship at the University of Michigan. He initiated Michigan's "Poets on Poetry" and "Under Discussion" series and served as the general editor of both until 1994. His recent books of poetry include *The One Day* (1988), which won the National Book Critics Circle Award; *Old and New Poems* (1990), *The Museum of Clear Ideas* (1992), *The Old Life* (1995) and

Without (1998), all published by Houghton Mifflin. A new volume entitled *The Painted Bed* expected in 2002. He was the guest editor of *The Best American Poetry 1989*.

Of "Her Garden," Hall writes: "For more than forty years Thomas Hardy has been one of my favorite poets in the language. But I never thought of trying to write the kind of stanza in which he often wrote: irregular lengths of iambic, all rhyming; the prosodic scheme repeated in further stanzas.

"Some of Hardy's best poems derive from the death of his first wife—a marriage which does not resemble Jane's and mine—and I don't believe I adopted his stanza because of subject matter. In the spring of 1998 I surprised myself by beginning to write these Hardyish poems, of which 'Her Garden' is the second. Stanzaic poems take much less time and effort, fewer drafts, than poems in free verse. The net determines some properties of the shot in tennis; free verse requires a net but its net is arbitrary. I continue to write free verse."

ANTHONY HECHT was born in New York City in 1923. He received the Pulitzer Prize in poetry in 1968, the Bollingen Prize in 1983, the Wallace Stevens Award from the Academy of American Poets in 1999, and the Robert Frost Medal in 2000. Among his published books are *Collected Earlier Poems* (Knopf, 1990), *The Transparent Man* (Knopf, 1990), *On the Laws of the Poetic Art* (Princeton), and *The Hidden Law: The Poetry of W. H. Auden* (Harvard, 1981). He lives in Washington, DC.

Of "Sarabande on Attaining the Age of Seventy-Seven," Hecht writes: "When I was twenty-nine, I read in an anthology, *A Little Treasury of Modern Poetry,* edited by Oscar Williams, a poem by George Santayana called "Minuet on Reaching the Age of Fifty." It began:

> Old age, on tiptoe, lays her jewelled hand
> Lightly on mine.—Come, tread a stately measure
> Most gracious partner, nobly posed and bland.
> Ours be no boisterous pleasure . . . .

I'm sure that at twenty-nine, fifty must have seemed very elderly, and I had a number of white-haired aunts whose jewels could not divert my glance from the large, worming blood vessels in their hands. There was something vaguely Spenserian about Santayana's poem, with its personifications and inverted word orders and dated vocabulary. Nevertheless, it had a certain charm that I recalled when I was far older than Santayana when he wrote it. The idea of a solitary dance (the sarabande can be danced alone) seemed right for someone my age, and without any further reference to Santayana's poem I set off to write one for myself. Moreover, I am not a good dancer, and the better for dancing alone."

LYN HEJINIAN was born in the San Francisco Bay Area in 1941 and lives in Berkeley. Her books include *My Life* (1987), *The Cell* (1992), and *The Cold of Poetry* (1994), all from Sun & Moon Press. The University of California Press has just published a collection of her essays entitled *The Language of Inquiry*. She has collaborated on projects with many poets and artists, among them Leslie Scalapino, Michael Davidson, Ron Silliman, and Barrett Watten. In 2000 she received the fellowship of the Academy of American Poets.

Hejinian writes: "The group of short poems entitled 'Nights' is part of a long-term project, a collection of night thoughts intended as an homage to Scheherazade. The work in its entirety is meant to give an account of nocturnal adventures, most of them entirely imaginary. These adventures take the form of somniloquys, insomniac lyrics, lullabies, fables, ghost stories, etc., and involve nighttime philosophizing, fretting, hallucinations, fantasies, eroticism, dreams, fear, and nonsense. The nonsense in question erupts with dark hilarity and is often ominous."

BRENDA HILLMAN was born in Tucson, Arizona, in 1951. She serves on the faculty of Saint Mary's College in Moraga, California. Her six collections of poetry—*White Dress* (1985), *Fortress* (1989), *Death Tractates* (1992), *Bright Existence* (1993), *Loose Sugar* (1997), and *Cascadia* (2001) are from Wesleyan University Press; she has also written three chapbooks, *Coffee, 3 AM* (Penumbra Press, 1982), *Autumn Sojourn* (Em Press, 1995), and *The Firecage* (a+bend press, 2000). Hillman has edited an edition of Emily Dickinson's poetry for Shambhala Publications, and, with Patricia Dienstfrey, has coedited *New Writings on Poetics and Motherhood*.

Of "The Formation of Soils," Hillman writes: "The strata in this poem are wide, mobile, soft, as when the story had been restless but isn't anymore. I was thinking about the making of soil in the middle of a state, as distinct from the making of dirt. In relation to something like an era, love or insight seems like air, and human times of making (or, as we sometimes say, *having*) experiences are so brief compared to how long it takes for rocks to crumble. All the kinds of significance are layered in an unknown order."

JANE HIRSHFIELD was born in New York City in 1953. She is the author of five collections of poetry, most recently *Given Sugar, Given Salt* (HarperCollins, 2001). Her other books include a collection of essays, *Nine Gates: Entering the Mind of Poetry,* and two anthologies collecting the work of women poets from the past. She has received fellowships from the Guggenheim and Rockefeller foundations, the Poetry Center Book Award, the Bay Area Book Reviewers Award, and other honors. This is her second appearance in the *Best American Poetry* series. A resident of the San Francisco Bay Area, she teaches in the low-residency Bennington MFA Writing Seminars.

Of "In Praise of Coldness," Hirshfield writes: "It has long seemed to me that one of the defining qualities in a human life is the tension between the path of the passions and that of a certain nonattachment to one's own fate. The advice the poem quotes (from one of Chekhov's letters) strikes me as somehow related to a solution 'If you want to move your reader, write more coldly.' The underbelly of that sentence is what interests: the point is not the coldness, but the way that a restraining coldness can in fact contain heat, can move the reader more than would a simple explosive outpouring. In art, in life, a certain coldness (the emotional distance of classical tragedy, the technical use of perspective in a Renaissance canvas, the capacity a person might have to step back sometimes from the pulses' racing) allows, paradoxically, greater feeling, greater range, increase of compassion, but it cannot so dominate as to deny human feeling, human life. Heat alone is narcissism; coldness alone is fatal. And so a dying man daydreams of travel, of eating, knowing all the while that he dreams the contemplation of Chekhov's allegiance to the world of the living, right to the end, both breaks and awakens the heart.

"The Japanese call the human realm 'the world of the middle,' or 'the world of betweenness.' One task then of a human life is to find a way of being that seats itself between—that falls neither into a plummeting, arid coldness nor into unrestrained heat. (It is only because we humans lean by nature toward warmth that the title of this poem leans toward the cold.) What I've written here, I must add, are the thoughts that came to mind while looking at the poem in retrospect. In writing it, one line simply followed the next onto the page, and I only discovered in the reading and revising of those lines what the poem was exploring in its words and musics. That discovering, and its consequent clarifying, are the reason I write."

JOHN HOLLANDER was born in New York City in 1929. He has published eighteen books of poetry, the most recent being *Figurehead* (Knopf, 1999) and a reissue with added notes and commentary of his *Reflections on Espionage* (Yale University Press, 1999). He has also published several books of criticism and theory, most recently *The Work of Poetry* (Columbia University Press, 1997) and *The Poetry of Everyday Life* (University of Michigan Press, 1998). Among the awards he has received for his work are the Bollingen Prize, the Levinson Prize, and a MacArthur Fellowship. He lives in Connecticut and is Sterling Professor of English at Yale University. He was the guest editor of *The Best American Poetry 1998*.

Of "What the Lovers in the Old Songs Thought," Hollander writes: "In this bit of play with the poetry of love (love-poetry, love-making, love's made-up stories about itself) I took up a form of story about Origins that had puzzled me since later childhood, the opening of the Fourth Gospel: 'In the beginning was the Word, and the Word was with God, and the Word was God.' Before I knew what the *Logos* might be, I'd puzzled at how something that was *with* something else might be said to be identical to what it was with. (Not being a Christian, I had had no educational guidance in the matter.) In college, I came across Faust's great sequence of revisions (and, finally, Trotsky's footnote to the last revision. 'In the Beginning was the Deed. The word followed as its phonetic shadow.'). My feelings about the revisionary sequence, and about claims of origination in religion, poetry, and love, found their place in this poem."

RICHARD HOWARD was born in Cleveland, Ohio, in 1929. He was educated at Columbia University and the Sorbonne. The most recent of his eleven books of poems is *Trappings* (Turtle Point Press, 1999); for his third, *Untitled Subjects,* he was awarded the Pulitzer Prize in 1970. He has translated more than 150 works from the French, including Stendhal's *The Charterhouse of Parma* for the Modern Library, and he received the American Book Award for his translation of Baudelaire's *Les Fleurs du mal*. He is a member of the American Academy of Arts and Letters and served as the Poet Laureate of New York State from 1994 to 1995. In 1996 he was named a Fellow of the MacArthur Foundation. He is poetry editor of both *The Paris Review* and *Western Humanities Review,* and teaches in the writing division of the School of the Arts at Columbia University. A chancellor of the Academy of American Poets, he was guest editor of *The Best American Poetry 1995*.

Of "After 65," Howard writes: "The poem was published five years late—it was written for a project of 'Poets Then and Now' by photographer Rollie McKenna, who asked for a poem of comment on her images thirty years apart."

FANNY HOWE was born in Buffalo, New York, in 1940, and grew up in Boston. She is a professor of writing and American literature at the University of California, San Diego. Her most recent novels are *Nod* (Sun & Moon, 1998) and *Indivisible* (Semiotext(e)/MIT Press, 2001). Her most recent collections of poems are *One Crossed Out* (Graywolf, 1997) and *Selected Poems* (University of California Press, 2000).

Howe writes: " 'Doubt' was written for a conference on Simone Weil two years ago at Columbia University. I ended up reading poems instead, because the atmosphere was contentious. . . . Originally I thought of this as a lyrical essay, but increasingly *all* my writing tends toward poetry, including my most recent novel, *Indivisible.* I can no longer make distinctions between the genres. This must have developed naturally over time, though I think it always created a problem for my prose, which might have had a happier life if I had called it poetry."

OLENA KALYTIAK DAVIS was born in Detroit in 1963. Her first book, *And Her Soul Out of Nothing,* was published by the University of Wisconsin Press in 1997. Her work has recently been anthologized in *The New American Poets: A Breadloaf Anthology; American Poetry: The Next Generation; The Best American Poetry 2000;* and *Pushcart Prize XXV.* She is currently living in Alaska, raising a family, and slowly finishing her second manuscript, *Shattered Sonnets Love Card and Other Off and Back Handed Importunities.*

Kalytiak Davis writes: " 'Sweet Reader, Flanneled and Tulled' was inspired by the opening sentence of the final chapter of *Jane Eyre:* 'Reader, I married him.' Not only did I want that kind of intimate and immediate relationship with my reader, I wanted to see just how intimate and immediate 'we' could actually become. It took me a long time to figure it out, as is the case with any emotional/sexual pairing. Naturally, it turned into a love/hate thing.

"Following my usual method, I sought help, by which I mean blatantly stole, from numerous and miscellaneous sources ranging from Milton's description of the good angel Abdiel to "Nessmuk"'s *Woodcraft and Camping.* (Speaking of craft, this poem was intentionally crafted to be read aloud; I also remember at the time being interested in Allen Grossman's premise of repetition as the absence of rhyme.) I saved nothing when writing 'Sweet Reader . . .', I put everything in it including my hang-ups and infidelities, my tea and my crumpets. This was several years ago. I sometimes feel I still haven't restocked my mental or poetic arsenals. Then again, it could be all these babies I seem to be suddenly having. . . ."

SHIRLEY KAUFMAN was born in Seattle, lived in San Francisco, and has resided in Jerusalem since 1973. Among her seven books published in the United States are *The Floor Keeps Turning* (University of Pittsburgh Press, 1970), *Rivers of Salt* (Copper Canyon Press, 1993), and *Roots in the Air: New and Selected Poems* (Copper Canyon Press, 1996). She has also translated several volumes of Hebrew poetry by Israeli poets Abba Kovner, Amir Gilboa, and Meir Wieseltier (forthcoming, University of California Press); and also a selection of poems from the Dutch of Judith Herzberg. Kaufman's *Selected Poems,* translated into Hebrew by Dan Pagis and Aharon Shabtai, was published by the Bialik Press in Jerusalem in 1995.

Of "The Emperor of China," Kaufman writes: "This poem grew and kept changing for almost two years. I began it in a study-bedroom at Kresge College of the University of California at Santa Cruz, where I wrote every morning for a week in August, looking out the window at the sunlit forest and the proprietary deer nibbling at the shrubs and leaves. I thought I was writing about this dreamy California scene, but my home in Jerusalem immediately intruded (as it always does when I'm writing in the U.S.A.) together with the memory of our friend's eightieth birthday party a month earlier. I realized how much I was 'enjoying my life' at that very moment.

"When I write, my personal life is usually mixed up with political events, daily news, conversations, associative memories, and a range of sensory detail that often overwhelms me. I don't sort all this out while the words keep coming. I'm happy when the random images keep rolling faster than I can write them down. I'm not at all sure at such an early stage where they are going, and what they will mean in the end. When I discover that, often much later, I can begin to shape the poem. "When I returned to Israel, to the very different world where I live most of the time, there was another window, in my study facing the street, the flats and gardens across from me. I watched the first clouds come after a long blue summer. Always the man across the street is cleaning his garden and sweeping the stone path from the sidewalk to the door of his home with such obsessive compulsion that he must be crazy. Summer and winter in the same khaki shorts and sandals. In the winter he adds socks.

"There's a thin curtain blowing across my vision much of the time (especially now as I write this at the end of January 2001). So that acts of kindness, pleasure in spring and gardening, a children's choir, even love keep dissolving into unease, anger, sometimes fear—and memories of Kieslowski's film, or the Holocaust, or the Gulf War, every war. Human suffering takes over.

" 'The Peace and Other Dreams Writers' Conference' was really the name of that Beersheva University conference. It took me a long time to weave it all together."

GALWAY KINNELL was born in Providence, Rhode Island, in 1927. He received a B.A. at Princeton University and an M.A. at the University of Rochester. His early books include *The Book of Nightmares* (1971) and *The Avenue Bearing the Initial of Christ into the New World* (1974), both from Houghton Mifflin. He won the Pulitzer Prize in 1983. His most recent books are *The Essential Rilke,* translated with Hannah Liebmann (Ecco Press) and *A New Selected Poems* (Houghton Mifflin). He lives in Vermont and New York, where he teaches in the graduate writing program at New York University.

Of "The Quick and the Dead," Kinnell writes: "My one regret in witnessing the events that are recounted in the poem is that I didn't photograph the creatures involved, or measure them, for better identification later. But in fact I was so enthralled by the burial and by the arrival of the female and some spectators that identification was the last thing on my mind. When the drama was over I felt I had been present at something like a medieval miracle play. As for the uncommon words, I like inventing words, using words that are still ahead of us, but just as much I like trying to save some of those that are falling off behind us."

DAVID KIRBY was born in Baton Rouge, Louisiana, in 1944. He is currently the W. Guy McKenzie Professor of English at Florida State University. His poems appear in *The Best American Poetry 2000* and *Pushcart Prize 2001,* and his books of poetry include *Big-Leg Music* (1995), *My Twentieth Century* (1999), both from Orchives Press, and, most recently, *The House of Blue Light* (Louisiana State University Press, 2000). He is married to the poet Barbara Hamby and lives in Tallahassee, Florida.

Of "Dear Derrida," Kirby writes: "A lot of poets can't stand theory, but I guess I believe in everything. Or, as Picasso said, I don't care who influences me as long as it isn't myself.

"Actually, there is one problem with deconstruction, which is that it's a French idea that amounts to an all-out assault on the masterpiece-kissing educational system in that country. Over here, of course, we aren't all that well-constructed in the first place. After you've been through our public schools, you're not really weighed down with all this information that needs to be taken apart, so deconstruction is kind of silly for Americans.

"On the other hand, a little indeterminacy isn't a bad thing. When my friend decided to put that gun barrel in his mouth, I just wish he hadn't been so sure of himself."

CAROLYN KIZER was born in Spokane, Washington, in 1925, and was educated in Spokane public schools. Her father was a noted civil liberties lawyer and urban planner. She has three children and is married to John Marshall Woodbridge, FAIA, also a city planner. She graduated from Sarah Lawrence College in 1945, and then became a fellow of the Chinese government at Columbia University; she subsequently went to China, where her father directed Chinese relief. Founder of the poetry quarterly *Poetry Northwest,* she was the first director of literature for the National Endowment for the Arts. *Cool, Calm and Collected: Poems 1960–2000* has just been published by Copper Canyon Press. In 1985 she received the Pulitzer Prize in poetry for *Yin: New Poems* (BOA Editions, 1984). She lives in Sonoma, California, and part-time in Paris.

Of "The Ashes," Kizer writes: "Periodically, I circle back to China, where I first lived in 1947–48. Evidence of the coming revolution was everywhere, as was the corruption of the Kuomintang warlords and the misery of the common people. It was such a traumatic year that I've rarely been able to cope with the memories. This poem comes as close as anything I've written. It is dedicated to William Gass because he also attended a meeting of Chinese and American poets and translators that took place a couple of years ago. My encounters with the older Chinese poet took place at that event."

KENNETH KOCH was born in Cincinnati, Ohio, in 1925. He lives in New York City and teaches at Columbia University. His most recent books of poetry are *New Addresses* (2000), *Straits* (1998), *One Train* (1994), and *On the Great Atlantic Rainway: Selected Poems 1950–1988* (1994), all from Knopf. Also published recently were two books about poetry: *The Art of Poetry* (University of Michigan, 1996) and *Making Your Own Days* (Scribner, 1998). A book of plays, *The Gold Standard,* was published by Knopf in 1996; and an opera for which he wrote the libretto (*The Banquet,* music by Marcello Panni) is being performed in Genoa, Rome, and Florence in 2001.

Of "To World War Two," Koch writes: "I spent about three years in the army during World War Two, some of it in combat in the Philippines. I wrote a few poems about being in the war when I was still a soldier, but hadn't written any since then until the device of talking to World War Two as if it were a person—or at least someone or something that could understand what I said—somehow enabled me to do so. Without this odd device of directly addressing the war I couldn't imagine how to get the right tone in talking about my experience of it. I found I had something to say and was happy to be able to say it. The poem was originally two poems, one 'To the United States Army' and the other 'To World War Two.' Neither by itself got enough of the subject to be quite what I wanted."

NOELLE KOCOT was born on November 14, 1969, in Brooklyn, where she now lives with her husband of eight years, composer/pianist Damon Tomblin. She graduated from Oberlin College and the University of Florida, and works as a training administrator. She has received the S. J. Marks Memorial Award from *The American Poetry Review* (1997) and a fellowship from the National Endowment for the Arts (2001). Her first book of poetry, *4,* was published in May 2001 by Four Way Books. She has no hobbies to speak of.

Of "Consolations Before an Affair, Upper West Side," Kocot writes: "I wrote this poem the morning after the experience in the poem, that is, having dinner on New York's Upper West Side with someone, a married poet, who was contemplating having an affair with another married poet. She asked me what I thought, and I told her that I thought it would only make her unhappy, which it did actually wind up doing.

"The poem is far more narrative and grounded and overtly confessional than most of my work and for that reason alone, it is one of my favorites, it really is the exception that proves the rule. The title is based on a poem that I love by James Tate, 'Consolations After an Affair.' The poem ends a line before I thought it should, but the editors of *Another Chicago Magazine* thought it should go (it is extremely melodramatic: 'Who has faltered, continually, on the upswing') and I thought maybe they were right. In any case, what is, is."

JOHN KOETHE was born on December 25, 1945, in San Diego, and was educated at Princeton and Harvard Universities. He has published five books of poetry, most recently *The Constructor* (HarperCollins, 1999), which was a finalist for the Lenore Marshall Prize and *The New Yorker* Book Award, and *Falling Water* (HarperCollins, 1997), which received the Kingsley Tufts Award. He is also the author of *Poetry at One Remove: Essays* (University of Michigan Press, 2000) and *The Continuity of Wittgenstein's Thought* (Cornell University Press, 1996). He is professor of philosophy at the University of Wisconsin, Milwaukee. "Songs of the Valley" will be included in *North Point North: New and Selected Poems,* to be published by HarperCollins in early 2002.

Of "Songs of the Valley," Koethe writes: "Though Wallace Stevens is one of the principle influences on my work, I almost never set out to write a poem in Stevens's manner (a partial exception is a long poem called 'The Secret Amplitude,' which was included in *The Best American Poetry 1998*). But a few years ago I was reading an article in which Helen Vendler talked about him, and the opening lines of 'Songs of the Valley' popped into my head, and I decided to write a short poem using some of Stevens's rhetoric and his sense of dualities and oppositions. Actually, the opening line is not the one that originally occurred to me, which was 'There are two choirs, one sung in space.' But several people to whom I showed the poem complained that choirs aren't sung, and while the idea still seemed fine to me, I didn't want readers to get hung up on the first line of the poem, so I changed it."

YUSEF KOMUNYAKAA was born in Bogalusa, Louisiana, in 1947. He received the Bronze Star for his service as a correspondent in Vietnam. His most recent books include *Pleasure Dome: New and Collected Poems, 1975–1999* (Wesleyan), *Talking Dirty to the Gods* (poems, Farrar, Straus and Giroux), and *Blue Notes: Essays, Interviews and Commentaries* (Poets on Poetry Series, University of Michigan Press), both in 2000. Among his other titles are *Thieves of Paradise,* a finalist for the 1999 National Book Critics Circle Award, and *Neon Vernacular: New and Selected Poems 1977–1989,* winner of the 1994 Pulitzer Prize in poetry. He wrote the lyrics for *Thirteen Kinds of Desire* (Cornucopia Productions, 2000), sung by jazz singer Pamela Knowles. Elected to the Board of Chancellors of the Academy of American Poets in 1999, he teaches at Princeton University.

Asked about his "relationship to form, particularly the 'sixteen-line approach,'" Komunyakaa replied: "It tells me I can write about anything and basically collapse whatever my observations and meditations are into a structure—if it's on metaphysics, a scientific principle, or the ritual of an insect or an animal—I can collapse it into that sixteen-line structure and, hopefully, through that compression be surprised. I'm saying more than I could say in thirty lines."

MARK LEVINE was born in Flushing, New York, in 1965. He grew up in Toronto and was educated at Brown University and the University of Iowa. He has published two books of poems: *Debt* (William Morrow, 1993) and *Enola Gay* (University of California Press, 2000). He is a member of the permanent faculty of the University of Iowa Writers' Workshop, where he teaches each fall. The rest of the year he lives in Brooklyn and works as a journalist for *The New Yorker* and other magazines.

Levine writes: "In 'Wedding Day,' the last poem in my book *Enola Gay*, some of the images that accumulate over the course of that book—craters, debris, marshes, ships, trumpets, atoms, trains—reappear in a setting that is essentially personal, even, obliquely, autobiographical. To me, it is a poem that tries to think about having 'an appointment with elsewhere,' with the place that is not the altar, not the book of poems one might have just read, not the site from which one is speaking. The desire to be here—the need to be elsewhere—the fact of being unreconciled. And the mislaid plans for a wedding ceremony on the longest day of the year."

SARAH MANGUSO was born in Newton, Massachusetts, in 1974. She received a B.A. from Harvard University and an M.F.A. from the University of Iowa, where she was a Truman Capote Fellow in creative writing. She is the author of *The Captain Lands in Paradise*, forthcoming from Alice James Books, and her poems have appeared in *American Letters & Commentary*, *The American Poetry Review*, *The Iowa Review*, and *The New Republic*. She works as a copy editor and book critic and lives in New York City.

Of "The Rider," Manguso writes: "The low prairie in the last line is the low prairie of western South Dakota, a state I drove across in 1999. At the time, it seemed like the end of the world."

J. D MCCLATCHY was born in Bryn Mawr, Pennsylvania, in 1945. He lives in New York City and in Stonington, Connecticut. He is editor of *The Yale Review* and has taught at Yale, Princeton, UCLA, and Columbia. He has written four books of poems: *Scenes from Another Life* (Braziller, 1981), *Stars Principal* (Macmillan, 1986), *The Rest of the Way* (Knopf, 1990), and *Ten Commandments* (Knopf, 1998). Two collections of his essays have appeared: *White Paper* (1989) and *Twenty Questions* (1998), both from Columbia University Press. In addition, he has written four opera libretti and edited many books, including *The Vintage Book of Contemporary American Poetry* (1990) and *The Vintage Book of Contemporary World Poetry* (1996). He is a chancellor of the Academy of American Poets.

Of "Tattoos," McClatchy writes: "Poems in their own way—ornamenting the white page—are tattoos: Their ink at its most precise can draw blood and make a moment endure. We admire tattoos, as we value poems, equally for their respect of convention and their impulse toward innovation. This poem—all in syllabics—is itself a set of patterns, that of its first section mirroring its third in matching anecdotes and scaffolding, and its middle part a discursive run of lines in limping, odd-numbered pairs. With a pointed but, I hope, forgivable swagger, I've used some insider lingo here, from a reference to the Great Lakes Naval Training Center and parlor slang like 'flashes' (predesigned emblems) or 'sleeve' (a tattooed scene that covers one's arm, wrist to shoulder) all the way to the Maori creation myth. The first part tiptoes around what used to be called 'unspoken desires.' The third part plunges into their cosmic depths. The middle part, I trust, turns inside out what the other, more melodramatic sections struggle to conceal. And two footnotes: 1) George Seferis, in his diary: 'In essence, the poet has only one theme: his living body,' and 2) I should add, of course, that I don't myself have a tattoo."

COLLEEN J. MCELROY lives in Seattle, Washington. Her most recently published book of poems is *Travelling Music* (Story Line Press, 1998). Other recent publications include her travel memoirs, *A Long Way from St. Louie* (Coffee House Press, 1997), and a work of creative nonfiction, *Over the Lip of the World: Among the Storytellers of Madagascar* (University of Washington Press, 1999). She has received a Before Columbus American Book Award. McElroy is editor in chief of the *Seattle Review* and teaches at the University of Washington in Seattle. She is currently working on a novel, teaching, and planning her next journey to some far-flung corner of the globe that will force her travel agent to pull out yet another map.

Of "Mae West Chats It Up with Bessie Smith," McElroy writes: "I could start with my grandmother's attic and the years during World War II when I was an only child dancing to tunes on the Victrola. I loved the ladies of torch songs and blues, so Bessie and Mae have been in my head for years. The poem is out of a collection of love poems, my second such collection. As with my first collection, I am the skeptic who doesn't 'know what love is' but has much to say about its regrets. What better voices than the seasoned comments of experience, like Mae West and Bessie Smith, *les femmes d'un certain âge,* living a little dangerously, always outrageous, outspoken, and out to get the most from life. They are my heroes, and more often than not, speak to me when I've once again ventured into that place where my heart beats too loudly. But most of all, they give me wit in those times when I could be flattened by the Blues. It took me half a century to get here, but I can't say it's been boring."

HEATHER MCHUGH was born in California in 1948. She is a professor of poetry at the University of Washington in Seattle; she frequently teaches in the low-residency MFA program at Warren Wilson College. Her most recent books are *The Father of the Predicaments* (poems, Wesleyan University Press/University Press of New England, 1999); *Broken English: Poetry and Partiality* (literary essays, Wesleyan University Press, rpt. 1999); and a cotranslation with her husband, Nikolai Popov, of *Glottal Stop: 101 Poems by Paul Celan* (Wesleyan University Press, 2000).

Of "My One," McHugh writes: "The poem proceeds from an anagrammatical insight into the relation between love and possessiveness. I'm not sure whether *homo* or *sui* is the generis of *cide* (some things a poet must not decide); but the poem's ecstatic coinages are, I trust, sufficiently ironized to take some of the shine off the romantic occasion. The old yearning of lovers to ask 'How much?' is as ruinous as it is revealing."

HARRYETTE MULLEN was born in Florence, Alabama, birthplace of blues man W. C. Handy, and grew up in Fort Worth, Texas, home of jazz leader Ornette Coleman. Mullen teaches English and African American Studies at UCLA. She is the author of five books of poetry: *Tree Tall Woman* (Energy Earth Communications, 1981), *Trimmings* (Tender Buttons Books, 1991), *S*PeRM**K*T* (Singing Horse Press, 1992), *Muse & Drudge* (Singing Horse Press, 1995), and *Sleeping with the Dictionary* (University of California Press, 2001). Parts of *Muse & Drudge* have been set to music in T. J. Anderson's *Seven Cabaret Songs* and Christine

Baczewska's *O Rose*. "Music for Homemade Instruments" is included in *Sleeping with the Dictionary*.

Of "Music for Homemade Instruments," Mullen writes: "A few years ago, I had the pleasure of performing with Douglas Ewart at Woodland Pattern Book Center in Milwaukee. Imagining a program divided between his music and my poetry, I looked forward to meeting this acclaimed jazz musician, who plays and creates many instruments, including bamboo flutes and didgeridoos. However, I was startled when our hosts suggested that we try a spontaneous collaboration before a live audience. Our performance was also to be recorded for a local radio broadcast. Douglas Ewart is a master of improvisation, but I was out of my depth. Usually, I just read the poetry. This was my first experience attempting a verbal-musical duet with an instrumentalist, but I survived that baptism, thanks to Doug's reassuring presence, expertise, and grace. The title of my poem is borrowed from Music for Homemade Instruments, an ensemble of classically trained musicians who invent, build, compose for, perform on, and teach with musical instruments built from found objects. This prose poem of recycled language, my tribute to Douglas, is a playful transformation of words into other words, as the jazz player improvises with musical notes and the jazz vocalist doodles with nonsense syllables."

CAROL MUSKE DUKES was born on December 17, 1945, in St. Paul, Minnesota. She directs the graduate program in creative writing at the University of Southern California. She is the author of six books of poems, most recently, *An Octave Above Thunder* (Penguin, 1997); three novels, most recently, *Life After Death* (Random House, 2001); and two books of criticism: *Women and Poetry* (University of Michigan Press, 1997) and the forthcoming *A Poet in Hollywood* (Random House, 2002).

Muske Dukes writes: " 'Our Kitty' is my way of imagining the return of John Keats—in the persona of a showgirl named Kitty. The 'untaken hand' turns up in a poem fragment by Keats, and seems to me to represent the proffered hand of Poetry itself."

ALICE NOTLEY was born in Bisbee, Arizona, on November 8, 1945, and grew up in Needles, California. She was educated at Barnard College and the University of Iowa Writers' Workshop. She lived a peripatetic poet's life until settling in New York's Lower East Side for sixteen years beginning in the early 1970s. Her book-length poem *The Descent of Alette* was published by Penguin in 1996. Her last book, *Mysteries of Small Houses*

(Penguin, 1998), was a finalist for the Pulitzer Prize and won the *Los Angeles Times* Book Award for Poetry. A book-length poem, *Disobedience,* is forthcoming from Penguin in the fall of 2001. Notley lives in Paris, where she teaches creative writing at the British Institute.

Notley writes: " 'Where Leftover Misery Goes' is from a very long manuscript (over three hundred pages) entitled *Reason and Other Women.* The book is intended to show the author herself in the process of thought; thus typos and mistakes are left in as standing for 'mind fuzz,' and repetition both maintains momentum and indicates stasis, in the way the two combine in thinking. However the book is also tied in with the concept of a Byzantine Church with all its icons and mosaics: permanent images or stories one never shakes, also the little dots or pieces of thinking, also the sacrality of consciousness. This particular poem dwells on events and dreams that occurred fifteen years before the writing of the poem but can never be lost: they are unpleasant but iconic. They have perhaps become beautiful."

SHARON OLDS was born in San Francisco in 1942. She teaches at New York University and lives in New York City. Her most recent books are *The Wellspring* (1996) and *Blood, Tin, Straw* (1999), both from Knopf.

Of "His Costume," Olds writes: "When I stop a moment and look at a poem of mine, not to rewrite it but to try to see it, it's the texture—the rhyme and beat—that come forward for me: the four-beat lines, and the sounds the strong accents fall on. And I see how this poem, when it gets its run on, is really more two-beat: so the sort of hearts or cores of it (as in geologic sea-floor readings) for me are

> dress . . . . . tennis
> breasts . . . breasts
> blonde . . . . lip
> body . . . . . . grace

and

> skirt . . . . . book
> nurse . . . . . drink
> round . . . . . care (mas*car*a)
> salt . . . . . . mother

—lots of liquidness, drooling, lipping, nourishing. (By 'core' I guess I mean structural beam-work of music, and density of image—form:content::costume:core.) (A poem *is* its music, that's the main thing.)"

KATHLEEN OSSIP was born in Albany, New York, in 1959. She received an M.F.A. from the New School University, where she now teaches a poetry workshop. Her poems have appeared in *The Antioch Review, American Letters & Commentary, The Journal,* and *Barrow Street.* She works as a writer of educational materials and lives with her husband and daughter in Westchester County, New York.

Of "The Nature of Things," Ossip writes: "One of the many pleasures of working with Susan Wheeler was the opportunity to peer at the Robert Lostutter painting that hung in the hallway of her apartment. The painting showed a man morphing into an exotic bird—the artist's constant subject. To my eye, the man looked slightly tormented and utterly quotidian.

"I wanted to create a narrative frame for the picture and I wanted to talk soothingly to the man. From those impulses came my first-and-only ekphrastic poem. (In some of Lostutter's paintings, there are two figures: thus the pal.)"

GRACE PALEY was born in the Bronx in 1922 to Russian Jewish immigrants. She has two grown children and three grandchildren and is now married to Robert Nichols—Russian, Yiddish, and English are all spoken in her home. She went to Hunter College and New York University; she finished neither. After spending most of her life in New York, she moved to Vermont fifteen years ago; she loves both places and continues to visit New York frequently. Her books of stories include *The Little Disturbances of Man* (1959), *Enormous Changes at the Last Minute* (1974), *Later the Same Day* (Penguin, 1986), *Long Walks and Intimate Talks* (Feminist Press, 1991), *The Collected Stories* (Farrar, Straus and Giroux, 1994), and *Just as I Thought* (Farrar, Straus and Giroux, 1998). Her books of poems include *New and Collected Poems* (Tilbury Press, 1992) and *Begin Again: Collected Poems* (Farrar, Straus and Giroux, 2001).

Of "Here," Paley writes: "I have always been a political person and have described myself as a combative pacifist and cooperative anarchist. The poem, I guess, is a love poem to my old man, who is as interested in this harsh world as I and even more eager to change it. We are both old and hate to leave the world even worse than we found it."

MICHAEL PALMER was born in New York City in 1943 and has lived in San Francisco since 1969. He has published nine collections of poetry and taught at many universities. He has worked extensively with contemporary dance for twenty-five years and has collaborated with numerous visual artists and composers. His most recent collections are *At Passages* (New Directions, 1995), *The Lion Bridge (Selected Poems 1972–1995)* (New Directions, 1998), and *The Promises of Glass* (New Directions, 2000). A prose work, *The Danish Notebook,* was published by Avec Books in 1999. With Régis Bonvicino and Nelson Ascher, he edited and helped to translate *Nothing the Sun Could Not Explain: 20 Contemporary Brazilian Poets* (Sun & Moon Press, 1997). Among his other translations are *Theory of Tables* by Emmanuel Hocquard (o-blek editions, 1992) and Alexei Parshchikov's *Blue Vitriol* (Avec Press, 1994). His own writings have been translated into more than twenty languages.

Of "Untitled (February 2000)," Palmer writes: "Not much I would wish to add to what is there / not there, visible / not visible in the poem. A chance encounter ('objective chance'?) with an air of unreality about it. Composed over a couple of weeks, the final chance element being its completion on Leap Year Day. This fact, as it suddenly dawned on me, seemed to confirm the out-of-time character of the entire experience. The poem goes out for a walk. What does it see and hear, and when, and who is to say?"

JOHN PECK was born in Pittsburgh, Pennsylvania, in 1941, and is now divorced, with one daughter, Ingrid. Currently he works as a freelance and contract editor, a Jungian analyst, and occasionally as an adjunct professor. A professional reshuffle at mid-career took him to Switzerland, where he worked for eight years as an editor, professor, and jack-of-all-trades while training in Jung's complex psychology (to use his own name for it). His eight books include *Shagbark* (Bobbs-Merrill, 1972), *The Broken Blockhouse Wall* (Godine, 1978, and Carcanet, 1979), *Poems and Translations of Hi-Lo* (Carcanet, 1991, and Sheep Meadow, 1993), *Argura* (Carcanet, 1993), *Selva Morale* (Carcanet, 1995), *Orestes* (Euripides: Oxford, 1995, with Frank Nisetich), *M and Other Poems* (Northwestern, 1996), and *Collected Shorter Poems 1966–1996* (Carcanet, 1999). An interview with Clive Wilmer appears in *Poets Talking* (Carcanet, 1994). For six of the past eight years he has worked in private practice in southern Vermont.

Of "A Metal Denser Than, and Liquid," Peck writes: "Albert Speer had fascinated me long before Gitta Sereny published her exhaustive portrait of the man, but only on happening to peer again through her microscope (at a public-library book sale) did the fascination recolonize its uncomfortable virus in me. This poem is my homemade antibiotic. While its task is a venerable one—the *examen de conscience*—its very gradual entrance into that task was my experiment. In the course of writing I discovered that the saving prompting which spoke to me—*discernment is not judgment*—I had heard at least five times over the course of several decades: from an Anglican priest, a former Catholic priest turned analyst, two teachers of Theravada meditation, and my fellow poet Teresa Iverson. So I am happy to acknowledge this small band of furtherers in the art of right-targeting. Their point not only helped me in my minor wrestle with a mightily destructive *artiste manqué,* whose only valid work, he said, was his design for a street lamp in Berlin. It also offers help, I would surmise, to any artist or museum-quality liberal who admires the work of W. B. Yeats, Djuna Barnes, or Marguerite Yourcenar while acknowledging the discomfiting engagement of their sensibilities with themes and atmospheres (or with the spiritual entrails, perhaps?) of what collectively we call 'fascism.' We are not yet able to handle such terms cleanly, and I suspect that we shall succeed in doing so only once we are able to face, while pointing the finger at others, our own mirrors."

LUCIA PERILLO was born in 1958 and grew up in the suburbs of New York City. Her latest book of poems is *The Oldest Map with the Name America* (Random House, 1999). She has taught at Southern Illinois University and now lives in Washington State.

Of "The Ghost Shirt," Perillo writes: The ghost shirt—that which we naively believe protects us—was something that I had often used naively as a poetic trope. I finally stumbled on a real one in the Museum of Natural History in New York while on a trip back east, where I was camping for a few days on various friends' couches, estranged from my usual encounters with newspapers and TV. As I made my way home to my parents' house in the suburbs, I found myself engulfed in a day-of-the-locust style human crush, and it was only as I waited on the train that I learned what was happening: the officers who'd assaulted Rodney King had been acquitted, and the city was emptying out. It was one of the few times in my life that I've truly felt swept up in capital-H History.

"I wrote the poem a few years later while studying Dante's *Inferno* under the tutelage of Dr. Edward Brunner at Southern Illinois University, and that was what impelled me to use the terza rima form to describe what was partly an underground experience. I should also say that a Native American woman has chastised me for using the word Sioux instead of the more accurate Lakota, and for my contention that belief in the ghost shirt was naive. Perhaps I merely cannot understand the mechanism of its effect."

CARL PHILLIPS was born in Everett, Washington, in 1959. He is the author of five books of poetry: *The Tether* (Farrar, Straus and Giroux, 2001), *Pastoral* (Graywolf, 2000), *From the Devotions* (Graywolf, 1998), *Cortège* (Graywolf, 1995), and *In the Blood* (Northeastern, 1992). A recipient of the Morse Prize and awards and fellowships from the Guggenheim Foundation, the Academy of American Poets, and the Library of Congress, he teaches at Washington University, St. Louis.

Of "The Clearing," Phillips writes: "At one point in Homer's *Iliad,* the Greek general Agamemnon is given instruction by the gods in a dream. He trusts the dream, he believes the gods. The result is disaster, for the gods have deliberately given Agamemnon a false dream, in order to tip the scales in favor of the Trojan army.

"*The Iliad* wasn't on my mind while writing, but the concerns that arise from that incident are the concerns of my poem: the capacity for deception in what we trust most, be it a deity, a lover, or (more distressing) the self; the distance that—swiftly, subtly—can come to exist between our actual selves and those that we construct, either out of a longing not to see the truth of ourselves or from an inability to do so; and that space in which to know what is 'wrong' is not necessarily to understand what is 'right,' even as understanding is rarely the same as doing, or so I have found.

"Another way to put it: not knowing where to turn, instead I built myself a wall against what I would and would not turn from. The poem is the result."

ROBERT PINSKY was born in Long Branch, New Jersey, in 1940. He served three terms as Poet Laureate of the United States. His most recent book of poems, *Jersey Rain,* was published by Farrar, Straus and Giroux in 2000. He has translated Dante's *Inferno.* He teaches at Boston University and is coeditor of *Americans' Favorite Poems,* an anthology of poems introduced by readers who selected them, published by Norton in 1999.

Of "Jersey Rain," Pinsky writes: "The past has certain resemblances to rain. Rain is a source of life, a fundamental replenisher. It makes things grow. It transforms our vision, making things we look at blurrier or sharper, less visible or more stark. It can be beautiful.

"And it can ruin a weekend. It can be depressing. It can make us feel confined.

"My poem is a pretty straightforward account of these similarities between rain and the past. And for me, the rain is in some ways always a New Jersey rain, just as the past is most certainly first of all a New Jersey past."

CLAUDIA RANKINE was born in Kingston, Jamaica, in 1963, and now lives in New York City. She is the author of three volumes of poetry, most recently *PLOT* (Grove Press, 2001). Her earlier books were *Nothing in Nature Is Private* (Cleveland State, 1994) and *The End of the Alphabet* (Grove Press, 1998). She has coedited with Juliana Spahr a collection of essays entitled *American Women Poets in the 21st Century*, which will be published by Wesleyan University Press in fall 2001. The collection includes essays by and about Rae Armantrout, Mei-mei Berssenbrugge, Lucie Brock-Broido, Jorie Graham, Barbara Guest, Lyn Hejinian, Brenda Hillman, Susan Howe, Ann Lauterbach, and Harryette Mullen. She teaches at Barnard College, and is the director of Women Poets at Barnard.

Rankine writes: "Katie Couric of the *Today* show on NBC interviewed a doctor who argued that women were intended to have children and that, because more and more women were choosing not to have them, all kinds of things were going awry in their bodies. He contended that a childless woman should stay on birth control pills all the time, including the week she normally bleeds. I forget now what this was supposed to achieve. Another doctor—Doctor Love from Santa Cruz perhaps, beamed into the studio via satellite—was outraged. This five-minute interview remained with me in the form of a warning to those women and had something to do with my writing 'A short narrative of breasts and wombs.' "

ADRIENNE RICH was born in Baltimore, Maryland, in 1929. She graduated from Radcliffe College in 1951, the year her first book, *A Change of World,* was chosen by W. H. Auden for the Yale Series of Younger Poets. She has published fifteen books of poetry and five of prose, including *Blood, Bread and Poetry* (Norton, 1986), *What Is Found There: Notebooks on Poetry and Politics* (Norton, 1993), and *Arts of the Possible: Essays and Conversations* (Norton, 2001). "Architect" appears in her most recent book of poems, *Fox* (Norton, 2001). For the past fifteen years she has lived in California. She was guest editor of *The Best American Poetry 1996.*

Of "Architect," Rich writes: "Let's say this architect was going through a bad, a degraded period. His work depends on popularity and nostalgia and the dictates of wealth; more literally, on the physical labor of others. He had done better in the past and perhaps his future work will redeem this shoddy interval. To what extent is his work determined by his time, to what extent does he collaborate? For better or for worse, architecture is the most social of the arts, most reflective of power and money relationships. Many of the other poems in *Fox* allude to art's stubborn transfusions of hope and energy, even in periods of social disintegration."

JAMES RICHARDSON was born in Bradenton, Florida, in 1950, and grew up in Garden City, New York. He is professor of creative writing and English at Princeton University, where he has taught since 1980. His collections of poems include *Reservations* (Princeton University Press, 1977); *Second Guesses* (Wesleyan University Press, 1984); *As If* (Persea Books, 1992), which was selected by Amy Clampitt for the National Poetry Series; *A Suite for Lucretians* (Quarterly Review of Literature Poetry Series, 1999); and *How Things Are* (Carnegie Mellon University Press, 2000). He has also written two critical studies, *Thomas Hardy: The Poetry of Necessity* (University of Chicago Press, 1977) and *Vanishing Lives: Tennyson, Rossetti, Swinburne, and Yeats* (University Press of Virginia, 1988).

Of "Vectors: Forty-five Aphorisms and Ten-second Essays," Richardson writes: "Back in 1993, I was looking at Montaigne for an essay to be called 'On Likeness.' A note sent me to the maxims of La Rochefoucauld, which I read not only with delight, but with eager disagreement. 'Wait, that's not right,' I'd mutter, or 'That's not *all*,' scribbling some correction or rotation of one of his insights. Soon, aphorisms were fizzing up in response to whatever I was reading—which was, more and more, Antonio Porchia, Marie von Ebner-Eschenbach, and *The Oxford Book of Aphorisms*—and I hardly had the attention span for longer thought. This was a distracting, obviously useless, and vaguely guilty pleasure, like playing video games or eating corn chips. Who'd want to hear my strictures and paradoxes? What about 'Show, don't tell'? What about 'negative capability'? If they mean anything, I suppose, they mean a writer had better be content not knowing exactly what he's doing, and I certainly didn't. And, after all, the best time is stolen time. Though I sometimes struggled heroically not to write it, *Vectors: Five Hundred Aphorisms and Ten-second Essays* will be published by Chase Twichell's new Ausable Press in fall 2001. As for that essay, it's . . . in progress."

RACHEL ROSE is a dual Canadian/American citizen who was born in Vancouver, Canada, in 1970. She has lived on Hornby Island in Canada, Fidalgo Island in Washington State, as well as in Seattle, Vancouver,

Montreal, and Maebashi, Japan, and is both drawn to and repelled by the intricacies of island life. She is currently a housewife and stay-at-home mother in Vancouver, where she lives with her partner, Isabelle, and son, Benjamin. Her first book of poetry is *Giving My Body To Science* (McGill/Queen's University Press), which was a finalist for the Gerald Lampert Award, the Pat Lowther Award, the Grand Prix du Livre de Montréal, and which won the Quebec Writer's Federation Poetry Award for 2000.

Rose writes: "Like any good foreigner living in another country, while I lived in Japan I read as much as I could about Japanese culture and traditions, both in books written by other foreigners and books written by the Japanese themselves for the purpose of educating visitors. The contradictions in these books were intriguing enough, but then, as the only American representative to which they had access, I was expected to answer all the questions my Japanese students posed: Why were we Americans so dangerously armed? Why couldn't we stay married?

"I went to Japan just after graduating from university, with the unspoken assumption that North America, despite its faults, was the most advanced area in the world. From the moment of my arrival, I was challenged by the steadfast belief of most Japanese that Japan was, despite its faults, superior to any country on earth. It was from these challenges and contradictions that these poems emerged, as I wrestled with the very concept of anthropology."

MARY RUEFLE was born in McKeesport, Pennsylvania, in 1952. She has received a National Endowment for the Arts Fellowship, a Whiting Writer's Award, and an award in literature from the American Academy of Arts and Letters. Her publications include five books of poems: *Memling's Veil* (University of Alabama Press, 1982), *Life Without Speaking* (University of Alabama Press, 1987), *The Adamant* (University of Iowa Press, 1989), *Cold Pluto* (Carnegie Mellon University Press, 1996), and *Post Meridian* (Carnegie Mellon University Press, 2000). She lives in Massachusetts and teaches in the MFA writing program at Vermont College. Her work appeared in *The Best American Poetry 1997*.

Of "Furtherness," Ruefle writes: "I look at this poem and I don't know what to say: when was it written, and where? I know the opening stanza is a description of the funeral of William Morris, and the sixth a description of Emily Dickinson's. The others—made up—though the third could be Stalin or Snow White, couldn't it? I always wanted to write a poem with the word *excelsis* in it—funny that it wound up in a poem with so many deaths. Ordure—what does that mean? My mother had a stainless steel coffin covered with photographs, but she died after the poem was written—would I add that now? No, I would add a stainless steel coffin covered with the flag of an obscure nation: so it goes. Poetry is murderous and off-kilter in all the ways those pies are, there at the end—all the while necessary and good—whatever it takes to sustain life, which will always go on its way."

JAMES SCHUYLER was born in Chicago in 1923. *Freely Espousing,* his first collection of poems, did not appear until he was forty-six. His subsequent books include *The Crystal Lithium* (1972), *Hymn to Life* (Random House, 1974), *The Morning of the Poem* (Farrar, Straus and Giroux, 1980), *A Few Days* (Random House, 1985), and the posthumous *Collected Poems* (Farrar, Straus and Giroux, 1993). *The Morning of the Poem* won the Pulitzer Prize. He was also the author of three novels, one of them, *A Nest of Ninnies,* written in collaboration with John Ashbery. Schuyler died in New York City in April 1991. *The Diary of James Schuyler,* edited by Nathan Kernan, was published in 1997, and Schuyler's *Selected Art Writings,* edited by Simon Pettet, in 1998, both from Black Sparrow Press. A paperback edition of *Alfred and Guinevere* (1958), Schuyler's first novel, is newly available from The New York Review of Books. Douglas Crase has written that he regarded Schuyler as his "moralist of the everyday": "The exciting thing about knowing as well as reading Jimmy was to observe how his ethics seemed to emerge directly from the life around us. . . . One evening after dinner at our apartment he was admiring the pink cover Robert Dash had done for John Koethe's book *The Late Wisconsin Spring.* It was, he said, 'a very fine pink.' But Jimmy, I warned, Bob says it's the wrong pink. Jimmy regarded me silently for a moment, then in that voice of sudden gravity he said, 'Only if you had another pink in mind.' "

"Along Overgrown Paths" was discovered in the John Ashbery archive of the Houghton Library at Harvard University. It had been lost twice. Schuyler sent a typed copy of the poem, dated April 23, 1968, to Ashbery in a letter four years later. "The other day I moved my filing cabinet and under it was this poem," Schuyler explained. "It's nothing much, but it does memorialize a notable trip to Pultneyville" (the upstate New York town where Ashbery's mother then lived). Librarians may have found the letter and its contents difficult to file; the letter is addressed to "Lotta Crust" from "Miss American Pie," though it is signed "Jimmy" and the initials "JS" appear beside the date on the typescript of the poem.

CHARLES SIMIC was born in Belgrade, Yugoslavia, in 1938, and immigrated to the United States in 1954. As a poet and translator, he has published more than sixty books in this country and abroad since 1967. He teaches American literature and creative writing at the University of New Hampshire. Among his numerous awards are the MacArthur Fellowship and the Pulitzer Prize. *Jackstraws,* a new book of poems, and *Selected Early Poems* were published by Harcourt Brace in 1999. He writes criticism regularly for *The New York Review of Books.* His book of memoirs, *A Fly in the Soup,* appeared from the University of Michigan Press in 2000. He was the guest editor of *The Best American Poetry 1992.*

Of "Night Picnic," Simic writes: "Before one thinks or says anything, I suppose, one ought to look at the sky at night first. For almost thirty years I have lived in the country surrounded by miles of woods. In the summer we usually dine outdoors or just sit late past bedtime, talking and sipping wine in the dark. The poem comes out of the memory of many such nights."

LARISSA SZPORLUK was born in Ann Arbor, Michigan, in 1967. She is the mother of two young children and lives with her husband, Carlo Celli, in Bowling Green, Ohio, where she sometimes teaches creative writing at Bowling Green State University. She is the author of *Dark Sky Question* (Beacon Press, 1998) and *Isolato* (University of Iowa Press, 2000), and has just completed her third manuscript, *The Wind, Master Cherry, The Wind.*

Szporluk writes: " 'Meteor' is unusually frank. It felt good to write. The metaphor came easily. There is a tremendous need, after bearing children, to be wickedly selfish and perhaps that's why even 'Nero' entered the poem naturally. Because the poem was guided by fury rather than the more typical patching and plodding, I am refreshingly detached from any artistic concerns—I wouldn't change a thing."

SUSAN STEWART was born in York, Pennsylvania, in 1952, and is the author of three books of poems, most recently *The Forest* from the University of Chicago Press. She teaches at the University of Pennsylvania and in 2000 delivered the Beckman lectures at the University of California at Berkeley. Her four books of criticism include *On Longing* and the forthcoming *Poetry and the Fate of the Senses,* and she often writes on contemporary art. Her translation with Brunella Antomarini of the poems of the Scuola Romana painter Scipione will appear from Charta in Milan in the coming year, as well as a translation with Wesley Smith of Euripides' *Andromache* in the new Oxford series of classical tragedies.

Stewart writes: " 'Apple' is the 'A' in an alphabet of georgics and their shadows that makes up my next book of poems. The georgics are poems of instruction from one generation to another and in writing 'Apple' I talked with everyone I knew about memories of, and names for, and advice about growing, apples. The poem is an archive of the voices of others, including by now the voices of the dead."

JAMES TATE was born in Kansas City, Missouri, in 1943. His most recent book of poems, *Memoir of the Hawk,* was published by Ecco/Harper-Collins in 2001. He is the author of fourteen previous books of poetry, among them *Shroud of the Gnome* (Ecco, 1997), *Worshipful Company of Fletchers* (Ecco, 1994), and *Selected Poems* (Wesleyan University Press, 1991). He has won the Pulitzer Prize and the National Book Award. He teaches at the University of Massachusetts in Amherst and was the guest editor of *The Best American Poetry 1997*.

Asked about his prose poems, Tate once replied, "The only thing that matters in a prose poem is the absolute quickness of telling this contained story. It's anecdotal, very brief, and to the point. There's no reason to break off those lines and call it verse."

BERNARD WELT was born in Houston, Texas, in 1952, and grew up in Arlington, Virginia. He received an M.A. in writing from the Johns Hopkins University and a Ph.D. in literary studies from the American University. As a professor of academic studies at the Corcoran College of Art and Design in Washington, DC, he teaches courses in cinema and interdisciplinary humanities studies. His essays for the Los Angeles journal *Art issues* were collected in *Mythomania: Fantasies, Fables, and Sheer Lies in Contemporary American Popular Art* (Art issues Press, 1996). In 1992, he was a one-show champion on the television game show *Jeopardy!,* a twenty-two-minute effort that garnered more attention than any writing he has ever done. He is the author of one book of poems, *Serenade* (Z Press, 1979).

Welt writes: " 'I stopped writing poetry . . .' almost didn't get written, because—well, *I'd stopped writing poetry.* Most of the testimony, explanations, and excuses offered in the poem are honest, or sincere, or authentic, or whatever you are left having to call it when you are genuinely trying to account to yourself for your own behavior. As a lot of your better poets, from Catullus to Joe Brainard, must have discovered, the first person enforces a strange duality, opening up the floodgates of real emotion and memory while leaving you in the uncomfortable position of experiencing yourself as a literary character. That discomfort is the main thing I think of when people speak of a poet's *voice*.

"When I saw Judith Hall of the *Antioch Review* at the St. Mary's Poetry Festival in Maryland and she encouraged me to contribute to a special issue on poetry in the year 2000, I was not only very grateful but happy, because I discovered that my ideas for an essay worked better as a sort of self-consuming poem (which Judith then had to talk me into actually writing). I blurted out on the page whatever half-baked idea popped into my head, then I'd get interested in why it came out in those words rather than any others. If I were writing an essay I'd stop at that point and remind myself that I'm more concerned with developing my ideas than obsessing about the aroma of words and phrases. But in writing a poem I surrender to my fascination with the *totality* of the powers of words, not just their denotative faculty; I'm thinking of how language works rather than what I want from it (which always misleads me). And then I really do fall in love with the stanza all over again, and enjambment, and internal rhyme, and I can imitate other writers' styles intentionally and ironically instead of just stealing from them, and I get to feeling that the strange hesitation I often display at line breaks isn't only a tic (though it is) but something I actually have to say."

DEAN YOUNG was born in Columbia, Pennsylvania, in 1955. He has received a fellowship from the Fine Arts Work Center in Provincetown, a Wallace Stegner fellowship from Stanford University, and two fellowships from the National Endowment for the Arts. He has published four books of poems including *Strike Anywhere,* which won the Colorado Poetry Prize, and *First Course in Turbulence* (University of Pittsburgh Press, 1999).

Of "Sources of the Delaware," Young writes: "First off, I have to note that I wrote this poem before the story broke about our President Clinton's oral activities in the oval office. I was trying to get a bunch of rather disparate material to fly in some kind of formation, weird art-world events, pseudo-myth, something I'd written about a phone conversation with a friend. What seemed to be wanted to hold this stuff together for me on the page was a sense of current, of unavoidable and unopposable forward flood. So of course it turned into a love poem."

RACHEL ZUCKER was born in New York City in 1971. She grew up in Greenwich Village, the only child of a storyteller/writer and a gem dealer/writer, and was educated at Yale and the Iowa Writers' Workshop. After working as a photographer, day care teacher, and gem dealer, she taught composition at NYU and poetry at Yale as an adjunct professor. Her poems have appeared in various journals such as *American Poetry Review, Colorado Review, Epoch, Iowa Review,* and *Pleiades.* She publishes *Boomerang! A Contributors' Journal,* now in its tenth issue. She lives in Manhattan with her husband and two young sons.

Zucker writes: "I wrote the first draft of 'In Your Version of Heaven I Am Younger' in September 1998. It was just after the crash of Swiss Air Flight 111 off the shore of Peggy's Cove, Nova Scotia, in which all 229 people aboard died. News of the crash upset me. I remember being particularly disturbed by a report that many of the bodies recovered were wearing life jackets. I became obsessed with imagining the twenty or so minutes during which the passengers knew it was likely that the plane was going to crash. In those same weeks, my husband and I started trying to conceive our first child. Somehow the intersection of these two events—imagining myself full of life, imagining myself about to die—as well as an annoying but typical comment my otherwise endearing husband made ('sometimes I wish you were exactly like you except blond and perky') caused the poem to spark into being. Thinking about it now, I suspect that the language and form of the poem were influenced by the clinical, declarative style of the newspaper articles about the crash."

MAGAZINES WHERE THE POEMS
WERE FIRST PUBLISHED

AGNI, ed. Askold Melnyczuk. Boston University, 236 Bay State Rd., Boston, Massachusetts 02215.

American Letters & Commentary, ed. Anna Rabinowitz. 850 Park Avenue, Suite 5B, New York, New York 10021.

American Poetry Review, eds. Stephen Berg, David Bonanno, and Arthur Vogelsgang. 1721 Walnut Street, Philadelphia, Pennsylvania 19103.

Another Chicago Magazine, eds. Lee Webster and Barry Silesky. 3709 N. Kenmore, Chicago, Illinois 60613.

The Antioch Review, poetry ed. Judith Hall. P. O. Box 148, Yellow Springs, Ohio 45387.

The Atlantic Monthly, poetry ed. Peter Davison. 77 North Washington St., Boston, Massachusetts 02114.

Barrow Street, eds. Patricia Carlin, Peter Covino, Lois Hirschkowitz, and Melissa Hotchkiss. P. O. Box 2017, Old Chelsea Station, New York, New York 10113.

Boston Book Review, ed. Theoharis Constantine Theoharis. 30 Brattle Street, Cambridge, Massachusetts 02138-0372.

Boston Review, poetry eds. Mary Jo Bang and Timothy Donnelly. E53-407, MIT, 30 Wadsworth Street, Cambridge, Massachusetts 02139-4307.

Callaloo, ed. Charles H. Rowell. Dept. of English, 322 Bryan Hall, University of Virginia, Charlottesville, Virginia 22903.

Chain, eds. Jena Osman and Juliana Spahr. Dept. of English, 1733 Donaghho Road, University of Hawai'i. Manoa, Honolulu, Hawaii 96822.

Colorado Review, poetry eds. Jorie Graham and Donald Revell. Dept. of English, Colorado State University, Ft. Collins, Colorado 80523.

Conjunctions, ed. Bradford Morrow. Bard College, Annandale-on-Hudson, New York 12504.

Crab Orchard Review, poetry ed. Allison Joseph. English Dept., Faner Hall, Southern Illinois University, Carbondale, Illinois 62901-4503.

Evansville Review, ed. Dan Walker. 1800 Lincoln Ave., Evansville, Indiana 47722.

Facture, eds. Lindsay Hill and Paul Naylor. P. O. Box 337, Cedar Ridge, California 95924.

Faucheuse, Oakland, California.

Fence, poetry eds. Caroline Crumpacker and Matthew Rohrer. 14 Fifth Avenue, #1A, New York, New York 10011.

Harper's, ed. Lewis H. Lapham. 666 Broadway, New York, New York 10012.

Jubilat, eds. Robert N. Casper, Christian Hawkey, Kelly LeFave, and Michael

Teig. Dept. of English, 482 Bartlett Hall, University of Massachusetts, Amherst, Massachusetts 01003-0510.

The Journal, eds. Kathy Fagan and Michelle Herman. Dept. of English, Ohio State University, 164 W. 17th Ave., Columbus, Ohio 43210.

The Kenyon Review, ed. David Lynn. Kenyon College, Gambier, Ohio 43022.

LIT, editors at large Mark Bibbins, Liz Brown, and Rebecca Reilly. New School University, Writing Program, 66 W. 12th St., #508, New York, New York 10011.

Massachusetts Review, poetry eds. Martín Espada, Anne Halley, and Paul Jenkins. South College, University of Massachusetts, Amherst, Massachusetts 01003.

McSweeney's, ed. Dave Eggers. 394A Ninth Street, Brooklyn, New York 11215.

The Nation, poetry ed. Grace Schulman. 72 Fifth Ave., New York, New York 10011.

The Nebraska Review, poetry ed. Susan Aizenberg. Creative Writing Program, University of Nebraska, Omaha, Nebraska 68182-0324.

New American Writing, eds. Paul Hoover and Maxine Chernoff. 369 Molino Avenue, Mill Valley, California 94941.

The New Republic, poetry ed. Charles Wright. 1220 19th Street NW, Washington, DC 20036.

The New York Review of Books, eds. Barbara Epstein and Robert Silvers. 1755 Broadway, 5th Floor, New York, New York 10019-3780.

The New Yorker, poetry ed. Alice Quinn. 4 Times Square, New York, New York 10036.

Northwest Review, ed. John Witte. 369 PLC, University of Oregon, Eugene, Oregon 97403.

The Paris Review, poetry ed. Richard Howard. 541 E. 72nd St., New York, New York 10021.

Pequod, ed. Mark Rudman. Department of English, New York University, 19 University Place, Room 200, New York, New York 10003.

Ploughshares, eds. Don Lee and David Daniel. Emerson College, 100 Beacon St., Boston, Massachusetts 02116.

Poetry, ed. Joseph Parisi. 60 W. Walton St., Chicago, Illinois 60610-3380.

Quarter After Eight, eds. Tom Noyes, Imad Rahman, and Andrew Touhy. Ellis Hall, Ohio University, Athens, Ohio 45701.

Seneca Review, ed. Deborah Tall. Hobart and William Smith Colleges, Geneva, New York 14456-3397.

Southern Review, poetry eds. James Olney and Dave Smith. 43 Allen Hall, Louisiana State University, Baton Rouge, Louisiana 70803-5005.

Southwest Review, ed. Willard Spiegelman. 307 Fondren Library West, P. O. Box 750374, Southern Methodist University, Dallas, Texas 75275-0374.

The Texas Review, ed. Paul Ruffin. Sam Houston State University, Dept. of English and Foreign Languages, Huntsville, Texas 77341-2146.

Threepenny Review, poetry ed. Wendy Lesser. P. O. Box 9131, Berkeley, California 94709.

Times Literary Supplement. Admiral House, 66–68 East Smithfield, London E1 W 9BX England.

Tin House, poetry ed. Amy Bartlett. P. O. Box 10500, Portland, Oregon 97296.
TriQuarterly, ed. Susan Hahn. 2020 Ridge Ave., Evanston, Illinois 60208-4302.
Verse, eds. Brian Henry and Andrew Zawacki. English Dept., University of Georgia, Athens, Georgia 30602.
Volt, ed. Gillian Conoley. P. O. Box 657, Corte Madera, California 94976-0657.

ACKNOWLEDGMENTS

The series editor wishes to acknowledge his invaluable assistant, Mark Bibbins. Ideas or suggestions contributed by John Diamond-Nigh, Jennifer Factor, Stacey Harwood, Martha Kinney, Christine Korfhage, Rebecca Livingston, and Susan Wheeler were greatly appreciated. Warm thanks also go to Glen Hartley and Lynn Chu, of Writers' Representatives, and to Gillian Blake, Rachel Sussman, Giulia Melucci, Kim Hilario, Erich Hobbing, and Jay Schweitzer of Scribner.

Grateful acknowledgment is made of the editors of the publications from which the poems in this volume were chosen. Unless specifically stated otherwise, copyright to the poems is held by the individual poets.

Nin Andrews: "Notes for a Sermon on the Mount" appeared in *Another Chicago Magazine*. Reprinted by permission of the poet.

Rae Armantrout: "The Plan" appeared in *American Poetry Review*. Reprinted by permission of the poet.

John Ashbery: "Crossroads in the Past" from *Your Name Here*. Copyright © 2000 by John Ashbery. Reprinted by permission of the poet and Farrar, Straus and Giroux. First appeared in *New York Review of Books*.

Angela Ball: "Jazz" appeared in *The Nebraska Review*. Reprinted by permission of the poet.

Mary Jo Bang: "Crossed-Over, Fiend-Snitched, X-ed Out" appeared in *New American Writing*. Reprinted by permission of the poet.

Cal Bedient: "When the Gods Put on Meter" appeared in *Colorado Review*. Reprinted by permission of the poet.

Elizabeth Bishop: "Vague Poem" was first published in *The New Yorker*. Reprinted by permission of *The New Yorker* and of Farrar, Straus and Giroux.

Robert Bly: "The French Generals" from *The Night Abraham Called to the Stars*. Copyright © 2001 by Robert Bly. Reprinted by permission of the poet and of HarperCollins. The poem first appeared in *The Paris Review*. "Jesus at the Well" appeared in the *Times Literary Supplement* and is reprinted here by permission of the poet.

Lee Ann Brown: "Sonnet Around Stephanie" appeared in *Verse*. Reprinted by permission of the poet.

Michael Burkard: "Notes About My Face" from *Unsleeping*. Copyright © 2001 by Michael Burkard. Reprinted by permission of the poet and Sarabande Books. First appeared in *American Poetry Review*.

Trent Busch: "Heartland" appeared in *The Nation*. Reprinted by permission of the poet.

Amina Calil: "Blouse of Felt" appeared in *Faucheuse*. Reprinted by permission of the poet.

Bernard Welt: "I stopped writing poetry . . ." appeared in *The Antioch Review*. Reprinted by permission of the poet.

Dean Young: "Sources of the Delaware" appeared in *Volt*. Reprinted by permission of the poet.

Rachel Zucker: "In Your Version of Heaven I Am Younger" appeared in *American Poetry Review*. Reprinted by permission of the poet.